Close-up

TUDENT'S BOOK **A2**

Angela Bandis
Diana Shotton

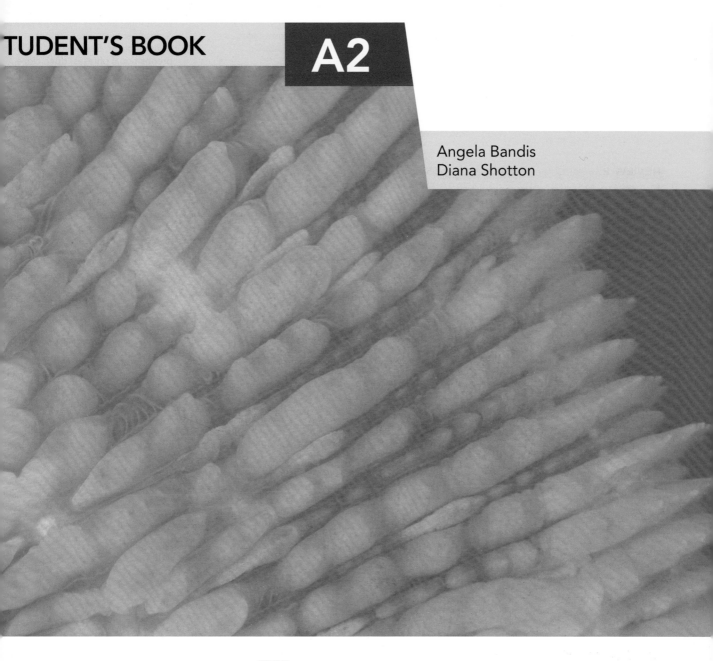

NATIONAL GEOGRAPHIC

L E A R N I N G

Australia · Brazil · Mexico · Singapore · United Kingdom · United States

Contents

Listening	Speaking	Writing	Video
gap-fill (dialogue), listening to instructions	asking & answering questions, giving details about yourself, talking about yourself	completing a form, focusing on accuracy, understanding & completing forms	Animal Families
multiple-choice, identifying the wrong answers	asking & answering questions, giving a description of a friend, describing a person	an email, writing about personality, answering all the questions, giving examples, describing personality & appearance	Happy Elephants
multiple-choice (pictures), choosing the correct picture	asking & answering questions, talking to a partner, asking for details about events, checking information	a poster, writing important information, finding the correct information, expressing time, giving contact details	Fat Tuesday
multiple-choice, understanding what to listen for	prompt cards, asking questions correctly, eating out, taking an order, ordering food & drink	an informal email, using adjectives in emails, using short forms, punctuation & greetings, talking about plans, giving opinions, inviting	A Grizzly Encounter
multiple-matching, identifying the two incorrect options	asking & answering questions, making your descriptions interesting, describing different rooms, describing my bedroom	a note, explaining why, checking your spelling, making excuses	The Horse Nomads of Mongolia
gap-fill monologue, listening for days, times & numbers	asking & answering questions, understanding what people say, asking for & giving directions, checking understanding	a formal email, using formal language, sequencing, describing a route	One of a Kind
matching, listening for clues	prompt card activity, answering in complete sentences, giving detailed information	an advert, making suggestions & persuading, understanding who & what, suggesting & persuading	Mechanical Lizard Car
gap-fill (monologue), listening for numbers & dates	asking about likes, making & responding to suggestions, asking about likes, giving advice, responding to advice	a blog, using the correct tense using appropriate vocabulary, positive emotions & negative emotions	A Muni Adventure
multiple-choice (pictures), getting ready to listen	asking & answering questions, getting information about places, asking about a holiday, describing a holiday	a social media post, making your writing flow, using correct punctuation, greetings, saying where you are, arriving, talking about activities	The Travelling Photographer
gap-fill (dialogue), predicting the answers before listening	prompt card activity, asking for & giving travel information	an invitation, using modals, responding correctly to questions, inviting, accepting & declining an invitation, explaining why, responding to a request	Travelling in India
gap-fill (monologue), listening for numbers, adjectives & common words	asking & answering questions, expressing differences & similarities, asking questions	a postcard, using a variety of tenses, planning your answer, talking about present, past & future activities	Snow on Tigers
multiple-choice, preparing to choose the right option	asking & answering questions, formulating questions, wh- questions, other questions	a report, structuring a report, reading both texts, giving background information, recommending	Mega Green Museum

1 Who Am I?

Reading:	right, wrong, doesn't say, reading for main ideas
Vocabulary:	numbers, dates, months, nationalities, family, word completion, identifying a set of words
Grammar:	present simple, adverbs of frequency, question words, present continuous, multiple-choice cloze, choosing the missing words
Listening:	gap-fill (dialogue), listening to instructions
Speaking:	asking & answering questions, giving details about yourself
Writing:	completing a form, focusing on accuracy, understanding & completing forms

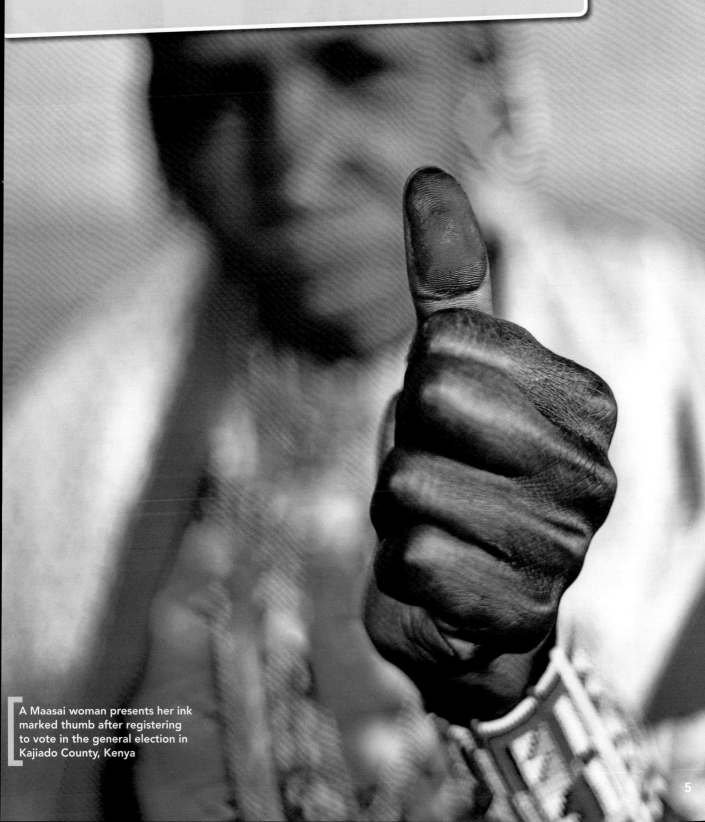

A Maasai woman presents her ink marked thumb after registering to vote in the general election in Kajiado County, Kenya

Reading

A Write the correct free-time activities under the pictures.

> playing football photography painting
> playing cricket playing in a band swimming

B Work with a partner. Tell each other which activities in A you like doing.

C Read Jack's online profile and write in the correct headings. Then take turns to tell your partner about Jack.

> Hobbies / Activities Age Country Dream Pets Name

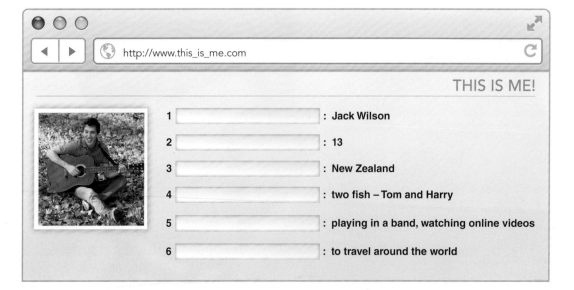

THIS IS ME!

1 _____ : Jack Wilson

2 _____ : 13

3 _____ : New Zealand

4 _____ : two fish – Tom and Harry

5 _____ : playing in a band, watching online videos

6 _____ : to travel around the world

Quickly read the text below. What information from the headings in C does it give about the girl?

Lucky Mbele

Lucky Mbele is a 10-year-old high school student. She lives in Cape Town, in South Africa. She is <u>brilliant</u> at drawing and painting, and her dream is to be a <u>well-known</u> artist in the future. She loves nature and her paintings of the sea and the forest are <u>incredible</u>.

Lucky has some <u>close</u> friends. When she isn't busy with her art, she spends time with her friends after school and at the weekend. 'We go to the beach in the summer and we swim. We love sport. In the winter, we play football and basketball. We also play cricket. Cricket is a <u>popular</u> sport in South Africa, England, Australia, New Zealand and India, but I don't think people play it in a lot of European countries! My friends and I also like the cinema and we go to cafés, too, just to hang out together. But I always make sure that I have time for my paintings.'

Lucky sells her paintings in <u>crowded</u> street markets. Tourists buy them because the paintings are about South Africa, and they are good souvenirs to have from their holiday. 'One day, when I am famous, I want to see my paintings in galleries all around the world!'

E **Read the *Exam Close-up*. Write key words in your notebooks for each paragraph in the text. Use ideas from the profile in C.**

Paragraph 1: name, age…

F **Now complete the *Exam Task*. Use your key words to help you answer the questions.**

Exam Task

Read the article about a young girl. Are sentences **1–8** **'Right' (A)** or **'Wrong (B)**? If there is not enough information to answer **'Right' (A)** or **'Wrong' (B)**, choose **'Doesn't say' (C)**.

1 Lucky's hobby is art. ☐
2 Lucky is a good student at school. ☐
3 Lucky draws and paints her dreams. ☐
4 Lucky does many things with her friends. ☐
5 In summer, Lucky plays football. ☐
6 People in Europe don't watch cricket. ☐
7 Lucky's paintings are in souvenir shops. ☐
8 Tourists pay a lot of money for Lucky's paintings. ☐

Exam Close-up

Reading for main ideas

- It's easier to understand a text if you find the most important information.
- Read each paragraph for the main ideas.
- Write key words next to each paragraph to help you remember.

G **These words are underlined in the text. Find them, and then circle the correct meanings.**

1 brilliant — new / excellent
2 well-known — famous / rich
3 incredible — amazing / colourful
4 close — near / good
5 popular — well-liked / unusual
6 crowded — noisy / busy

Ideas Focus

- Should everyone have a hobby? Why? / Why not?
- Is it better for young people to do sport or creative hobbies (e.g. painting, music)? Why?

Vocabulary

A Write the numbers as words in each gap.

1 5 + 7 = 12
   _____five_____ and _____seven_____ is _____twelve_____

2 8 + 16 = 24
   _____ and _____ is _____

3 9 + 29 = 38
   _____ and _____ is _____

4 19 + 26 = 45
   _____ and _____ is _____

5 21 + 38 = 59
   _____ and _____ is _____

6 33 + 44 = 77
   _____ and _____ is _____

7 11 + 85 = 96
   _____ and _____ is _____

8 43 + 57 = 100
   _____ and _____ is _____

B Write the dates of the national holidays for ten European countries.

	Date	Day and month	Country
1	2/6	the second of June	Italy
2	25/3		Greece
3	12/10		Spain
4	14/7		France
5	15/2		Serbia
6	21/9		Malta
7	1/12		Portugal
8	3/5		Poland
9	1/8		Switzerland
10	28/11		Albania

C Write the twelve months of the year from first to last in your notebooks. Which months are not in B?

D Circle the correct words.

1 It's in Greece / Greek.
   It's a Greece / Greek island.

2 It's from Chinese / China.
   It's a Chinese / China dragon.

3 It's from Italian / Italy.
   It's Italian / Italy spaghetti

4 She's from Spanish / Spain.
   She's a Spanish / Spain dancer.

5 It's in France / French.
   It's a France / French symbol.

6 He's from England / English.
   He's an England / English bulldog

7 It's from Swiss / Switzerland.
   It's a Swiss / Switzerland
   cuckoo clock.

8 They're in Dutch / The Netherlands. They're
   Dutch / The Netherlands tulips.

A windmill in a field of tulips
in Lisse, Holland

Can you think of any other nationality adjectives?

Complete 1–4 with words from below that have the same meaning. Then circle the correct words in 5 and 6.

> dad   grandma   mum   granny   daddy   grandpa   grandad   mummy

1   grandmother, _____, _____
2   grandfather, _____, _____
3   mother, _____, _____
4   father, _____, _____
5   The people in 1 and 2 are
    parents / grandparents.
6   The people in 3 and 4 are
    parents / grandparents.

Complete the text with these words.

> brother   family   grandchildren   granddaughter
> married   sister   surname   twins

My family

Hi, I'm Elsa. I'm 14 years old and I live in England. This is a photo of my (**1**) _____. I'm not in the photo because I'm the photographer!

My mum's name is Carol and she's 37 years old. She's with Becky. Becky is my (**2**) _____ and she's 10 years old. Next to them is my dad, Kevin. He's 38 years old and he's with our dog, Sam. My little (**3**) _____ Oscar is with my grandparents, John and Kathleen – they're my dad's parents. They have five (**4**) _____ altogether – me, Becky, Oscar and our two cousins in Australia, Jenny and Jessica Spano. They're (**5**) _____ and they're 16.

Their dad is from Italy so their (**6**) _____,

Spano, is Italian. He is (**7**) _____ to my dad's sister.

Grandma and grandpa say I'm their favourite (**8**) _____, but I think they say the same thing to all of their grandchildren!

Read the *Exam Close-up*. Then read the *Exam Task* and underline the topic in the instructions.

Now complete the *Exam Task*.

Exam Task

Read the descriptions of some words for family members. What is the word for each one? The first letter is already there. There is **one** space for **each letter** in the word.

1   This child is a boy.   s _ _
2   This child is a girl.   d _ _ _ _ _ _ _
3   A woman who is married to a man.   w _ _ _
4   A man who is married to a woman.   h _ _ _ _ _ _

Exam Close-up

Identifying a set of words

- Read the instructions and underline the vocabulary topic.
- Read the definitions of the words carefully.
- The answers you write should all link. Check them carefully against each other and the topic.
- Check your spelling.

5   He is your mother's or father's brother. u _ _ _ _
6   She is your mother's or father's sister.   a _ _ _
7   This is your mother's sister's child.   c _ _ _ _ _

- Would you like to go back to a date in your past? Why? / Why not?
- 'A big family is better than a small family.' Do you agree? Why? / Why not?

Ideas Focus

Grammar

Present Simple

A Read the sentences and underline the verbs in the Present Simple.

1 My grandparents live in Cyprus.
2 His mother drives to work.
3 Water freezes at 0°C.
4 I go to my photography class on Wednesdays.

B Which sentences in A ... ?

a talk about facts
b talk about routine activities

C Read this dialogue. Underline the Present Simple verbs, then choose the correct words to complete the rule.

A Do you walk to school?
B No, I don't walk. My mum drives me.
A Lucky you! My parents don't have a car.
B Oh. So, do you walk or cycle to school?

We use the auxiliary verb *be* / *do* in Present Simple questions and negatives.

Adverbs of Frequency

D We often use adverbs of frequency with the Present Simple. Underline the adverbs of frequency in these sentences.

1 People <u>often</u> get up late at weekends.
2 John never walks to school because he's lazy.
3 The baby usually cries at night.
4 Rita sometimes drinks coffee but she prefers tea.
5 Maria's birthday is always in the holidays.
6 I hardly ever see my Australian cousins.

E Complete the rule about adverbs of frequency. Then write the adverbs from D in the correct place on the line.

Adverbs of frequency go _____ main verbs but _____ the verb *be*.

0% |—————|—————|—————|—————▶ 100%

never _____ _____ _____ _____

Question Words

F Read the questions. Underline the question words we often use with the Present Simple.

a What time do the shops close today?
b When do the pupils have exams?
c Where does the family spend their weekends?
d Who do you often invite to your house?
e What does your teacher do after school?
f Why do we learn English?

G Which question word do we use for?

1 people _____
2 things or ideas _____
3 a specific time, e.g. 10.30 a.m. _____
4 a reason _____
5 a general time _____
6 a place _____

▶ Grammar Focus p. 161 (1.1 to 1.2)

H Choose the correct answers.

1 Where ____ your uncle come from?
  a do   b does
2 The baby ____ in his parents' room.
  a sleeps   b sleep
3 ____ is your birthday?
  a What time b When

4 I ____ a hat.
  a never wear b wear never
5 ____ do some Canadians speak French?
  a What   b Why
6 The bus ____ late.
  a arrives always b is always

I Read these answers and write the questions.

1 *Where do usually you go on holiday?* I usually go on holiday to Italy.
2 _____ I like pasta, pizza and ice-cream.
3 _____ I usually go to bed at 11 p.m.
4 _____ I walk to school.
5 _____ I hang out with Luke at break times.

Present Continuous

J Read these Present Continuous sentences. Then choose the correct words to complete the rule.

'I am studying English. My teacher is helping me. My friend is sitting next to me. My classmates are listening to me. They aren't writing.'

We use the Present Continuous to describe actions that are happening *soon / now*. We form the Present Continuous with the verb *be / do* and the infinitive / *-ing* form.

K Read these sentences and underline any examples of the Present Continuous.

1 We're English, but we're living in Dubai until next September.

2 We're lying next to our swimming pool. We're reading books and listening to music.

3 My dad is working in Dubai for a year.

4 We're studying Arabic every day.

5 My parents are making dinner in the kitchen right now.

L Match the sentences in K with uses a–c.

a an action happening at the time of speaking ☐2☐ ☐

b an action happening around the time of speaking ☐

c a temporary situation ☐ ☐

> **Be careful**
> Watch out when spelling verbs in the Present
> ● Continuous.
> * Verbs ending with a vowel before a consonant, e.g. *hit*, *shop*, *run* = double the consonant + *-ing*, e.g. *hitting*, *shopping*, *running*.
> * Verbs ending in *–e*, e.g. *write* = lose the *-e* and add *-ing*, e.g. *writing*.

▷ Grammar Focus p. 161 (1.3)

M Complete the dialogues with the Present Continuous.

1 A: I'm doing my homework.
B: Which subject _____ you _____ (study)?

2 A: Sssh!! I'm on the phone!
B: Who _____ you _____ (speak) to?

3 A: Are you busy right now?
B: Yes, I _____ (have) lunch with my family.

4 A: Where are you?
B: I _____ (sit) at the bus stop.

5 A: Are you working at the moment?
B: No, I _____ (take) a break.

6 A: Why isn't Dad answering his phone?
B: He _____ (fly) to Greece now.

7 A: Who are you talking to?
B: We _____ (chat) to our cousin.

8 A: Why aren't your parents here?
B: They _____ (not feel) well.

N Read the *Exam Close-up*. Then read the email in the *Exam Task* and think about what type of word should go in each gap.

Exam Close-up

Choosing the missing words
* Read the text first and try to get the general idea.
* Look at each gap. What type of word do you think goes in the gap?
* Read again and complete the text. Check your answers make sense.
* If you are not sure, try to make a guess. Answer all the questions.

O Now complete the *Exam Task*.

Exam Task

For questions **1–8** read the email and choose the best word (**A**, **B** or **C**) for each gap.

● ○ ○	Email Message	⤢

From: Jenny
To: Granny

Hi Granny,

I'm sorry you're in hospital and I hope you get well soon. I **(1)** _____ enjoying my birthday today. Right **(2)** _____, I'm having a great time with my best friends. I **(3)** _____ the present from you! Thanks! The T-shirt is really cool and I'm wearing it **(4)** _____ the moment and everyone likes it. The party is starting **(5)** _____ and my brother's dancing. He's a great dancer! He **(6)** _____ dances at parties! Dad is **(7)** _____ dancing, he's taking photos. I'm **(8)** _____ you one now on the mobile.

Wish you were here.

Love,
Jenny

1	**A** do	**B** really	**C** am
2	**A** now	**B** moment	**C** time
3	**A** loving	**B** love	**C** loves
4	**A** at	**B** in	**C** just
5	**A** now	**B** always	**C** often
6	**A** hardly ever	**B** never	**C** always
7	**A** never	**B** not	**C** sometimes
8	**A** send	**B** sent	**C** sending

Listening

A [1.1] Listen and write the places or names.

1 _____ 2 _____

3 _____ 4 _____

5 _____ 6 _____

B [1.2] Listen and choose the correct words.

1 a Taylor   b Tailor
2 a Cygnet   b Signet
3 a Lauren   b Lorraine
4 a Curry   b Carey
5 a Bristol   b Bristle
6 a Anna   b Anne

C Read the questions below. Decide which type of word from the options would be used to answer the question.

> a date   a name   a price   a time

1 When does the next course begin? _____
2 What time do the lessons start? _____
3 How much do the lessons cost? _____
4 Who is teaching the course? _____

D [1.3] Read the *Exam Close-up*. Then listen to the instructions for the *Exam Task* and decide if these sentences are true (T) or false (F).

1 You will hear two men speaking.
2 They will talk about art lessons.
3 You need to listen and choose the correct answer, a, b, or c.
4 You will hear the audio two times.

E [1.4] Now listen and complete the *Exam Task*.

A selection of paints and brushes

Exam Close-up

Listening to instructions

- Before a listening task begins, you will hear some instructions. Always listen carefully to these instructions.
- Note if the instructions tell you *who* you will listen to and *where* the speakers are.
- Check that you understand what you need to do and how many times you can listen.

Exam Task

You will hear a man asking a woman about art lessons. Listen and complete the form.

You will hear the conversation twice.

Art Club

Place: Spring Arts Centre

Lessons: painting and drawing

Teacher: (1) Mrs _____

Course of (2) _____ lessons

Starting date (3) _____ January

Time of lessons (4) _____ to 7pm Mon and Fri

Total cost of course (5) £_____

F [1.5] Now listen again and check your answers.

Speaking

A

B

Work with a partner and look at the families in the photos. Match the sentences to the photos. Which sentence can match to both photos?

1 'I live with my grandparents.'
2 'I live in an apartment with my parents.'
3 'I share a bedroom with my sisters.'
4 'We live in Oslo in Norway. Winters are very cold here.'
5 'We live in Hanoi. It's usually very hot here.'
6 'I'm learning English at school at the moment.'

Look at the statements from some students in a speaking exam. Which student, a or b, uses the correct language?

1 a My family is having five people.
  b There are five people in my family.
2 a I go to English school twice a week.
  b I'm going to English school two times the week.
3 a I'm going to the third class of high school.
  b I'm in the third year at high school.
4 a I'm not watching TV every evening.
  b I don't watch TV every evening.
5 a I meet my friends most weekends.
  b I'm meeting my friends at weekends.

Write the questions that the students answered in B in your notebooks. Follow this example.

1 How many people are in your family?

Read the *Exam Close-up* and complete the *Exam Task*. Use the *Useful Expressions* to help you.

Exam Close-up

Giving details about yourself
- When talking about yourself, don't just answer 'yes' or 'no'.
- Give extra information or explain why.
- Show interest in your partner's answers, too.
- Practise talking about yourself with your friends in class.

Useful Expressions

Talking about yourself
My favourite subject is …
In my free time I usually …
I've got one sister, she's older / younger than me …
I don't have any pets.

I've got a cat called Jasper.
I spend a lot of time with my (grandma).
I always (play football / watch TV) with my dad / friends.

Exam Task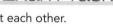

Work with a partner. Find out about each other. **Student A** should ask the questions in Quiz 1 and **Student B** answers them.

Quiz 1
Where / live? ☐
Brothers or sisters? If yes, how many? ☐
When / your birthday? ☐
What / favourite subject at school? ☐
What / do / in your free time? ☐

Then **Student B** should ask the questions in Quiz 2 and **Student A** answers them.

Quiz 2
Any pets? If yes, what? Name? ☐
When / your mum's birthday? ☐
Where / usually / go on holiday? ☐
What / favourite food? ☐
What / your hobbies? ☐

- Is it good to share hobbies with your family? Why? / Why not?
- Do you often see your cousins, aunts, uncles and grandparents? Why? / Why not?

Ideas Focus

13

Writing: completing a form

Learning Focus

Focusing on accuracy

When you complete a form, you often need to give the following information:

- title (e.g. Mr, Mrs, Ms, Miss)
- first name and surname
- age and / or date of birth (DOB)
- place of birth
- home address
- phone number
- email address
- interests

You must learn to write this information correctly in English.

A Which forms have you completed? Tick ✔ and then discuss questions 1–6 with a partner.

a An application for a passport ☐

b A membership for a club ☐

c To enter a competition ☐

d To buy something online ☐

e An online profile ☐

Which of the forms need your ...

1 name?

2 date of birth?

3 place of birth?

4 home address?

5 phone number?

6 email address?

B Which is the correct way to write the information? Circle *a* or *b* for the correct answer.

1 a Title: Ms
First name: Smith
Surname: Michael

b Title: Mr
First name: Michael
Surname: Smith

2 a DOB: 23st November, 2000

b DOB: November 23rd, 2000

3 a Home Address: 10 Main Street, Clayton

b Home Address: Street Main 10, Clayton

4 a Landline: (03) 543 2637
Mobile: 6977878903

b Landline: 6977878903
Mobile: (03) 543 2637

5 a Signature: M. Smith

b Signature: *M. Smith*

C Answer these questions with a partner.

1 Which title shows that a woman is married and which shows that she is unmarried?

2 What title can a woman use if she doesn't want to show whether she is married or not?

3 If your full name is Jason Ryan Reynolds, what is your surname?

4 In UK addresses what comes first, the name of the road/street or the house number?

D Read the writing task and answer the questions.

> *You want to order a monthly magazine. Complete the form.*
>
> On the form:
>
> - write your personal information correctly
> - say which magazine you want
> - ask a question about the price

1 What do you have to write?

2 Why are you writing?

3 What information do you need?

Read the example form. What does Christina want to know?

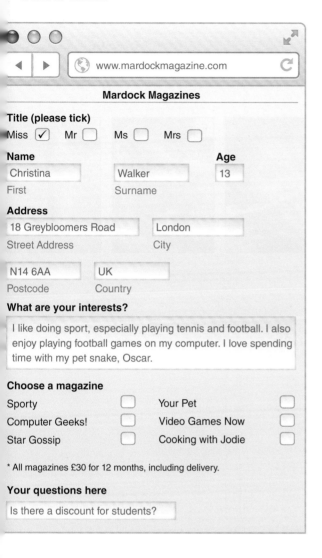

Mardock Magazines

Title (please tick)

Miss ☑ Mr ☐ Ms ☐ Mrs ☐

Name | **Age**

Christina | Walker | 13
First | Surname

Address

18 Greybloomers Road | London
Street Address | City

N14 6AA | UK
Postcode | Country

What are your interests?

I like doing sport, especially playing tennis and football. I also enjoy playing football games on my computer. I love spending time with my pet snake, Oscar.

Choose a magazine

Sporty ☐ Your Pet ☐
Computer Geeks! ☐ Video Games Now ☐
Star Gossip ☐ Cooking with Jodie ☐

* All magazines £30 for 12 months, including delivery.

Your questions here

Is there a discount for students?

Read the form again. Which magazines do you think Christina wants?

Useful Expressions

Expressing likes

I like + -ing
I enjoy + -ing
I love + -ing

I'm interested in …
I like … because …

Understanding & completing forms

- Check you understand what each part means.
- Make sure you write the correct information in each part.
- Make sure your handwriting is clear.
- Use a variety of expressions to talk about your interests. Don't just say 'I like …'.

G Read the *Exam Close-up* and the *Exam Task*. Then make a list of your interests.

H Now complete the *Exam Task*. Use the *Useful Expressions* to help you.

Exam Task

You want to enter a competition. Complete the form. On the form, you must:

- write your personal information correctly
- choose the prize you want
- answer a question to win a prize

www.mardockmagazine.com

10 Lucky Readers Will Win Great Prizes!

Title (please tick)

Miss ☐ Mr ☐ Ms ☐ Mrs ☐

Name | **Age**

First | Surname

Address

Street Address | City / Town

Postcode | Country

Choose your prize

The Happy Chappies CD ☐ FIFA 2018 ☐
'Strange Lives' DVD ☐ 'Smeli' perfume ☐
Epic headphones ☐

* We will announce the winners in the next issue.

Tell us about your interests.

Question: Why do you like *Sporty* magazine?

1 Animal Families

Before you watch

A Look at the photos. Which live in families?

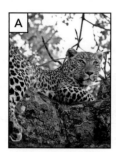

While you watch

B Watch the video to see if your answers in A are correct.

C Read the sentences below. Which pictures do they refer to?

1 Many animals live in family groups / teams as well. ☐
2 There are usually five to seven females / males in the group. ☐
3 In the group, there is usually only one female / male. ☐
4 He has long hair on his head / neck. ☐
5 There are 20–30 meerkats in the family / group. ☐
6 This is the alpha pair / parent. ☐
7 He has silver hair on his back / front. ☐
8 He is the father / leader of all the young gorillas. ☐

D Watch the video again and circle the words in the sentences above that you hear.

After you watch

E Complete the summary of the video below using these words.

| alone | daughters | hair | handsome | important | leader | mother | young |

Some animals live **(1)** _____, but many animals live in family groups. Lions usually live in families of about five to seven females and one male. The male lion has long hair on his neck and he is very **(2)** _____. All the young lions in the group are his sons and **(3)** _____. Meerkats also live in big families. There are 20–30 meerkats in a family. One pair, called the alpha pair, are the **(4)** _____ and father of all the young meerkats. Gorillas also live in families. The **(5)** _____ is a large male gorilla with silver **(6)** _____ on his back. He is the father of all the **(7)** _____ gorillas and the seven females in the group are their mothers. Families are **(8)** _____ for animals and people.

Ideas Focus

- Are your family the most important people in your life? Why? / Why not?
- Is the father usually the leader in a family? Why? / Why not?

2 Look At Me!

Reading:	multiple-choice, finding the information you need
Vocabulary:	appearance- and personality-related words, prepositions
Grammar:	past simple, *used to*, past continuous
Listening:	multiple-choice questions, identifying the wrong answers
Speaking:	asking & answering questions, describing a person, giving a description of a friend
Writing:	an email, writing about personality, answering all the questions, greetings & sign-offs, giving examples, describing personality, describing appearance

A Japanese bride in
traditional dress

17

Reading

A Work with a partner. Match these sentences with the correct photo.

1 Congratulations! You won a holiday!
2 Your best friend moved to another city.
3 Oh, no! There's a snake!!
4 Your brother broke your iPhone.
5 There's nothing to watch on TV.
6 I got an A+ in my English test!

B Match adjectives a–f with the situations in A.

a sad
b angry
c bored
d surprised
e happy
f scared

C Quickly read the text about three people and their jobs. What are their jobs? Can you find the adjectives from B in the text?

Word Focus

Aboriginal Australian: the first people in Australia

fringe: part of someone's hair at the front; it goes down to the eyebrows

didgeridoo: a long wooden instrument that you blow into to make music

professional: when you do something as a job, not a hobby

culture: the way of life of a group of people

snacks: small, tasty pieces of food eaten between meals

My Job

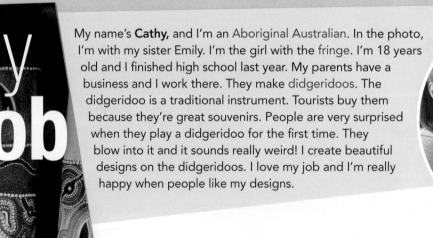

My name's **Cathy,** and I'm an Aboriginal Australian. In the photo, I'm with my sister Emily. I'm the girl with the fringe. I'm 18 years old and I finished high school last year. My parents have a business and I work there. They make didgeridoos. The didgeridoo is a traditional instrument. Tourists buy them because they're great souvenirs. People are very surprised when they play a didgeridoo for the first time. They blow into it and it sounds really weird! I create beautiful designs on the didgeridoos. I love my job and I'm really happy when people like my designs.

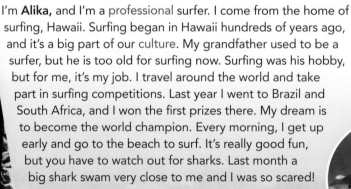

I'm **Alika,** and I'm a professional surfer. I come from the home of surfing, Hawaii. Surfing began in Hawaii hundreds of years ago, and it's a big part of our culture. My grandfather used to be a surfer, but he is too old for surfing now. Surfing was his hobby, but for me, it's my job. I travel around the world and take part in surfing competitions. Last year I went to Brazil and South Africa, and I won the first prizes there. My dream is to become the world champion. Every morning, I get up early and go to the beach to surf. It's really good fun, but you have to watch out for sharks. Last month a big shark swam very close to me and I was so scared!

A selection of didgeridoos with aboriginal designs

Read the *Exam Close–up*. Then read the *Exam Task* below and underline the key words in each question.

Exam Task

Read the text about three interesting jobs. For questions **1–7**, circle the correct letter **a**, **b** or **c**.

1 What does Cathy do now?
  a She has a business.
  b She goes to school.
  c She paints musical instruments.

2 Why do tourists buy didgeridoos?
  a They are surprised by the didgeridoos.
  b They want good souvenirs.
  c They think didgeridoos are weird.

3 Where did Alika win competitions?
  a In Hawaii and Brazil.
  b In South Africa and Hawaii.
  c In Brazil and South Africa.

4 What is true about Alika's grandfather?
  a He knew how to surf.
  b Surfing was his job.
  c He still enjoys surfing.

Exam Close-up

Finding the information you need
- Underline the key words in each question.
- Go back to the text and look for the key words or similar words.
- Look at the answer choices again and decide which is best.

5 What is Harry's job?
  a He is like a teacher.
  b He is a policeman.
  c He is an animal doctor.

6 According to Harry, why are dogs like people?
  a They like to work.
  b They have the same feelings.
  c They are like babies.

7 Who makes Harry angry?
  a People who are horrible to animals.
  b Most of the people he knows.
  c Police officers.

Now complete the *Exam Task*. Use the words you underlined to find the answers.

Find these adjectives in the reading text and match them to the correct definition. Then write six sentences in your notebooks using these adjectives.

traditional great weird beautiful smart unkind

1 Not nice; mean or horrible. _____
2 Very strange; not normal. _____
3 Very attractive; looks very nice. _____
4 Really good; excellent. _____
5 Something done in the same way for hundreds of years. _____
6 Clever; intelligent. _____

My name's **Harry**, and I've got the best job in the world. Every day I work with German Shepherd dogs. I train them to be police dogs! It takes quite a long time to train them and I have to use a lot of snacks and toys to help me! I love dogs – they're very smart and each one has a different personality. Like people, they can get angry, sad or bored. My favourite police dog, Tom, is in the picture with me. He's now a very successful working police dog. At home I have a Labrador called Dennis. He's my best friend – we look after each other when we're sad or ill. Animals are my life. I get really angry when people are unkind to them. Animals are better than some people I know!

- What jobs do people in your family do? Would you like to do those jobs? Why? / Why not?
- Would you like to do one of the jobs in the text? Why? / Why not?

Ideas Focus

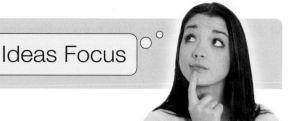

Vocabulary

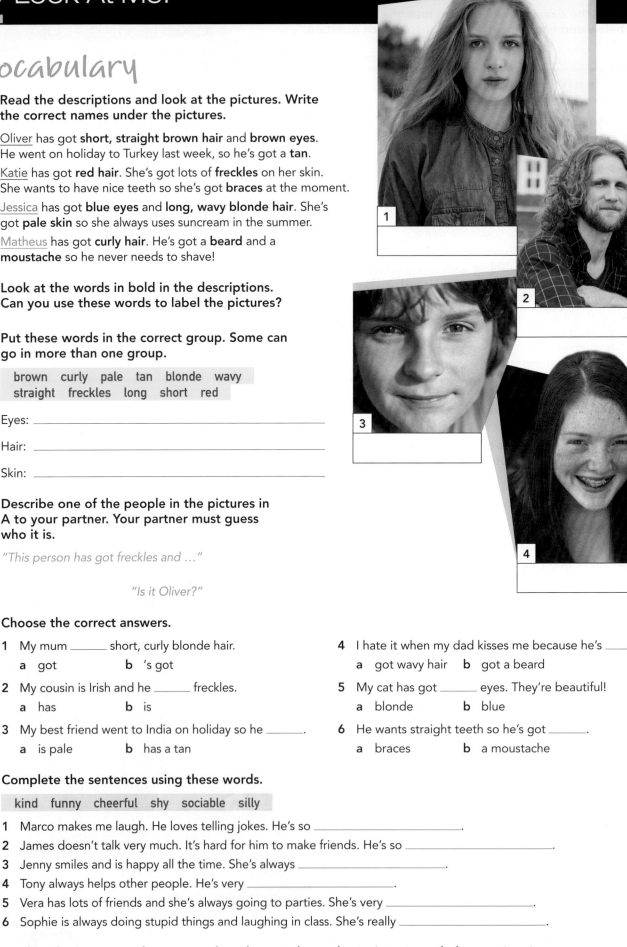

A Read the descriptions and look at the pictures. Write the correct names under the pictures.

Oliver has got **short, straight brown hair** and **brown eyes**. He went on holiday to Turkey last week, so he's got a **tan**.

Katie has got **red hair**. She's got lots of **freckles** on her skin. She wants to have nice teeth so she's got **braces** at the moment.

Jessica has got **blue eyes** and **long, wavy blonde hair**. She's got **pale skin** so she always uses suncream in the summer.

Matheus has got **curly hair**. He's got a **beard** and a **moustache** so he never needs to shave!

B Look at the words in bold in the descriptions. Can you use these words to label the pictures?

C Put these words in the correct group. Some can go in more than one group.

> brown   curly   pale   tan   blonde   wavy
> straight   freckles   long   short   red

Eyes: _____

Hair: _____

Skin: _____

D Describe one of the people in the pictures in A to your partner. Your partner must guess who it is.

"This person has got freckles and …"

"Is it Oliver?"

E Choose the correct answers.

1 My mum _____ short, curly blonde hair.
   a got   b 's got

2 My cousin is Irish and he _____ freckles.
   a has   b is

3 My best friend went to India on holiday so he _____.
   a is pale   b has a tan

4 I hate it when my dad kisses me because he's _____
   a got wavy hair   b got a beard

5 My cat has got _____ eyes. They're beautiful!
   a blonde   b blue

6 He wants straight teeth so he's got _____.
   a braces   b a moustache

F Complete the sentences using these words.

> kind   funny   cheerful   shy   sociable   silly

1 Marco makes me laugh. He loves telling jokes. He's so _____.
2 James doesn't talk very much. It's hard for him to make friends. He's so _____.
3 Jenny smiles and is happy all the time. She's always _____.
4 Tony always helps other people. He's very _____.
5 Vera has lots of friends and she's always going to parties. She's very _____.
6 Sophie is always doing stupid things and laughing in class. She's really _____.

G Work with a partner. Take turns to describe people you know (e.g. your dad, your sister).

"My dad's got brown hair and a beard. He's really kind because he helps me with my homework."

I Complete the table with the adjectives. Sometimes there is more than one possible answer.

Noun	Verb	Adjective
annoyance	annoy	**1** *annoying*
beauty	-	**2**
care	care	**3**
friend	-	**4**
laziness	-	**5**
love	love	**6**
shock	shock	**7**
worry	worry	**8**

Complete sentences 1–8 with the adjectives from H.

1 My little sister always comes into my room and uses my things. She's so _____.

2 Our neighbour talks to everyone on the street. He's really _____.

3 Our new teacher is so kind, helpful and beautiful. She's _____.

4 Mum says I'm _____ because I never clean my room or cook the dinner.

5 My brother looks ill because he's so _____ about his exams.

6 I was really _____ when I heard the terrible news about that car crash.

7 My brother thinks that singer is really _____ and he has pictures of her on his bedroom wall.

8 Julia always looks after her friends when they're sad or feeling ill – she's so _____.

J Circle the correct preposition.

1 I'm angry on / with Ben because he didn't call me.

2 Lisa is unhappy and I'm worried about / for her.

3 Rita loves animals and is always kind at / to them.

4 Are you scared from / of spiders, Samantha?

5 Jake took my phone and I'm angry about / on it.

6 I was very shocked by / for Julia's news.

7 I'm so annoyed on / with Luke for taking my phone without asking.

8 I'm sad about / for the school holidays – they finished yesterday!

K Choose the best word, a, b, or c, for each space.

My Uncle Ed
My uncle Ed is my **1**_____ younger brother. He's got curly brown **2**_____ and a beard. He often comes to visit us. He always makes me laugh – he's so **3**_____. And he's always doing **4**_____ things. On his last visit he danced around my bedroom and jumped on my bed. My mum was really annoyed **5**_____ him – she didn't want him to break the bed. My mum says she's really **6**_____ about Uncle Ed because he hasn't got a girlfriend. I'm really surprised that he hasn't because he's so kind and **7**_____ – he's always helping other people. He's certainly not **8**_____ – he talks to everyone. I hope he finds a lovely girlfriend soon.

1 a sister's	b aunt's	c mum's
2 a moustache	b hair	c freckles
3 a funny	b cheerful	c lazy
4 a beautiful	b silly	c shy
5 a for	b on	c with
6 a scared	b worried	c angry
7 a caring	b annoying	c surprised
8 a friendly	b cheerful	c shy

A greenbottle blue tarantula

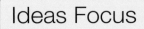

- Would you like to change your hair style? Why? / Why not?
- 'Beautiful people are happier than kind people.' Do you agree? Why? / Why not?

Ideas Focus

Grammar

Past Simple

A Read these sentences. <u>Underline</u> the verbs in the Past Simple.

   a In 1990 mum bought a house in London.

   b My parents both worked in London.

B Which sentence in A …

   1 uses a regular past simple verb (ending -ed)? ☐

   2 uses an irregular past simple verb? ☐

   3 talks about a past situation that lasted for while (a past state)? ☐

   4 talks about a past action that happened once (a past event)? ☐

C Read the two conversations and <u>underline</u> all the verbs in the Past Simple.

   A: I didn't see you at swimming lessons yesterday. Were you ill?

   B: No, I wasn't. I left my swimming costume at home!

   A: Did you see that Harry Potter film on TV last night?

   B: No, I didn't. I went out for dinner with my parents.

D Look at the sentences in C then circle the correct answers in 1–3.

   1 To make a negative sentence in the Past Simple, use *did* + *not* + past simple verb / infinitive verb.

   2 To make a question in the Past Simple, use *did* / past simple verb + subject + infinitive verb.

   3 We don't use *did* in Past Simple questions and negatives with the verb *to do* / *to be*.

Used to

E Read the sentences below and answer the questions.

   1 The family **used to live** in London, but they moved to Scotland 5 years ago.

   2 Dad **used to go** to work by train every day, but he works from home now.

   3 '**Did he use to read** on the train?' 'Yes, he did.'

   4 Mum **didn't use to work**, but now she manages her own shop.

   a Do the family live in London now? _____

   b Does dad go to work by train now? _____

   c What did dad do on the train? _____

   d Does mum work now? _____

F Circle the correct answers to complete the rules.

   1 We use *used to* to talk about habits or routines in the past that are not true now / yesterday.

   2 Form = subject + *used to* + verb (infinitive without to) / verb (-*ing* form).

   3 To make a question, use *did* + subject + *use to* / *used to* + verb (infinitive without *to*).

   4 To make a negative, use *didn't* + *use to* + past simple verb / verb (infinitive without *to*).

> ▶ Grammar Focus pp. 161 & 162 (2.1 to 2.2)

G Complete the table with the Past Simple forms of these irregular verbs.

Infinitive	Past Simple
bring	brought
buy	
catch	
eat	
drink	
go	
teach	
think	

H Find the mistakes with the Past Simple or *used to* and then write the sentences correctly in your notebooks.

   1 My grandad use to play tennis, but he stopped when he broke his arm.

   2 'Used you to like One Direction when you were little?' 'No, I didn't!'

   3 Where did you went on holiday last year?

   4 I eated a cheese and tomato pizza at the restaurant yesterday.

   5 I didn't used to like coffee, but I love it now.

   6 'Did you be at school yesterday?' 'No, I wasn't.'

Past Continuous

Read the sentences and <u>underline</u> examples of the Past Continuous. The first one is done for you.

1 I <u>was making</u> breakfast at 7 o'clock this morning when I got a message.
2 It was snowing and the TV was showing pictures of roads and the cars weren't moving.
3 When I read the message, I knew that nobody was going to school because the school was closed.

Complete the rules with these words.

> information   past   action   *to be*   the same time

a We use the Past Continuous to describe actions that were happening at a specific time in the _____.
b We also use it to show one or more actions that were happening at _____ in the past.
c We also use it to give background _____ in a story.
d We also use it with the Past Simple to show an action that was interrupted by another _____.
e We form the Past Continuous with past tense of the verb _____ and the *-ing* form.

Can you find examples of rules a–d in sentences 1–3 in I?

▶ Grammar Focus p. 162 (2.3)

Complete the dialogues with the Past Continuous of the verbs in brackets.

1 A: Why did you go home early?
   B: Because I _____ (not feel) well.
2 A: Why didn't you answer your phone last night?
   B: I _____ (swim) in the pool.
3 A: What did Sam do at the weekend?
   B: He _____ (work) all weekend.
4 A: Why _____ you _____ (drive) so fast last night?
   B: We were going to the hospital.

5 A: Ben, can you read your story to the class, please?
   B: The sun _____ (shine) and the wind _____ (blow) through his long wavy hair, when suddenly he saw an angry man running towards him …
6 A: What happened to our lunch?
   B: I _____ (play) on the computer, and when I looked in the oven, lunch _____ (burn)!

M Circle the correct words.

A family photo

Look at this old photo! We look really bad! Dad **(1)** took / was taking this picture in the 90s. I **(2)** used to have / was having long blonde hair, and I used to have braces. I **(3)** didn't like / wasn't liking them! My brother **(4)** used to think / was thinking he looked really cool. He **(5)** never had / had never short hair and he **(6)** always listened / was listening always to heavy rock music. I don't know why my sister **(7)** wasn't smiling / didn't use to smile in the photo. Perhaps because she **(8)** used to hate / was hating family photos. What **(9)** was she wearing / did she wear? I remember that jacket, she used to wear it all the time and it **(10)** looked / was looking horrible!

Listening

A Read these sentences.

1 Jack's eyes are _____.
   a blue   **b** big

2 The girl's brother is _____.
   a tall   **b** blonde

3 John is wearing _____.
   a glasses   **b** a uniform

4 The boy finished his homework _____.
   a before 8 pm   **b** before he went to bed

5 Where did the dog sleep last night? _____.
   a In the hall.   **b** In the garden.

6 The boy likes the teacher because _____.
   a he doesn't get much homework   **b** she is very funny

B `2.1` ▶‖ Now listen to the speakers but don't choose your answers yet.

C `2.1` ▶‖ Listen again, and this time choose your answers for 1–6 in A.

D Read the *Exam Close-up*. Are these sentences true (T) or false (F)?

1 Read only the first question before you listen.

2 You will probably hear words from all the answer options.

3 You should choose your answers as quickly as possible.

4 You should listen to the complete conversation before you choose your answer.

Exam Close-up

Identifying the wrong answers

- Read the questions first and look at the options.
- For each question you usually hear all the words from the different options so you need to identify which of those are incorrect.
- The first time you listen, don't decide on the answer too quickly.
- Listen to the complete conversation first, then listen again and choose your answer.

E `2.2` ▶‖ Listen and complete the *Exam Task*.

Exam Task

Listen to Lisa talking to her friend Sue about a video. For each question choose the right answer (**A**, **B** or **C**).

You will hear the conversation twice.

1 What colour is the singer's hair?
   A blonde
   B red
   C black

2 The singer is wearing...
   A a dress.
   B trousers.
   C a skirt.

3 The singer is...
   A little.
   B tall.
   C twenty.

4 The girls are listening to...
   A dance music.
   B a slow song.
   C an old song.

5 Who went to the concert?
   A Sue
   B Lisa
   C Sue's brother

F `2.3` ▶‖ Now listen again and check your answers.

Speaking

A Work with a partner. Student A: choose a person from the pictures, but don't tell Student B. Student B: use yes/no questions to find out who Student A chose. Then change roles.

"Is he / she wearing ...? / Has he / she got ...?"

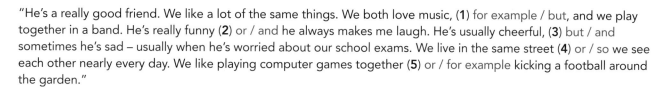

B Read the questions. Decide if they are asking about personality (P), appearance (A), or likes/activities (L).

1 What is your best friend like? ☐
2 Do you like doing the same things? ☐
3 What kind of music does your friend like? ☐
4 What does your friend look like? ☐
5 How often do you see your best friend? ☐
6 Where do you go together? ☐
7 Is your best friend different or similar to you? ☐
8 Are you both at the same school? ☐

C Read the *Exam Close*-up. Then work with a partner and choose the correct words to complete this description.

"He's a really good friend. We like a lot of the same things. We both love music, (**1**) for example / but, and we play together in a band. He's really funny (**2**) or / and he always makes me laugh. He's usually cheerful, (**3**) but / and sometimes he's sad – usually when he's worried about our school exams. We live in the same street (**4**) or / so we see each other nearly every day. We like playing computer games together (**5**) or / for example kicking a football around the garden."

D Complete the *Exam Task*. Use the *Useful Expressions* to help you.

Exam Task

Work in pairs. **Student A** should ask **Student B** the questions in Task 1.

Task 1
Tell me about your best friend.
What does your best friend look like?
What is your best friend like?
How do you spend your time when you are together?
Do you have the same interests? What are they?
What do you like best about your friend?
What do you and your friend disagree about?

Student A should think about **Student B's** answers and complete Task 2 by ticking ✔ what **B** did.

Task 2
The student answered the questions. ☐
The student was easy to understand. ☐
The student used the right vocabulary. ☐
The student answered with more than one word. ☐
The student used adjectives and linking words. ☐

Discuss your answers and then swap roles.

Exam Close-up

Giving a description of a friend
- If the examiner says, *tell me about your friend,* describe your friend's appearance, personality, likes and dislikes.
- If the examiner says, *What is your best friend like?*, describe your friend. Do not answer *My best friend likes …*
- Use lots of adjectives to describe your friend.
- Try to 'speak in a paragraph', this means using words like *and, but* and *so* to link your ideas.

Useful Expressions

Describing a person
She's … tall / blonde / quiet.
He's got … red hair / braces.
She usually wears … jeans / black.
He's really funny … but he gets angry if …
He understands me / listens to my problems.
She loves … animals / parties / volleyball.
He doesn't like … homework / shopping / winter.

- Do you prefer to spend your time with one friend or many? Why?
- Do believe that friendships can last a lifetime (best friends forever)? Why? / Why not?

Ideas Focus

Writing: an email

Learning Focus

Writing about personality

- When you describe someone's personality, you can write about their good and bad qualities.
- Give an example to support your description.
- Use linking words and phrases to connect your descriptions and examples (*so, and, but, because, that's why, for example*).

A Choose the correct linking words to complete the sentences.

1 Anna is a bit shy, so / but it's hard for her to make friends.

2 Jack makes everyone laugh, but / because he's really funny.

3 Matilda is very reliable and / for example is there when you need her.

4 Harry is lazy, because / that's why his room is always messy.

5 Sofia is really mean, for example / but she always makes her sister cry.

6 Jane is usually a cheerful person, so / but she was really sad yesterday.

B Read the writing task below and circle the correct words in 1–3.

Read the email from your friend, Alice.

> **Email Message**
>
> From: Alice
> To: Julie
>
> Hi Julie,
>
> I'm really looking forward to meeting your cousin Chloe at your party on Saturday. When did she arrive from London? What does she look like? What's she like?
>
> Love
> Alice

Write an email to Alice and answer the questions.
Write 25–35 words.

1 You have to write an email / a letter / a party invitation.

2 Alice / Chloe / Julie will read it.

3 You have to answer 2 / 3 / 4 questions.

C Read the example email. What are the answers to Alice's questions?

1 When did Chloe arrive?

2 What does she look like?

3 What is she like?

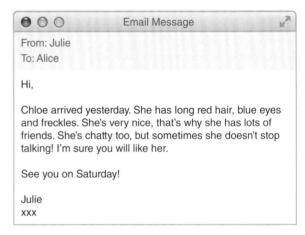

> **Email Message**
>
> From: Julie
> To: Alice
>
> Hi,
>
> Chloe arrived yesterday. She has long red hair, blue eyes and freckles. She's very nice, that's why she has lots of friends. She's chatty too, but sometimes she doesn't stop talking! I'm sure you will like her.
>
> See you on Saturday!
>
> Julie
> xxx

D Read the email in C again and underline the linking words.

Read the example email again and tick the things Julie does in her reply.

She …

1 says when her cousin arrived. ☐
2 says something positive about Chloe's personality. ☐
3 tells Alice what Chloe likes. ☐
4 describes Chloe's appearance. ☐
5 mentions something negative. ☐
6 tells Alice what Chloe is doing. ☐
7 gives examples in her description. ☐
8 asks Alice to see them on Saturday. ☐

Complete the sentences about Chloe with your own examples or descriptions. Be careful which linking words you use.

1 Chloe is a good student …
2 Chloe loves animals …
3 She's very friendly …
4 Everyone likes her …

Look at the example email in C again and put this plan in the correct order, 1–5. What greeting and sign-off does Julie use?

☐ Say what Chloe is like
☐ Sign off
☐ Say when Chloe arrived
☐ Greet
☐ Say what Chloe looks like

Read the Exam Close-up and the Exam Task. Then make a plan.

Now complete the Exam Task. Remember to answer all of the questions.

Read the email from your friend, Max.

● ● ●	Email Message	↗

From: Max
To:

It's great you can come to my street party and of course you can bring your friend Pedro. When did you meet him? What does he look like? What's he like?

Max

Write an email to Max and answer the questions.

Write 25–35 words.

Useful Expressions

Greetings
Hi Jack
Hello!
Dear Jack

Sign-offs
Love, Emily
See you soon!
See you on Saturday!
Best wishes

Giving examples
that's why
because
so
for example
but
and

Describing personality
He's / She's very …
He / She likes …
He / She seems …

Describing appearance
He's / She's tall / short …
He's / She's got … hair …
  eyes … skin
His / Her hair is … / eyes
  are …

Exam Close-up

Answering all the questions

- There are usually three questions and you must answer all of them.
- Underline the question words to make sure you understand each question.

A diamond jubilee street party in Bristol, England

2 Happy Elephants

Before you watch

A Look at the photos. What are the differences and similarities between them? Match a–d with 1–4.

1 Working elephant with driver ☐
2 Elephant in captivity in a zoo ☐
3 Elephant in captivity in a circus ☐
4 Elephants in the wild ☐

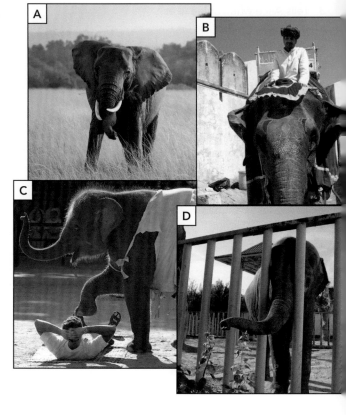

While you watch

B Watch the video and decide if these statements are T (True) or F (False).

1 Elephants and people have worked together for over 2,000 years. ☐
2 Mike Hackenberger, an elephant trainer, talks to his elephants. ☐
3 Not everyone is sure that animals feel happiness. ☐
4 Mike Hackenberger says elephant training is worse than in the past. ☐
5 The elephant called Limba was happier alone. ☐
6 Elephants love swimming. ☐

After you watch

C Complete the summary of the video below using these words.

closely   feelings   happier   happiness   intelligent   normal   similar   wild

Elephants are large, gentle and **(1)** _____ animals. When they work with people, they are not in the **(2)** _____. How can elephants be happy in captivity? Mike Hackenberger, an animal trainer at Baltimore zoo, believes he knows the answer. His elephants are very healthy and seem to be happy. He talks to his elephants and says they make happy sounds! Many people who work **(3)** _____ with animals say that animals have **(4)** _____ and can experience **(5)** _____. Others are not certain, but everyone agrees that elephants seem safer and **(6)** _____ when their home in captivity is **(7)** _____ to life in the wild. Their lives are happier and more **(8)** _____ when they are with other elephants than when they are alone.

Ideas Focus

- Is it right to keep animals in captivity? Why? / Why not?
- Is it right for people to use animals for work and transport? Why? / Why not?
- Do you think animals have feelings? Why? / Why not?

Vocabulary

A Write the dates as words.

1 21/1 _____
2 15/3 _____
3 2/7 _____
4 23/8 _____
5 4/10 _____
6 30/12 _____

B Complete the sentences with the correct nationality adjective.

1 I've got an _____ car. It's a red Ferrari! **(Italy)**
2 In Athens, I heard _____ music on the radio. **(Greece)**
3 I think the _____ language is easy to learn. **(England)**
4 Did you eat a lot of _____ food in Beijing? **(China)**
5 Barcelona is a famous _____ football team. **(Spain)**
6 Did you know that _____ people are very tall? **(Netherlands)**

C Circle the correct words.

Hi. My name's Nick and I'm 13. My **(1)** brothers / sisters are Emma and Helen. My **(2)** brother / sister is George, and he's 10. Our **(3)** parents / grandparents are Kelly and James. They got married 20 years ago. My **(4)** parents / grandparents are Michael and Jenny. They've got two children – my dad James is their **(5)** son / daughter, and my **(6)** aunt / uncle Betty is their **(7)** son / daughter. Betty's **(8)** wife / husband is my **(9)** aunt / uncle Tim, and their children are my **(10)** cousins / twins.

D Complete the sentences with the words.

| beard blue braces freckles moustache pale short straight tan |

1 Samantha has got long, _____, brown hair. Her eyes are _____ and she's got _____ all over her face.
2 Tania's skin is usually_____, but she went on holiday to Spain and now she's got a lovely _____. She's also got _____ on her teeth.
3 Jack's 21 years old. He's got _____ dark hair and a funny _____ under his nose. He's also got a _____ and sometimes food falls into it!

E Circle the correct words.

1 My brothers annoy / annoying me all the time!
2 My cousin Sophia is very beauty / beautiful.
3 Jo would be a good nurse because she's really care / caring.
4 Everyone likes Max because he's friend / friendly.
5 I love / lovely my family very much.
6 Don't worry / worried – everything is OK.

F Complete the sentences with these prepositions.

| about by of to with |

1 My granny is kind _____ everyone.
2 I'm angry _____ my twin brothers!
3 Are you shocked _____ the news?
4 What are you worried _____, Tom?
5 I'm scared _____ spiders and snakes!

Grammar

A Circle the correct words.

1 Do you like / likes French food?
2 They not want / don't want to go to school.
3 Are / Do the children eating now?
4 Harry doesn't / isn't know the answer.
5 My cousin Catherine lives / live in Australia.
6 I'm study / studying for my exams this week.
7 People buy / buying clocks in Switzerland.
8 The dogs aren't / don't running in the park.

B Write the adverbs of frequency in the correct place.

1 I get up early in the morning. (**usually**)
2 She is late for school. (**hardly ever**)
3 The Smith family goes to Spain in July. (**always**)
4 My friends are busy on Saturdays. (**often**)
5 Uncle Bill visits us in summer. (**never**)
6 My friends go to the cinema. (**sometimes**)

C Complete the questions with the words. Sometimes more than one answer is possible.

Who	Why	When	What	Where	What time

1 _____ is your sister?
2 _____ are they doing?
3 _____ does she work?
4 _____ do you start school?
5 _____ are your friends?
6 _____ are you crying?

D Complete the sentences with the Past Simple or the Past Continuous of the verbs in brackets.

1 They _____ to the shops when I _____ them yesterday. (**walk, see**)
2 I _____ the dishes while my mum _____ pizza. (**wash, make**)
3 He _____ in his bedroom, but he _____. (**be, not sleep**)
4 When my friends _____ me, they _____ to a football match. (**call, go**)
5 She _____ to the supermarket, but she _____ milk. (**go, not buy**)
6 The sun _____ and the birds _____ that morning. (**shine, sing**)
7 When I _____ home from school, my dad _____ TV. (**come, watch**)
8 _____ your phone when you _____ the house? (**you / forget, leave**)

E Circle the correct words.

1 Used you / Did you use to live in Manchester a few years ago?
2 I didn't use / wasn't used to have short hair, but now I do.
3 We are used / used to go to France every year for our holiday.
4 When I was younger, I never / didn't use to read, but I love it now.
5 Did your cousins used / use to come to England to stay with you?
6 I'm a good student now, but I didn't use to be / being.

3 Let's Get Together

Reading:	multiple-choice & matching, understanding the context
Vocabulary:	party- and technology-related words, phrasal verbs, multiple-choice sentences, identifying collocations
Grammar:	present continuous for future plans & arrangements, prepositions of time, place, direction & prepositional phrases, open cloze, choosing the correct preposition
Listening:	multiple-choice (pictures), choosing the correct picture
Speaking:	asking & answering questions, talking to a partner, asking for details about events, checking information
Writing:	a poster, writing important information, finding the correct information, expressing time, giving contact details

Two horned puffins sat on a rock. Round Island, Alaska

Reading

A Read the information in 1–5. What do they have in common? Choose the best option from a–c.

a thank yous   b invitations   c asking for help

1

Email Message

From: Waverley High School
To: All students
Subject: School Summer Fair

Dear students

Don't forget! The school fair is on next Saturday at 3 p.m.

We hope to see everyone there.

2
Hi, Cathy. Do u want 2 come 2 my sleepover on Friday night? It will be a lot of fun!!!

Read 15:45

3

Dear Tom

It's a Fancy Dress Party!
Saturday 8 p.m. at 10 Smith Street

Best costume wins a prize!

4

New Message

To:
Message: Hey everyone! It's the Champions League final next Saturday! Want to watch it at my place? The address is 23 Mawron Street. See you there!

Send   Cancel

5

Anna, I'm having a New Year's Eve party. Would you like to come?

B What different ways of inviting someone to an event are used in A?

C Invite a friend to a party. Use a method from A (e.g. email). Include the following.

- what the event is
- where it is
- what time it starts
- who is going

D Quickly read the article and write the correct heading for each paragraph.

How do they celebrate?
When is this special day?
What do they celebrate?

Do people work on that day?
What do they usually eat?

Word Focus

settler: a person who arrives from another country to live in a new place and use the land

harbour: a closed area of water where boats are safe

spectacular: very exciting to look at

Aussie: something or someone Australian

backyard: an open space at the back of a house

invade: to go to a place and take it from others

Australia Day

1 _____

Australia Day is the national day of Australia and it is on January 26. That was the day in 1788 when the British ships arrived with the first white settlers.

2 _____

It's a public holiday, so people take a break from work. Banks, post offices, and most businesses are closed. The schools are already closed then for the summer holidays.

3 _____

People go swimming, spend time with family and friends, go to concerts, watch sports events, have parties and relax. In many places there are firework displays. The fireworks over Sydney Harbour are spectacular and thousands of people go there at night to enjoy the fun. Many people arrive at the harbour in the morning to get the best places to sit and watch the fireworks.

4 _____

Food is important at this celebration. At picnics across the country Aussies enjoy traditional meat pies, sandwiches with colourful sprinkles, and little square cakes with chocolate and coconut on them called *lamingtons*. It's also popular to have a barbecue on Australia Day. People invite friends and family and spend the day cooking, eating, having fun and playing cricket in their backyards.

5 _____

However, it's important to understand that not all Australians celebrate this day. Many Aboriginal Australians are still unhappy because the British invaded their country and they took the aboriginal land. But today, Australia Day celebrates modern Australia: its freedom, its lifestyle and cultures, the land and its beauty and its future.

Read the *Exam Close-up*. Then read the short dialogues in Part 1 and the longer dialogue in Part 2 of the *Exam Task* below and decide what is happening in each.

Now complete the *Exam Task*. Remember to think about the context.

Exam Task

Part 1

Complete the five conversations. Choose **A**, **B**, or **C**.

1 Why didn't you watch the fireworks?
   A I was studying for an exam.
   B It was spectacular.
   C I was worried about you.

2 I can't come to the barbecue at your house.
   A How amazing.
   B That's a pity.
   C Good luck.

3 Would you like to have a picnic with us?
   A Yes, I did.
   B I hope not.
   C That'd be lovely.

4 Who made these delicious lamingtons?
   A Why not?
   B My dad did.
   C Yes, I did.

5 Shall we play cricket?
   A Good idea.
   B Yes, I do.
   C I hope so.

Part 2

Complete the telephone conversation. What does Gino say to Nick? Choose the correct answer **A–H**. There are three letters you do not need to use.

Nick: Hi, Gino. Would you like to come to a party next Sunday?

Gino: (6) _____

Nick: It's Australia Day, our national day.

Gino: (7) _____

Nick: I know. I want you to enjoy it with us because you are a new Australian.

Gino: (8) _____

Nick: At Bondi beach. A lot of Aussies go to the beach that day.

Gino: (9) _____

Nick: We usually have some food and drinks, we swim and surf.

Gino: (10) _____

Nick: It is. It's a great way to celebrate our country!

A Thanks. Where are you having the party?
B Why are you going there?
C I'd love to. What are we celebrating?
D What do you do there?
E Well, I'm not sure about that.
F It sounds like a lot of fun.
G Is it difficult to surf?
H Oh yes! This will be the first time for me.

---

6 Complete the sentences with the verbs to make collocations. Look back at the text for help if necessary. There are two verbs you do not need to use.

| do go have make give spend take |

1 The school holidays are boring! I don't know how to _____ my time!

2 Do you want me to _____ a cake for the party?

3 Every summer I travel to Greece and I _____ swimming at fantastic beaches.

4 It's really hot today and I can't walk any more. I need to _____ a break.

5 I can buy some meat and sausages today and we can _____ a barbecue.

- 'National celebrations make everyone feel happy.' Do you agree? Why? / Why not?
- Which is your favourite celebration? Why is it special to you?

Ideas Focus

Vocabulary

A Match the words from the list with the pictures.

Things to take to Becky's party

balloons – pink and blue if possible

candles – 12 for the cake

confetti – enough for kids to throw over Becky

presents – for Becky

sparklers – 20; one for each kid to hold

streamers – pink and blue to put on tables

B Circle the correct answers.

1 **A:** Why do you hang out / hang up with Melanie?
  B: Because we get on / get together very well.

2 **A:** Did you go around / go out with your friends last night?
  B: No, I stayed in / stayed up and went to bed early.

3 **A:** Why did you ask about / ask for Jane's phone number?
  B: I want to take her away / take her out on a date.

4 **A:** We have to call back / call off the picnic.
  B: Oh, no! I was looking forward to / looking up to it.

C Match the phrasal verbs you didn't use in B with their meanings.

1 _____ : go on holiday with someone
2 _____ : visit someone at their home
3 _____ : respect someone
4 _____ : not go to bed
5 _____ : end a phone call
6 _____ : phone someone that phoned you first
7 _____ : ask how someone is
8 _____ : meet someone socially

D Complete the expressions with the correct words.

having	friend	make	great time	getting	free	have	company	fun	sharp

1 'Did you have _____ at Juan's fancy dress party?'
  'Yes, I had a _____.'

2 Elizabeth is my best _____. I really like spending time with her because she's good _____.

3 'Are you _____ on Saturday night? I'm having a party and it starts at seven _____.'

4 'Welcome, Harry. Come in and _____ a seat. Please, _____ yourself at home.'

5 I have to go now, it's _____ late. Thanks for _____ me. I hope to see you soon.'

Read and answer the questions.

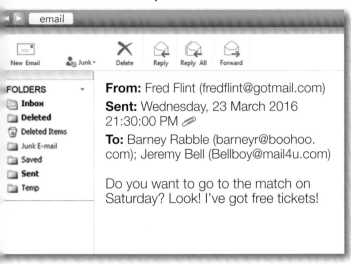

◄ ► □ email	

New Email   Junk ▾   Delete   Reply   Reply All   Forward

FOLDERS ▾
- Inbox
- Deleted
- Deleted Items
- Junk E-mail
- Saved
- Sent
- Temp

From: Fred Flint (fredflint@gotmail.com)
Sent: Wednesday, 23 March 2016 21:30:00 PM 📎
To: Barney Rabble (barneyr@boohoo.com); Jeremy Bell (Bellboy@mail4u.com)

Do you want to go to the match on Saturday? Look! I've got free tickets!

1 Which of Fred's folders is the email in?
_____

2 Who received the email?
_____

3 Which of their folders is the email in?
_____

4 What can they do if they don't want to keep the email?_____

5 Is there an attachment?
_____

6 What do you think it is?
_____

7 Read out the email addresses of all the boys.

Circle the correct words.

A modern grandmother

My grandmother says that I am very lucky to have so many useful (**1**) devices / computers that make life easy. When she was a teenager, there was no (**2**) digital / mechanical technology. She didn't have a mobile phone. She used a (**3**) landline / handline to call her friends and everyone at home could hear what she said. Now, she has a smartphone so she can (**4**) do / make calls and send texts.

There was no internet, so she couldn't go online or send emails. She had to send everything by (**5**) letter / post. When she sent letters to her cousins in Canada, the letters took a long time to arrive. She laughed when I told her that we call it (**6**) 'fail / snail mail' because it's slow! Recently, she bought a small (**7**) desktop / laptop computer that she takes with her. Now, she uses the internet to (**8**) communicate / contact her family and friends overseas. She says it's amazing that she can (**9**) click / tick 'Send' and her mail can go anywhere in the world. The computer has a (**10**) net / web cam too, and she chats with her sisters in Canada. She checks her email every day. She's a very modern woman!

Read the Exam Close-up. Then read the Exam Task and think of the words that can go in each gap.

Now complete the Exam Task.

Exam Task

Read the sentences about using the internet. Choose the best word (**A, B** or **C**) for each answer.

1 Julie usually goes _____ in the evening.
  A computer   **B** internet   **C** online

2 First, she _____ her email for any new mail.
  A checks   **B** reads   **C** sees

3 After that, she _____ the net for a little while.
  A skis   **B** surfs   **C** swims

4 Julie doesn't like to _____ time on the internet.
  A keep   **B** use   **C** waste

5 But she thinks it's a great way to stay in _____ with people.
  A touch   **B** company   **C** close

Exam Close-up

Identifying collocations

- Collocations are words that go together (often a verb and a noun).
- Some tasks have gaps in the texts – they sometimes remove one of the words from the collocations.
- Look at the sentence and at the words before and after the gap.
- If you think you know the answer, look at the choices. Is it there?
- If it isn't, look at the choices and try each one in the gap and say the sentences to yourself. Choose the one that you think fits best.

- Do you like social network sites? Why? / Why not?
- How much time do you spend online? Is it too much? Why? / Why not?

Ideas Focus

Grammar

Present Continuous for future plans & arrangements

A Read the conversation below and underline examples of the Present Continuous.

A: What are you doing at the weekend?

B: We're going to Sue's party. Are you coming?

A: No, I'm not. I'm visiting my aunt.

▷ **Grammar Focus p. 162 (3.1)**

B Look at the sentences in A and answer these questions.

1 They're talking about the present / the future.
2 They're talking about plans / something that might happen.
3 We can / can't use the Present Continuous to talk about future, if we are talking about plans or arrangements.
4 We make a Present Continuous question with be / do + subject + verb + -ing and a negative with subject + be / do + not + verb + -ing.

C Look at Sue's diary for next week. Complete the sentences and questions with the Present Continuous. Use the verbs in brackets.

Mon	Tues	Weds	Thurs	Fri
study for tests!	do tests at school ☹	go shopping at the mall, get new jeans	download music for party	buy food and drink for party

Sat	Sun
PARTY!!! ☺ from 8 till late!	Help Mum tidy up! ☹

1 Why ——————— for tests on Monday? **(study)**
2 She's studying on Monday because ——————— tests at school on Tuesday. **(do)**
3 ——————— shopping on Tuesday? **(go)**
4 No, ——————— shopping on Wednesday. **(go)**
5 Where ——————— new jeans on Wednesday? **(get)**
6 ——————— new jeans at the mall. **(get)**
7 ——————— food for the party on Thursday. **(not buy)**
8 ——————— music on Thursday. **(download)**
9 ——————— the food for the party on Friday. **(buy)**
10 The party ——————— at 8 pm on Saturday. **(start)**
11 Who ——————— on Sunday? **(help)**
12 ——————— her mum; they ———————. **(help, tidy up)**

D Circle the activities below that you are doing this weekend. Then talk to a partner about your weekend plans.

go shopping	go swimming	go to a party
do homework	meet friends	play basketba
play computer games	tidy my room	visit relatives

"What are you doing this weekend?"

"I'm going shopping with my mum"

E Look at the tickets and answer the questions in your notebook using the Present Continuous.

1 Where is the band playing?
2 When is the band playing?
3 When is the match starting?
4 Where are the teams playing?
5 Is the passenger flying business class or economy class?
6 Where is the passenger sitting?

T001 $39.00	An evening with **PEARL JAM**
ROW **M** SEAT **8**	**U.S Bank Arena** 100 Broadway St/Cincinnati OH
10/01/15	WED Oct 01 2015 7:30PM

NEW YORK JETS vs **MIAMI DOLPHINS**

GATES OPEN 12:3
KICK OFF 14:30
ENTER VIA **E**
Block **300**
ROW **10**
Block **58**

10 OCTOBER
WEMBLEY STADIUM

UNITED FLIGHT U3054 — ANNA PETERSON

DEPARTURE GATE
E12
BUSINESS CLASS
BOARDS AT
2:10PM NOV 09
259 8712 4126 2

UNITED FLIGHT U3054
SEAT NUMBER
19A BUSINESS CL
ANNA PETERSON
PHOENIX AZ TO DENVE
DEPARTURE
2:50PM

▥ **UNITED** BOARDING PASS

Prepositions of time, place, direction & prepositional phrases

F **Read the sentences. <u>Underline</u> all the prepositions. The first has been done for you.**

1 The plane is leaving <u>at</u> midnight tomorrow.
2 They are having tests at school next week.
3 We are playing basketball on Monday evening.
4 My brother was writing on his desk.
5 The cat jumped onto my bed.
6 Dolphins live in the sea.
7 Sue is having a party in June.
8 The actor walked into the café for a drink.
9 What is inside the box?
10 The tourists are travelling to Greece next week.

G **Look back at the sentences in F and decide if each one refers to time (T), place (P) or direction (D).**

> **Be careful**
> When we describe movement (going from one place
> • to another), we use prepositions like *to, into, onto, towards* and *from*.
>
> When we describe position (where something is), we use prepositions like 'in', 'on' and 'at'.

H **Complete the rules with 'in', 'on' or 'at'.**

We use _____ with clock times and some time periods, e.g. 'night', 'weekends'.

We use _____ for longer periods of time, e.g. years, months, seasons, parts of the day (morning, afternoon, evening) and to describe how long before something happens in future.

We use _____ for days.

I **Read the sentences and underline the prepositional phrases. The first is done for you.**

1 We live in the house <u>at the end of</u> the street.
2 The teacher stood at the front of the class.
3 The photos are in the middle of the book.
4 The answers are at the back of the book.
5 The page number is at the bottom of the page.
6 The title is at the top of the page.
7 The photo is on the right / left of the text.

▶ Grammar Focus pp. 162 & 163 (3.2 to 3.5)

Complete the sentences with 'in', 'on' or 'at'.

1 It's starting _____ 8 _____ the evening.
2 The next holiday is _____ March 25th.
3 Our cousins are visiting us _____ March.
4 The weather is hot _____ summer.
5 The baby doesn't sleep much _____ night.
6 The family goes shopping _____ Saturdays.
7 Dad left school _____ 1990.
8 The plane is leaving _____ five minutes!
9 He usually has a sandwich _____ lunchtime.
10 We're meeting _____ Monday night.

K **Read the *Exam Close-up* and then complete the *Exam Task*.**

Exam Task

Complete the email from a manager at a museum. Write **ONE** word for each space.

> ● ● ●
>
> **Email Message**
>
> Re: the new exhibition 'The Mummy'
>
> Dear colleagues,
>
> The museum is opening a new exhibition
> **(1)** _____ a week. The main exhibit is the amazing Egyptian mummy. It will be in the middle
> **(2)** _____ the room, so that it is the first thing that visitors will see. The other objects from the tomb will be
> **(3)** _____ the back of the room **(4)** _____ glass cases. These include the jars and furniture **(5)** _____ the tomb. Some parts from the inside of the dead person's body were **(6)** _____ the jars. The furniture was there because Egyptians thought the dead person could take it with them **(7)** _____ the afterlife. On the right **(8)** _____ the mummy there will be a display, to show how ancient Egyptians created mummies.
> **(9)** _____ the opposite wall, visitors will see X-ray photos showing what is inside the mummy! We also need to update the website **(10)** _____ the morning!
>
> Regards, James

Exam Close-up

Choosing the correct preposition

• Before you complete a gapped text, quickly read the whole text first.

• Then go back and read each sentence carefully. Look at the word before and after the gap. Decide what type of word is missing (preposition, noun, etc.).

• If a preposition is missing, decide if it is connected to time, place, or direction.

• Write your chosen preposition, then read the complete sentence to yourself and check your answer.

Listening

A Look at the photos in 1–3. Work with a partner and discuss the similarities and differences between each set of three photos (a–c).

1

2

3

B Find a photo in A to match these words. Then work with a partner and brainstorm more vocabulary to describe the pictures in A.

> a month   a photograph   a sister

C Match questions a–c with 1–3 in A.

a What present are they giving? ☐

b When is the music festival? ☐

c Who is the boy taking to the party? ☐

D 3.1 ▶❙❙ Now listen and circle the correct pictures in Exercise A.

E Read the *Exam-Close-up*. Then look at the *Exam Task*. Note down any vocabulary connected to the pictures and think about any similarities and differences.

F 3.2 ▶❙❙ Now complete the *Exam Task*.

Exam Close-up

Choosing the correct picture

- Sometimes you have to listen and choose the correct picture from three options.
- Prepare by looking carefully at each set of photos. Brainstorm vocabulary connected to the photos.
- Think about the similarities and differences between each set of three pictures.
- You will hear each conversation twice. Make short notes when you listen the first time.
- Using your notes, choose the correct picture.

Exam Task

You will hear five short conversations. You will hear each conversation twice. There is one question for each conversation. For each question, choose the right answer (**A**, **B** or **C**).

1 Who is the girl bringing to the party?

a   b   c

2 What is the girl wearing to the wedding?

a    b   c

3 What are they giving to grandad?

a   b   c

4 What time will the concert finish?

a   b   c

5 When are they going to the music festival?

a   b   c

G 3.3 ▶❙❙ Listen again and check your answers.

Speaking

A Put the events in order, from favourite (1) to least favourite (6). Explain why to a partner.

- a family wedding ☐
- b end of school disco ☐
- c party to celebrate a team's win ☐
- d a child's birthday party ☐
- e New Year ☐
- f Christmas party ☐

B What information should you include on an invitation to an event?

- date
- _____
- _____
- _____
- _____
- _____

C Write an invitation to an event from A.

D Work with a partner. Ask questions about your partner's event and note down the information. Check your answers then change roles.

E Read the *Exam Close-up* then match sentences 1–4 with situations a–d.

1. OK, thanks … and when …?
2. The party is on Monday 17th April, from 5 pm till 11 pm.
3. Sorry, I didn't understand. Could you repeat that?
4. What I bring to the party?

a. You didn't hear what your partner said.
b. Your question wasn't grammatically correct.
c. You responded to the information your partner gave you.
d. You gave a full answer.

Exam Close-up

Talking to a partner

- Remember to listen to the instructions carefully and make sure you understand.
- Read through all of your prompt cards to help you prepare to ask or answer questions.
- Remember that this task is a conversation, so take turns and don't interrupt.
- Give full answers to the questions.
- If you don't understand your partner, ask them to repeat what they said.

F Now work in pairs to complete the *Exam Task*. Use the *Useful Expressions* to help you.

Useful Expressions

Asking for details about events
Where is it?
When time does it start / finish?
What should / shall I bring?
Is there a phone number / an email address?
Can I take my friend / boyfriend / girlfriend / partner?

Checking information
Sorry, I didn't understand.
Can you repeat that / say that again, please?
Can you spell that, please?

Exam Task

Task 1

Student A: Here is some information about Tom's birthday party.

Student B: You are invited to Tom's party but you don't know the details about the party, so ask **A** some questions about it. Turn to page 179.

> Come and help me celebrate my 14th Birthday party!
>
> Tom invites you to his swimming party on Saturday, 15th June at The Fairway Sports Centre, Dee Road, Liverpool.
>
> Time: 5pm till 7pm
> Please call or text 07795 2271167 to say if you are coming or not.
> Bring your swimwear … and a present!

Task 2

Student B: Here is some information about Mel and Luke's wedding.

Student A: You are invited to the wedding but you don't know the details about the wedding, so ask **B** some questions about it. Turn to page 178.

> Together with their families, Mel and Luke invite you (and a partner) to their wedding.
>
> 21 December 2016
>
> One thirty in the afternoon at St John's Church, Steeple Road, Cambridge.
>
> Followed by food and drink at the Duke Hotel, Cambridge.
>
> RSVP by email to Mel's parents, John and Wendy Baker: jwbaker@outlook.com

- Are birthdays important to you? Why? / Why not?
- Do you enjoy parties? Why? / Why not?

Ideas Focus

Writing: a poster

Writing important information

- When we create posters or write notes and notices, we write down important information in just a few words.
- This information is usually about dates, times, places, events, phone numbers, addresses, activities, etc.
- It's important to know how to write this kind of information correctly.

Lodge Field school fair in Shropshire, England

A Match the information to the headings.

1	20:30	a	date
2	21/01/16	b	price
3	surprise party	c	time
4	taxi	d	address
5	£10	e	event
6	12 Smith Street	f	transport

B Read the poster for a school fair and an email Lucy wrote to her friend about it. What kind of information is in the two texts? Use the list in the *Learning Focus* to help you.

C Two students used the poster and email to complete their notes. Which student completed them correctly?

Come to the school fair at

Waverley High School

Food
jewellery
CDs
DVDs
video games
and
more for sale

Sunday 12th June, 3 p.m. – 10 p.m.
Concert at 5 p.m.

◄ ► email

From: Lucy
To: Phoebe

Do you want to go to the school fair together? Joe's band, The Block Heads, are playing in the afternoon. We can meet in the town at 4.30 p.m. and then take the bus. Text me (0402604174) or ring me at home (6528421) to let me know.

Student 1	
Waverley High School fair	
Day:	12th June
Meeting time:	5 p.m.
Meeting place:	in the town
Travel by:	bus
Lucy's mobile phone number:	6528421

Student 2	
Waverley High School fair	
Day:	Sunday
Meeting time:	4.30 p.m.
Meeting place:	in the town
Travel by:	bus
Lucy's mobile phone number:	0402604174

D Now make a poster for a fair at your school. Include the following information.

- where it is
- the day and time
- what will be there
- price
- contact number / email

Read the *Exam Close-up*. Then look at the *Exam Task*. Which of the following will you need to find to complete your notes?

email address   name of something / someone
telephone number   place   time   date   price

Now complete the *Exam Task*.

Exam Task

Read Toby's notes and the email from Mr Watts. Complete the poster.

Oakford School Winter Fair

- School band 'The Oakford Gang' playing Christmas songs 3.30 p.m. – 4.15.p.m.
- Lots of rides.
- Dance competition for students 4.30 p.m. – 5.30 p.m.
- People should email me at toby.lane@oakford.com for information / tickets.
- Ask head teacher (Mr Watts) about where, food and drink, ticket prices.

◀ ▶ email

From: Mr Watts
To: Toby Lane

Dear Toby

I like your idea to have a School Winter Fair. You can use the school playground on that date: Saturday 19th December, between 3.00 p.m. and 6.00 p.m. We can sell hot chocolate, tea, coffee, cake and biscuits. Tickets should be £3 each for adults and £1.50 for children. You need to organise the rides and make a poster. Let me know if you need more help.

Best wishes
Mr Watts

Oakford School Winter Fair

When? (1) _____, from 3pm until 6pm.

Where? (2) _____

3.30pm–4.15pm: Come and listen to

(3) '_____' playing Christmas songs!

4.30pm–5.30pm: Watch Oakford students break-dance, waltz or do ballet in the dance competition.

Hot chocolate, tea, coffee, cakes and biscuits for sale.

Prices: (4) _____

Contact Toby for more information / tickets: (5) _____

Useful Expressions

Expressing time
a.m. (before 12 midday)
p.m. (after 12 midday)
in the morning / afternoon / evening
at night
from ... until
starts at ... and finishes at ...

Giving contact details
Email me at toby.lane@oakford.com.
Call me on 0402604174.

Exam Close-up

Finding the correct information

- There are five items to complete in the note-taking task and all of the information you need is in two texts.

- Read through the two texts first. Then focus on the gaps you need to complete and check that you understand the kind of information you need to find, e.g. a time, a place, a person, etc.

- Then go back to the texts and look for the kind of information you identified.

- You will often see lots of different options for each kind of information, so read the text carefully to find the correct answer.

41

3 Fat Tuesday

New Orleans, USA

Before you watch

A Match the words with their meanings.

1 Carnival	☐	**a** when people and vehicles move through the streets in a celebration
2 Lent	☐	**b** a celebration in spring before Lent
3 costume party	☐	**c** a vehicle that is decorated for a parade
4 parade	☐	**d** the period of 40 days before Easter Sunday
5 float	☐	**e** a party where people dress in unusual clothes and masks

While you watch

B Watch the video and decide if these statements are T (True) or F (False).

1 The Romans used to celebrate a spring festival. ☐
2 In 1780 French people came to New Orleans. ☐
3 Mardi Gras means 'Fat Thursday'. ☐
4 In 1857, the first Mardi Gras parade took place. ☐
5 The Mardi Gras colours are purple, green and gold. ☐
6 The Mardi Gras celebrations end at midnight. ☐

After you watch

C Complete the summary of the video below using these words.

> green   next   modern   biggest   French   cake   celebration   rich

Carnival started in Roman times as a **(1)** _____ of spring.
Later, it became a feast before Lent. This is when Christians stop eating
(2) _____ foods. The **(3)** _____ arrived in
New Orleans in 1718 with their Mardi Gras tradition and it soon turned into the
(4) _____ celebration. Mardi Gras means 'Fat Tuesday' in French and
this is when people eat all the rich food before the start of Lent. Today, the New
Orleans Mardi Gras is the **(5)** _____ in the United States. You can
buy special King Cakes, coloured purple, **(6)** _____ and gold. Each
(7) _____ contains a hidden toy baby. The person who finds this,
buys the **(8)** _____ cake. At midnight Mardi Gras is over until
next year.

Ideas Focus

- Do you enjoy celebrating in the streets? Why? / Why not?
- Are street celebrations a good idea for a city? Why? / Why not?

4 A Day in the Life

Reading:	multiple-choice, finding the right part of the text quickly
Vocabulary:	everyday jobs-, money-, shopping & food-related words
Grammar:	*be going to* & *will*, countable & uncountable nouns & quantifiers
Listening:	multiple choice, understanding what to listen for
Speaking:	prompt cards, eating out, taking an order, ordering food & drink, asking questions correctly
Writing:	an informal email, using adjectives in emails, using short forms, punctuation & greetings, talking about plans, giving opinions, inviting

A young inuit seen picking
ice for drinking water in
Kangertivatsiakajik, Greenland

Reading

A What is a typical day for you? Tell your partner about your everyday activities. Use the pictures and your own ideas.

"Everyday I get up at 7 o'clock …"

get up

brush my teeth

go to school

walk the dog

do my homework

play basketball

B Quickly read the article about Fu's day. Which of the activities in Exercise A does he talk about?

C Read the text again and answer these questions.

1 What does Fu eat for breakfast?
2 How long does it take him to get to school?
3 Where does he eat his lunch?
4 Does he like sport?
5 At what time in the evening does he have a snack?

Word Focus

the capital: the most important city of a country

porridge: a soft food cooked in water or milk and eaten hot for breakfast

break: a time for students to talk or play

physical education: a class at school where students do exercise and play sport

steamed: food that is cooked with the hot gas from boiling water

FU'S DAY

What's it like to live in China? This is how one boy spends a typical school day.

My name is **Fu Wang**. I am 12 years old. I live with my parents and grandparents in the capital, Beijing.

6:30 A.M.
I get up, wash and get dressed. My grandmother makes breakfast for me. I usually have congee for breakfast. Congee is a rice porridge.

7:15 A.M.
I walk to school. It takes about 15 minutes. I go to an international school and many foreign students study there.

D Read the *Exam Close-up*. Then read the *Exam Task* and underline the key words in the questions.

E Now complete the *Exam Task*. Use the words you underlined and scan the text for similar words.

Exam Task

Read the article about Fu. Are sentences **1–8** 'Right' **(A)** or 'Wrong' **(B)**? If there is not enough information to answer 'Right' **(A)** or 'Wrong' **(B)**, choose 'Doesn't say' **(C)**.

1 Fu makes breakfast before he goes to school. ☐
2 There are students at his school who are not Chinese. ☐
3 He learns a language in the morning. ☐
4 The students don't have a lot of time to eat lunch. ☐
5 Fu wants to become a basketball player. ☐
6 Fu goes home as soon as school finishes. ☐
7 He has dinner after five o'clock. ☐
8 Fu is tired when he goes to bed. ☐

Finding the right part of the text quickly

- Key words are the most important words in the question.
- Underline the key words in the first question, then scan the text quickly for any similar words and underline those too.
- Read that part of the text carefully and check that it answers the question. Then write your answer. Continue in the same way with the other questions.

F The verb *get* is used a lot in English. Look back at the text and circle every *get* you see. Look at the words that come after each *get*.

G Match these uses of *get* from the text with their definitions.

1 **get** up   a arrive at
2 **get** to school / **get** home   b become
3 don't **get**   c buy
4 **get** some snacks   d leave your bed
5 **get** tired   e receive
6 **get** a lot of homework   f (don't) understand

7:30 A.M.
When I get to school, I hand in my homework. Then I have three classes in the morning – Chinese, English and history.

11:30 A.M.
It's time for lunch and I eat in the school cafeteria. It's a long break, so after I eat, I usually hang out with my classmates. But we are going to have exams soon and our teachers want us to study during the break.

1:30 P.M.
Afternoon classes start. We have geography and physical education, which is my favourite. I really love sport and I want to be an athlete. Last year, I won a running race at my school's mini-Olympic Games.

3:30 P.M.
Classes finish, but I stay so that my teachers can explain anything that I don't get.

4:10 P.M.
I walk home with some of my friends. On the way, we get some snacks and chat. Sometimes, we stop to play football or basketball.

5:00 P.M.
I get home and I have a rest before dinner. For dinner, we usually have some rice or steamed bread, meat and vegetables. After dinner, I watch TV. I like movies and sports programmes.

6:30 P.M.
I do my homework. I get a lot of homework from my teachers. At 8:30 I have a snack, then I study again. Sometimes I get tired, but I really want to do well in my exams.

10:00 P.M.
I organise my school bag for the next day. Then it's time for bed.

- Is your typical day easier than Fu's? Why? / Why not?
- 'To get good marks, students should do four hours of homework every day.' Do you agree? Why? / Why not?

Ideas Focus

Vocabulary

A Match the everyday jobs we do at home to the pictures.

dusting   vacuuming the carpet   making the bed   doing the washing
sweeping the floor   ironing   doing the washing up   cleaning the bathroom

B Circle the correct words.

1 Every day from Monday to Friday, I get / rise / go up at 7 o'clock.

2 I start to get ready. First, I do / make / take a quick shower.

3 Then I brush / put / make my hair and I dry it with the hairdryer.

4 After that, I choose my clothes and be / get / put dressed.

5 Then I make / do / have my bed so that my bedroom looks tidy.

6 By this time, I'm hungry, so I do / make / take my breakfast.

7 I usually do / find / have a cup of coffee with my breakfast.

8 Then I help / make / do the washing up and after that I'm ready for school.

C Complete the dialogues about jobs at home with the correct words.

do   hang out   tidy   wash   water

1 **A:** Can you please _____ your bedroom, Joe? It's such a mess!
   B: Yes, mum. I'll do it in a minute.

2 **A:** I can do the washing, dad.
   B: Thanks. Can you _____ the clothes to dry, too?

3 **A:** Do you _____ the garden in the winter?
   B: No, I don't.

4 **A:** Who is going to _____ the car this week?
   B: I'll do it.

5 **A:** When do you _____ the housework?
   B: I'm too busy in the week so I do it on Saturday morning.

Use both words to complete the sentences.

1 **pay   spend**
   A: We _____ a lot of money at the supermarket.
   B: Yes, and we _____ a lot for some products.

2 **do   go**
   A: Let's _____ shopping. We need some bread.
   B: I don't want to _____ the shopping now. I'm busy.

3 **buy   rent**
   A: Do you _____ the flat that you live in?
   B: Yes, but we're going to _____ one soon.

4 **lend   borrow**
   A: Can you _____ me some money?
   B: Sure. How much do you need to _____?

5 **make   save**
   A: How can I _____ money?
   B: You can work hard and _____ it.

Choose the correct words to complete the text.

Lizzy's Saturday Job

My sister Lizzy is 16. She's a student, but she's also got a job. She works in a supermarket every Saturday. Sometimes, she the (**1**) till / cashier. She's very friendly and she likes talking to the (**2**) customers / shelves. She has a chat with them when they take their shopping out of the (**3**) receipt / trolley and she puts it into bags for them. Then they pay, she puts the money into the (**4**) till / trolley and she gives them a (**5**) cash / receipt. Other times, she puts products on the (**6**) shelves / customers. She says that's the most boring part of her job!

Look at the pictures and complete 1–10 with the correct words.

bottle   carton   jar   loaf   packet   tin   bar   can

A _____ of bread.

A _____ of water.

3
A _____ of cornflakes.

4
A _____ of cola.

A _____ of olives.

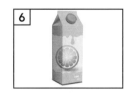
A _____ of orange juice.

A _____ of tomatoes.

A _____ of chocolate.

Complete the text with the correct words.

packet   go   customers   receipt   cans   carton   loaf   spend   jar   bars   till   buy   cashier   trolley

I only (**1**) _____ food shopping once a week because I hate it. I always (**2**) _____ the same things. I put everything into the (**3**) _____ as quickly as I can. First I get the drinks – six (**4**) _____ of lemonade and a (**5**) _____ of orange juice. Then I get the food for my breakfasts and lunches. A (**6**) _____ of bread, some cheese, a (**7**) _____ of jam, a (**8**) _____ of cornflakes, and some (**9**) _____ of chocolate. Then I look for a (**10**) _____ where there are no other (**11**) _____. I don't usually talk to the (**12**) _____ because I want to be quick. But I always take my (**13**) _____ because I like to know how much money I (**14**) _____ every week.

- Is it a good idea for students to have jobs? Why? / Why not?
- Are you careful with money? Do you save it or spend it?

Ideas Focus

4 A Day in the Life

Grammar

Be going to

A Read the dialogue below and underline all the examples of *be going to*.

Amy: We're going to visit Thailand in the summer.

Ben: Are you going to stay in hotels?

Amy: No, we aren't. We're going to take a tent.

Ben: With all your clothes, books, camera and a tent, you're going to need a big backpack!

B Read these questions about the dialogue in A and circle the correct answers.

1 When did Amy decide to go to Thailand?
   a Before she spoke to Ben.
   b When she was speaking to Ben.
2 Why does Ben think she's going to need a big backpack?
   a Because she's going away for a long time.
   b Because she has a lot of things to take.

C Complete the rules with the correct options.

1 We use *be going to* to talk about the future / the present.
2 We use *be going to* to talk about a decision before / at the time of speaking.
3 We use *be going to* to talk about a future event based on what we know or can see at the moment / in the past.
4 The form = subject + *be* + *going to* + verb + *-ing* / verb (infinitive without *to*).

Will

D Underline the all examples of *going to* or *will* in this dialogue.

Becky: I'm going to take this backpack on holiday.

Mum: I'll help you pack it!

Becky: Thanks! Will you drive me to the station, too?

Mum: Yes. What time is your train? Your dad will need the car at 9.

Becky: 8 o'clock, but I think I will need to arrive a bit earlier.

Mum: OK, that should be fine.

Becky: I'm feeling a bit scared about going away on my own, mum!

Mum: Don't worry. You'll have a great time!

E Match sentences 1–4 with rules a–d.

1 I'll help you pack it! ☐
2 Your dad will need the car at 9. ☐
3 I think I will need to arrive a bit earlier. ☐
4 You'll have a great time! ☐
a We use *will* with verbs like *think, know, be sure.*
b We use *will* to talk about a decision made at the time of speaking.
c We use *will* for predictions about the future (when we say what we think will happen).
d We use *will* to talk about a future fact.

▶ Grammar Focus pp. 163 & 164 (4.1 to 4.2)

F Complete the dialogues with the correct form of *will* or *be going to* and the verbs in brackets.

1 **A:** I'm going to watch my favourite team play tonight.
   B: Do you think they _____? (win)
2 **A:** Look at those black clouds in the sky!
   B: I know! It _____ very soon! (rain)
3 **A:** We're going to your favourite restaurant tonight.
   B: Yes, and I've already decided what I want. I _____ the steak. (order)
4 **A:** Oh no! I wanted to buy this ice-cream but I don't have any money!
   B: Don't worry! I _____ it for you. (buy)
5 **A:** Good evening. What would you like to order?
   B: Erm ... OK, I _____ the tuna pasta, please. (have)
6 **A:** Come in! I'm going to make coffee!
   B: I can't, I'm afraid. I _____ tennis with Rick. (play)

G Match 1–6 with a–f.

1 The doorbell's ringing!
2 Our team is playing badly.
3 I got up late.
4 I'm worried about the test.
5 I'm going to post a letter now.
6 The teacher looks angry.

a Oh no! They're going to lose!
b He's going to shout at us!
c I'm going to miss the bus.
d I'll answer it!
e I'll take it! I'm going to pass the Post Office today.
f Don't worry, I'm sure you'll pass.

Countable / Uncountable Nouns & Quantifiers

H Read the sentences. Circle the correct words.

1 They bought new furniture / furnitures.
2 The guidebook includes travel information / informations.
3 There's lots of fruit / fruits in the bowl.
4 I haven't got much / many money.

I Circle the correct word.

The nouns *furniture, information, fruit, research, money* are examples of **countable / uncountable** nouns.

J Write the words in the correct column.

~~banana~~ biscuit bus dollar food fun
furniture ~~fruit~~ game homework information
money table traffic

Countable	Uncountable
banana	fruit

Be careful
● Remember some very common words are uncountable in English: *money, information, advice, luggage, news, equipment.*

Some uncountable nouns end in -s: *maths, news.*

Some plural countable nouns are irregular and do not end in -s: *men, women, children, people, sheep.*

K Read the dialogue and underline all the nouns. Which are countable? Which are uncountable?

Harry: Can you lend me some money? I really want to buy a new game for my Xbox.

Mark: How much money do you need?

Harry: I've got some, but I need another ten euros.

Mark: Sorry, I've only got three euros. Ask Dan.

Harry: I have. He hasn't got any money! Oh, well. I think I'll do some homework instead.

Mark: Me too. Have we got a lot of homework?

Harry: No, we've only got a little homework so it won't take long.

Mark: Have you got any food? I'm really hungry?

Harry: I've got some fruit and I've got some biscuits.

Mark: How much fruit have you got?

Harry: Just a few strawberries.

Mark: Oh. How many biscuits have you got? Have you got any chocolate ones?

Harry: I've got lots of biscuits, all different kinds.

L Look at the dialogue in K again and the circle the correct words to complete the rules.

1 Countable nouns can / cannot be singular and plural. We can / cannot use them with numbers and indefinite articles: *ten euros, a chair, an egg.*

2 Uncountable nouns refer to things that we can / cannot count. We can / cannot use numbers or singular indefinite articles (*a/an*) with them. They have / do not have a plural form.

M Look at the dialogue in K again. Circle all examples you see of these words / phrases.

a few   how much   some   a little
how many   any   a lot of   lots of

N Complete the rules with 'countable', 'uncountable' or 'both countable and uncountable'.

1 We use **how much** with _____ nouns.
2 We use **how many** with _____ nouns.
3 We use **a lot of / lots of** with _____ nouns.
4 We use **any** in questions and negatives with _____ nouns.
5 We use **some** in positive sentences and questions with _____ nouns.
6 We use **a few** with _____ nouns.
7 We use **a little** with _____ nouns.

▶ Grammar Focus p. 164 (4.3 to 4.5)

O Choose the correct answers.

1 **A:** How many / much / little children are coming to the party?
  B: Ten, so we'll need lots of / many / a few food.
2 **A:** How many / any / much money have you got with you?
  B: Just a little / a few / much euros. I'll go home and get some more.
3 **A:** There isn't some / any / a few food in the cupboard.
  B: I'm going to buy any / a / some bread later.
4 **A:** Would you like a few / a little / many sugar in your coffee?
  B: I'll have two / many / lots of sugar, please.

4 A Day in the Life

Listening

A Read the questions and circle the question words. The first is done for you.

a (Who) is she going to travel with?
b When will they leave the hotel?
c How much money has she got now?
d Which city is she going to visit?
e How are they going to get to the museum?
f What does she order in the café?

Tourists travel on gondolas in Venice, Italy

B Match a question (a–f) from A with the information it is asking for (1–6).

1 some food or drink ☐
2 a person ☐
3 a city ☐
4 an amount ☐
5 a time ☐
6 a form of transport ☐

C Read the multiple choice answers. Write the correct question from A for each one.

1 _____
A Rome   B Milan   C Venice

2 _____
A mum and dad   B granny   C mum

3 _____
A an espresso   B a cappuccino   C some milk

4 _____
A 10 euros   B 4 euros   C 6 euros

5 _____
A walk   B bus   C boat

6 _____
A 9   B 10   C 8:45

D [4.1 ▶‖] Listen and choose the correct answers in C.

E Read the *Exam-Close-up*. Then read the *Exam Task*. Underline the question words and look at the options. Check you understand what kind of information you need to listen for.

F [4.2 ▶‖] Complete the *Exam Task*.

G [4.3 ▶‖] Listen again and check your answers.

Exam Close-up

Understanding what to listen for

- Before you listen, look at the question words in the questions (e.g. *When, How many, Why*) These words tell you the kind of information you need to listen for (e.g. a time/day, a reason, etc.).
- Make sure you are clear on what you need to listen for, so that you can focus on the key information needed to answer to the question.
- The questions follow the order of the dialogue. If you are not sure of one question, leave it and go back to it the second time you listen.

Exam Task

Listen to Dan talking to his friend Cate about going on a trip. For each question, choose the right answer (**A, B** or **C**). You will hear the conversation twice.

1 Who will take the cameras?
   A Dan   B Cate   C both Dan and Cate

2 What clothes will they need?
   A a lot of trousers   B a few clothes   C warm clothes

3 Why will they wear boots?
   A because perhaps there will be snakes   B because it will be wet   C because they are comfortable

4 How will they get to the village?
   A on foot   B by car   C by plane

5 What time do they hope to reach the gorillas?
   A 5 am   B 6 am   C 7 am

Speaking

A Match the words to the pictures. Then decide if each is a starter, main course, dessert or drink.

> ice-cream   olives   espresso   chocolate brownie   spaghetti with prawns
> sparkling water   orange juice   garlic bread   cheese and tomato pizza   still water

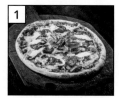    

B Complete the dialogues with the correct words.

1 **A:** What would / do you like to order?
   B: For my dessert / starter I'm going to have some olives, and then a pizza for my main course.
   C: Erm … I'll have / I have some garlic bread, and can / must I have the spaghetti, please?

2 **A:** Anything to drink?
   B: How many / much is a bottle of sparkling water?
   A: We have two kinds. The cheapest is 5 euros.
   B: We'll have / We're having that one, please.

3 **A:** Have you got any tiramisu?
   B: I'm afraid we haven't got any / some. We only have ice-cream or chocolate brownies.

4 **A:** What kind / cup of coffee do you have?
   B: We have espresso or cappuccino.

5 **A:** Should we leave a receipt / tip?
   B: Yes, let's leave 10%. I'll ask for the bill / cost.

C Read the *Exam Close-up*. Then read the *Exam Task* and try to prepare your questions.

Useful Expressions

Eating out
What time does the restaurant open?
Can I book a table?

Taking an order
What would you like to order?
Any drinks?
I'm afraid we don't have …

Ordering food and drink
Can I have / I'd like / I'll have the pasta, please?
Do you have any garlic bread?
What kind of ice-cream do you have?
How much is an espresso?
Can we have the bill, please?

D Now complete the *Exam Task* in pairs. Use the *Useful Expressions* to help you.

Exam Close-up

Asking questions correctly
- You will need to ask your partner five questions and you will only be given some key words.
- Before you start, prepare your questions.
- Think carefully about how you will form each question. Do you need to use a question word (e.g. *When …?*, *What …?*, etc.). What verbs will you need? Do you need an auxiliary verb (e.g. *do, be*)?

Exam Task

1 **Student A:** Turn to page 178 to see the menu for Mo's Bistro.

Student B: Ask A the following questions about the menu for Mo's Bistro.

- When / open?
- Any starters?
- How much / apple cake?
- Who / call to book a table?
- Telephone number?

2 **Student B:** Turn to page 179 to see the menu for Dave's Café.

Student A: Ask B the following questions about the menu for Dave's Cafe.

- What time / open?
- How much / garlic bread?
- Any desserts?
- What kind / coffee?
- Who / call for takeaway lunch?

- What is your favourite restaurant? Why do you like it?
- 'Young people can't cook. They eat junk food or go to restaurants.' Do you agree? Why? / Why not?

Ideas Focus

Writing: an informal email

Learning Focus

Using adjectives in emails

- When you write an email talking about past activities or future plans, try to use adjectives to make your writing more interesting.
- Using positive or negative adjectives (e.g. *it's fun, it was great, it's going to be boring*) helps you to explain your opinion on something.
- Adding adverbs before adjectives helps you to give a stronger opinion (e.g. *it was really good, it was very bad*).

Exterior of Salvador Dali Museum in St. Petersburg, Florida

A Order these weekend activities from the best (1) to the worst (10) in your opinion.

go to a restaurant ☐	cook dinner ☐
do homework ☐	do the washing up ☐
play volleyball ☐	visit a museum ☐
sunbathe ☐	go to a restaurant ☐
tidy your room ☐	watch TV ☐

B Work with a partner and talk about your answers in A. Did you have the same order as your partner? Explain your answers.

C Read Katie's email to her friend, Julie. Is Katie happy about her weekend plans?

> ● ● ○   Email Message
>
> From: Katie
> To: Julie
>
> Hi Julie
>
> How are you? I'm OK, but I'm not looking forward to the weekend.
>
> My parents are going to take me to the town museum on Saturday – I think it'll be really boring. After that we're going to eat dinner at a Japanese restaurant. I hate fish, so it's going to be awful! And when we get home they want me to tidy my room, make dinner, and do the washing up!
>
> Are you free on Sunday? Can we meet and do something exciting?
>
> Love
> Katie

D Now read Julie's reply and answer the questions.

1. When did Julie go to the museum?
2. Did Julie like the museum?
3. Who is Julie going to play volleyball with on Sunday?
4. What time are they going to meet and where?
5. What is she going to do after playing volleyball?
6. Can she meet Katie on Sunday?

> ● ● ○   Email Message
>
> From: Julie
> To: Katie
>
> Dear Katie
>
> Sorry to hear about your weekend! It won't be as terrible as you think. I went to the Museum last month and it was great fun. I'm going to play volleyball with my cousins on the beach on Sunday. I'm really looking forward to it. You can come too! We're going to meet at the beach café at 10 o'clock. After the volleyball I'm going to sunbathe and swim – it'll be really relaxing.
>
> Hope to see you on Sunday.
>
> Julie

E Find these adjectives and phrases in the emails in C and D, then write them in the correct column.

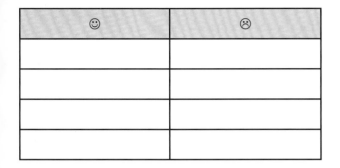

awful   really boring   great fun   exciting
I'm not looking forward to …   relaxing   terrible
I'm really looking forward to …

☺	☹

Exam Close-up

Using short forms, punctuation & greetings

- When you write an informal email (e.g. to a friend), you should use short forms, e.g. *It'll be fun. I'm going to the cinema.*
- You can use exclamation marks in emails (!) when you are excited or annoyed about something you're writing about, e.g. *I did 10 hours of homework at the weekend!*
- Use short greetings in informal emails, e.g. *Hi Jack, Hello, Dear Lucy.* You can sign off with just your name if you are near the maximum word limit.

F Read the *Exam Close-up* and the *Exam Task*. Look back at the emails in C and D and circle all the short forms and exclamation marks.

Exam Task

Read the email from your mum about plans for the weekend.

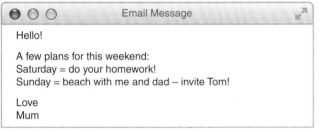

Email Message

Hello!

A few plans for this weekend:
Saturday = do your homework!
Sunday = beach with me and dad – invite Tom!

Love
Mum

Write an email to Tom.
- Tell him about your plans for Saturday. Are you happy / unhappy about the plans?
- Then tell him about Sunday. Are you happy / unhappy about the plans?
- Find out if he can come.

Write 25–35 words.

G Now complete the *Exam Task*. Use the *Useful Expressions* to help you.

Useful Expressions

Talking about plans
We're going to go to the cinema.
We're going to meet at 11 o'clock at the museum.
I'm going to tidy my room on Saturday.

Giving opinions
It'll be great fun.
It'll be really boring.

It's going to be really relaxing.
I'm really looking forward to it.
I'm not looking forward to it.

Inviting
Can you come?
You can come too!
Would you like to come with us?

Swanpool beach in
Cornwall, England

4 A Grizzly Encounter

Montana, USA

Before you watch

A How much do you know about grizzly bears? Look at the statements below and write T (True) or F (False).

1 A grizzly bear can eat about 16 kg of food a day. ☐

2 Grizzly bears hibernate during the winter and wake in spring. ☐

3 Grizzly bears live in Europe. ☐

While you watch

B Watch the video and circle the words you hear.

1 The staff at the Montana Grizzly Encounter look after the bears seven / six days a week. ☐

2 The first task of the day is to prepare Brutus' room / meal. ☐

3 The grizzly bear eats apples and bananas / oranges. ☐

4 The grizzly bear eats 35 / 16 kg of food a day. ☐

5 The Grizzly hotel is very comfortable / cold. ☐

6 Grizzly bears have powerful noses / eyes. ☐

After you watch

C Complete the summary of the video clip below using these words.

apples	chicken	day	hunt	meal	room
routine	treats				

At Montana Grizzly Encounter, staff take care of the grizzly bears 24 hours a **(1)** _____, 7 days a week. The first task of the day is to prepare a bear's **(2)** _____. The bear called Brutus eats a variety of food ranging from meat, including venison, beef, pork and **(3)** _____, to fruit such as **(4)** _____, oranges and even a pomegranate. The Grizzly hotel is very comfortable. Each bear has a private **(5)** _____ with a bed to lie on! Another daily **(6)** _____ for the staff is hiding **(7)** _____ for the bears to find. This helps to keep the bears mentally healthy . The bears use their powerful noses in their **(8)** _____ for the hidden food. It doesn't take long for them to find it!

Ideas Focus

- Do you think these grizzly bears live a natural life? Why? / Why not?
- Would you like to work somewhere like Montana Grizzly Encounter? Why? / Why not?

Vocabulary

A **Circle the correct words.**

1 Jackie burnt her hand while trying to light the sparklers / streamers.
2 Of course Tom has a lot of friends – he's really best / good company.
3 I'm sure I replied to your email, but let me check my inbox / sent folder.
4 I need to contact / communicate my friend, but I can't find my phone.
5 Don't forget to make / say a wish before you blow out the candles.
6 We need to leave now because it's becoming / getting very late.
7 It only takes me about half an hour to make / tidy my bedroom.
8 Katy quickly got / put dressed, ate her breakfast and went to school.
9 The cashiers / customers waited in a long line to pay for their shopping.
10 Kenny bought a can / carton of cola and a sandwich for his lunch.
11 I lent / borrowed money from my sister to buy the new video game.
12 Mum's going to the supermarket this afternoon to do / go the shopping.

B **Complete the sentences using these verbs.**

brush click do go have make pay stay surf waste

1 My sister and I always _____ our beds in the morning.
2 When I am bored, I usually _____ the net for a while.
3 Did you _____ fun at the party you went to last night?
4 Don't forget to _____ your hair before you go out!
5 First, attach the photos and then just _____ 'Send'.
6 Ian doesn't want to _____ a lot for his new smartphone.
7 Let's _____ the washing up before we watch television.
8 Some people _____ a lot of time on sites like Facebook.
9 The internet makes it easy to _____ in touch with friends.
10 I usually _____ online after I finish all of my homework.

C **Complete the sentences using these phrasal verbs in the correct form.**

ask for call back call off get on go around hang out
hang up look forward to stay in stay up

1 I rang Max, but he wasn't at home so I _____.
2 Why did Lisa _____ her party? Is there a problem?
3 Let's _____ to Bob's house and play video games.
4 I'm really tired, so I'm going to _____ tonight.
5 Dan _____ well with everyone because he's friendly.
6 The teens in this area usually _____ at the mall.
7 There's a good film on TV later, so let's _____ and watch it.
8 Are you _____ Tina's fancy-dress party?
9 Sorry, I'm busy now. Can I _____ you _____ later?
10 Tom _____ Mary's number and I gave it to him.

Grammar

A Complete the sentences with the present continuous tense.

1 I _____ (not meet) my friends this weekend because I _____ (study) for a test on Monday.

2 _____ (you / go) to the rock concert next week? I _____ (get) my ticket tomorrow.

3 I'm so excited! We _____ (fly) to Greece tomorrow and then we _____ (sail) in the Aegean.

4 The twins don't like Chinese food, so they _____ (not come) with us tonight. They _____ (stay) home instead.

5 Nigel _____ (not have) a party for his birthday next week because his parents _____ (take) him to New York!

B Complete the sentences with the words.

> at from in inside into on onto towards

1 When you come back _____ the shops, tidy your room.

2 The trolleys are _____ the front of the supermarket.

3 Sam's new phone is still _____ the box because he doesn't like it.

4 My cat jumped _____ the table and ate my dinner!

5 Jill was running _____ the bus stop when she fell over.

6 I was walking _____ the shop when I saw Sid and Nancy.

7 Harry's party is _____ Saturday night. Are you going?

8 My sister's birthday is _____ November, and mine is too.

C Complete the sentences with the correct form of *will* or *be going to* and the verb in brackets.

1 I've got the tickets! I _____ (go) to the concert!

2 Don't worry. I _____ (make) the food for the party.

3 We _____ (not send) the invitations at the end of the week.

4 You look tired Mum, so I _____ (do) the shopping for you.

5 Jack can't come with us because he _____ (wash) his dad's car.

6 I _____ (drive) very carefully, Dad. I promise.

7 The supermarket is full! It _____ (take) ages to do the shopping.

8 I'm sure Jason's birthday party _____ (be) fantastic!

D Circle the correct words.

1 How much / many eggs do we need to make a cake?

2 Who is going to eat all of this / these food?

3 Mandy is going to a few / a little parties this month.

4 I don't know why people think physics are / is hard.

5 She hasn't got many / much time to do the shopping.

6 Are you sure the information / informations is correct?

7 There was a few / a little traffic this morning, but I wasn't late.

8 We haven't got any / some biscuits for our coffee.

5 Home Sweet Home

Reading:	multiple-choice, justifying your answers
Vocabulary:	home- and room-related words, phrasal verbs, open cloze, focusing on words before & after the gap
Grammar:	present perfect simple, *for* & *since*, possessives, multiple-choice cloze, identifying the kind of word you need
Listening:	multiple matching, identifying the two incorrect options
Speaking:	describing different rooms, asking & answering questions, making your descriptions interesting, describing my bedroom
Writing:	a note, explaining why, checking your spelling, making excuses

Converted former water tower
'The house in the clouds' in
Suffolk, England

Reading

A What is the difference between 'needing' and 'wanting'? Discuss as a class.

B Look at the pictures and tell your partner which you need and which you want in your home. Explain why.

laptop

3D TV

bed

sofa

air conditioner

toilet

C Quickly read the article. Which of the items in B do you think is in each home?

Word Focus

running water: water that comes from a tap

animal skin: a big piece of fur from an animal

nomad: a person who does not have a permanent home

seasons: spring, summer, autumn and winter

wood stove: a piece of equipment that burns wood to make heat

chill out: relax

This is Where I Live

Hi. My name is **Sesi** and I'm 14 years old. I'm an Inuit. It's another name for 'Eskimo'. My people come from the Arctic and I live in Greenland.

My family lives in an igloo that my father built with my uncles. Our igloo is one big, round room. That's where we eat, sleep and cook. We don't have a bathroom or a kitchen because we don't have running water. We melt ice when we want to drink, cook or wash. Of course it's very cold in the north, but we can stay warm inside our igloo. When it is very cold, our dogs sleep in the igloo too. We don't have beds or carpets on the floor. Instead, we have animal skins. We use them as blankets when we sleep. I haven't got a phone, like teenagers in other countries. Why do I need it? Who would I call? This is how I have always lived, but I'm sure it seems strange to you!

My name's **Yisu** and I'm from Mongolia. Many Mongolians live in the capital city, Ulaanbaatar, but my family are nomads. We take our animals — goats, camels and horses — to new places when the seasons change.

Our homes come with us. We live in gers. A ger is a big, round tent. We spend a lot of time outdoors with our animals. For us, the ger is a dry, warm room in a large 'house', with most of the 'rooms' outside. We cook, wash and work outside. We sleep and eat in the ger, so there are beds and a table with chairs. It's cosy inside. There is a wood stove in the centre that makes the whole ger warm very quickly. We have a satellite dish and a solar panel that creates electricity from the sun. We use the electricity for our TV and radio. I'm happy about that because I can watch football matches!

Traditional Mongolian ger interior

Read the *Exam Close-up*. Then read the *Exam Task*.

Exam Task

Read the article about the homes of three teenagers. Choose the best answer (**A**, **B** or **C**) for each question.

1 Which is the only home that can be moved?
  A the igloo
  B the ger
  C the houseboat

2 Who doesn't sleep in a bed?
  A Sesi
  B Yisu
  C Femke

3 Who lives close to nature?
  A Sesi and Femke
  B Yisu and Femke
  C Sesi and Yisu

4 How does Sesi get water?
  A from the igloo
  B from the ice
  C from a tap

5 How many rooms are in the ger?
  A one
  B two
  C more

Exam Close-up

Justifying your answers
- When you think you have found the answer, try to justify it, i.e. explain to yourself why it is correct and the other options are not.
- If you cannot do this then your chosen answer is probably wrong.
- Look at the options again and try to find one that you can justify.

6 What is unexpected about Femke's home?
  A It sits on water.
  B She can't have any pets.
  C It's like other houses.

7 Which teenager doesn't care about modern technology?
  A Sesi
  B Yisu
  C Femke

8 Which teenager has to do work around the house?
  A Sesi
  B Yisu
  C Femke

Now complete the *Exam Task*. Remember to justify your answers.

Find these words in the article. Then complete the sentences with the correct words.

| blanket | carpet | wardrobe | satellite dish | floor |

1 We've got a _____ so that we can watch TV programmes from other countries.
2 A glass of juice fell on my bedroom _____ and it looks terrible now. I need a new one.
3 My mum is always asking me to put my clothes in my _____.
4 I usually leave my clothes on the _____ so I'm never sure if they are dirty or clean!
5 I was cold last night, so I got an extra _____ to put on my bed.

Hello. I'm **Femke**. I'm from Amsterdam, the capital of the Netherlands. My home is a houseboat. Well, it sits on water, but it doesn't move like a boat. When you go inside, you get a surprise. Why? Because it looks like a normal house. There's a kitchen, a bathroom, a living room and three bedrooms. There's a lot of room inside my home. In fact, mine is the same size as my friends' homes. I've never lived in a 'normal' house with a garden or a pet.

My brother and I help my parents with the jobs. Every Saturday morning when my mum does the shopping, we clean and tidy our rooms. We vacuum the carpets and put our clothes away in the wardrobes. Then we clean the rest of the house. When we finish, we sit down in front of the television and chill out!

- Do you need more things than you have now to make you happy? Why? / Why not?
- 'A woman's place is in the home.' Do you agree? Why? / Why not?

Ideas Focus

Vocabulary

A Circle the correct word. Then answer the questions.

1

cottage / house

2

flat / house

3

cottage / villa

4

flat / villa

B Which place in A would you like to live in most? Why? Tell a partner.

C Label the pictures with the words.

bathroom   bedroom   dining room   hallway   kitchen   living room

_____   _____   _____   _____   _____   _____

D Match the descriptions to the pictures.

utility room

patio

shed

1 "My dad spends a lot of time in there. Everything he needs for the garden is there. He's got some tools in there and that's where he fixes things that are broken. My old bike is in there, and there are loads of spiders, too!"

2 "We use it a lot in the summer. It's nice and shady there when the weather is warm. I always enjoy eating there because I can smell the flowers and the fruit trees in the garden. At night, we light some candles and put them on the table."

3 "It's about the size of a small bedroom. It's close to the back door so that it's easy to go outside and hang out the wet clothes. I don't spend spend much time in there, but my poor mum does."

E Where do these things go? Write the correct room / place. Some rooms can be used more than once.

utility room (x2)   kitchen (x2)   bathroom   living room (x2)   bedroom   dining room   hallway   patio   shed

1 tumble dryer   _____
2 cooker   _____
3 shower   _____
4 sofa   _____
5 wardrobe   _____
6 lawnmower   _____

7 armchair   _____
8 washing machine   _____
9 barbecue   _____
10 dining table   _____
11 fridge   _____
12 front door   _____

Work with a partner. Look at these rooms. Which one do you like best? Why?

Find these things in the pictures in F. Write the picture number/s next to each one.

a rug ☐☐   d poster ☐   g blinds ☐☐   j duvet ☐

b mirror ☐   e painting ☐☐   h lamp ☐☐   k shelves ☐

c mat ☐   f curtains ☐   i pillow ☐☐   l coffee table ☐

Complete the sentences with the correct phrasal verbs.

| put away   pull up   switch on   hang up   put up |

1 It's getting a bit dark – can you _____ the lamp?

2 Please _____ your toys – your bedroom is such a mess!

3 Dad told me to _____ my jacket in my wardrobe.

4 The first thing I do in the morning is _____ the kitchen blinds and look out at the garden.

5 Can you _____ this painting for me? I'd like it on that wall over there.

Read the *Exam Close-up*. Then read the *Exam Task* and look at the words before and after each gap. What kind of words are they?

Now complete the *Exam Task*.

Exam Task

Read the email Femke sent to her friend Maria. Write **ONE** word for each space.

◀ ▶ email

Well, you wanted to know about my houseboat. Most people find it unusual, but for me it's normal. I (**1**) _____ lived here all of my life. It's (**2**) _____ living in a flat because (**3**) _____ isn't a garden or a shed.

When I'm (**4**) _____ home I watch TV or I (**5**) _____ online. I've got my (**6**) _____ laptop computer in my room. You see, my home is just like (**7**) _____; I have everything that I need … but it's on water! Sometimes (**8**) _____ the evening it's a bit noisy outside. There are (**9**) _____ of tourists in Amsterdam and they all want to (**10**) _____ photos of my beautiful houseboat!

Exam Close-up

Focusing on words before & after a gap

• Some tasks include a gapped text. Only one word goes in each gap.

• This task tests what you know about grammatical structures and vocabulary.

• First, look at the gap. What words come before and after? What kind of words are they (e.g. verbs, nouns, prepositions, pronouns)?

• Look again at the words around the gaps. Can you think of words that often go together with them? Write your answer in the gap and then read the whole sentence to see if it fits.

• 'I love coming home at the end of a holiday.' Do you agree? Why? / Why not?

• Describe your ideal home. Why do you want to live there?

• Would you like to live on a houseboat? Why? / Why not?

Ideas Focus

Grammar

Present Perfect Simple

A Read the sentences below and underline examples of the Present Perfect Simple.

1 Jon has slept in this bedroom since he was a baby.
2 I've been to Peru, but I've never been to Chile.
3 I've just seen your mum in the library!

B Match the sentences in A to the rules.

a We use the Present Perfect Simple to talk about experiences, i.e. things you have done in your life.
b We can also use it to talk about something that happened in the recent past, e.g. only a few minutes ago.
c It can also be used to talk about something that started in the past and still happens today.

> **Be careful**
> We form the Present Perfect Simple with subject + has / have + past participle. Many common verbs have irregular past participles so you need to learn them!

C Underline the time expressions used with the Present Perfect Simple in these sentences. The first one is done for you.

1 A: Have you been to the shops today?
  B: Yes, I've just put the food in the cupboard.
2 A: Has he tidied his bedroom yet?
  B: Yes, he's already finished.
3 A: Have they ever painted the living room?
  B: No, they've never painted the living room.
4 A: Have you cleaned the kitchen floor yet?
  B: Yes, but I still haven't cleaned the windows.

D We often use *for* and *since* with the Present Perfect Simple. Read the sentences and circle the correct words in the rules.

I've lived in this house **for** 12 years.
I've lived in the house **since** 2004.

1 We use *for / since* to talk about a point in time.
2 We use *for / since* to talk about a period of time.

▷ Grammar Focus p. 165 (5.1 to 5.3)

E Complete the dialogues with these words.

> already   ever   just   never   still   yet (x2)

1 A: Have you _____ won any money?
  B: No, I've _____ been very lucky.
2 A: How do we turn on the oven?
  B: I've _____ told you, weren't you listening?
3 A: Haven't you left _____?
  B: No, I _____ haven't found my car keys.
4 A: How long have you been home?
  B: I've _____ got in, and I haven't sat down _____!

F Complete the text with the Present Perfect Simple of the verbs in brackets.

Explore More

Bored with traditional travel? Perhaps you **(1)** _____ (visit) similar places every year or **(2)** _____ (return) to your favourite hotel again and again. **(3)** _____ your trips _____ (be) the same since you were a small child? Your trips are boring because you **(4)** _____ (never try) anything new! You **(5)** _____ (never have) enough time to enjoy a different experience. Don't worry! You **(6)** _____ (just find) the answer to your problems! Our company **(7)** _____ (change) hundreds of people's lives. Our customers **(8)** _____ (stay) in traditional Gers in Mongolia, and **(9)** _____ (learn) about the Nomadic way of life. Others **(10)** _____ (choose) to discover a country by living on a boat for a month. There are plenty of options, but no five star hotels!

G Do we use *for* or *since* before these words / phrases?

> a few days   a long time   years   1991   November 5th   8 o'clock   yesterday   24 hours
> three minutes   last week

Possessives

H Read the sentences and circle the apostrophes (') that show that something belongs to someone (possession).

1 John's book is on the table.
2 The man's car is very fast.
3 The children's dinner is ready.
4 The boys' bikes are in the garage.
5 Jess' cat is 10 years old.

I Look at the sentences in H again and complete the rules with the words below.

> irregular   plural   -s   singular

a To show possession with nouns, we use an apostrophe followed by -s for _____ nouns.

b We use an apostrophe <u>after</u> a name ending in _____.

c We use an apostrophe <u>after</u> the 's' for regular _____ nouns and an apostrophe followed by –s for _____ plural nouns, e.g. *men*.

L Complete the sentences with 's, s' or '.

1 The dog_____ bed is in the hall.
2 This car park is only for visitor_____ cars.
3 Women_____ clothes are on the third floor.
4 James_____ new car is black and very expensive.
5 This is my sister_____ room; they share a bedroom!
6 His parent_____ names are Arthur and Mary.

N Read the *Exam Close-up*. Then read the *Exam Task* and note what kind of words you see in the answer options.

O Now complete the *Exam Task*.

Exam Task

Choose the best word (**A**, **B** or **C**) for each space.

Little Helpers

Children have helped adults with their daily jobs (**1**) _____ 100s of years. For example, where parents are farmers, children help on their (**2**) _____ farm. They often feed the family's animals or pick vegetables from (**3**) _____ fields. Many children have (**4**) _____ seen a tap for water. They have walked to a well to get water every day (**5**) _____ they were quite small. If a fisherman has a son, (**6**) _____ son will probably also go out on his fishing boat. It is hard for these families to survive without their children's help. When they grow up, they have (**7**) _____ learnt important skills that they need in everyday life. The lucky ones have also (**8**) _____ to school!

1 **A** for   **B** since   **C** when
2 **A** parents   **B** parent's   **C** parents'

J Read the dialogue and look at the words in bold. Which word comes before a noun? Which word is a pronoun?

A: Is this **your** book?
B: Yes, it's **mine**!

K Match the sentences in J with the uses below.

a We use a possessive pronoun to replace a possessive adjective and noun.
b We use a possessive adjective before a noun.

> **Be careful**
> Remember possessive adjectives and pronouns do
> ● **not** have apostrophes!

> ↻ **Grammar Focus p. 165 (5.4 to 5.5)**

M Circle the correct answers.

1 My sons' room: It's his / their room. It's theirs / his.
2 My mum's dog: It's her / hers dog. It's hers / her.
3 My dad's desk: It's his / her desk. It's hers / his.
4 My family's car: It's our / ours car. It's our / ours.
5 These cats belong to me. They're my / mine cats. They're my / mine.
6 This homework belongs to you. It's you're / your homework. It's yours / your.

Exam Close-up

Identifying the kind of word you need
- Read the whole text first.
- When you look at a gap, always read the sentences before and after it.
- Look at each set of three possible answers. What kind of words are they?
- If there are pronouns, make sure you choose the right person. If there are possessives, do they refer to one or many? If there are verbs, pay attention to the tense.

3 **A** their   **B** theirs   **C** they
4 **A** never   **B** yet   **C** still
5 **A** for   **B** since   **C** when
6 **A** his   **B** their   **C** him
7 **A** never   **B** already   **C** ever
8 **A** studied   **B** gone   **C** been

Listening

A Match 1–6 with a–f.

1 Whose job is it to wash up?
2 Who's going to clean the kitchen?
3 Are these your shoes?
4 This is my computer.
5 It's the children's job to feed the dog.
6 Where are their drinks?

a No, it's not yours; it's ours.
b John. It's his turn to clean it.
c They're there, on the table.
d It isn't mine. I did it yesterday.
e Its dinner's in the fridge.
f No, they're Dad's.

B 5.1 ▶❙❙ Listen to the dialogues. Circle the correct answer.

1 Jack / Mary
2 daughter / father
3 Jimmy / Mike

4 Sue / Tim
5 Dad / dog
6 Mrs Green's car / Mr Smith's car

C Read the *Exam Close-up* and then read the *Exam Task*. Does the question ask about where items <u>are</u>, or where they <u>should be</u>?

D 5.2 ▶❙❙ Now listen and complete the *Exam Task*.

Exam Task

Listen to a mother and father talking about tidying up. Where does each item belong?

For questions **1–5**, write a letter **A–G** next to each item. You will hear the conversation twice.

1 ketchup ☐
2 towels ☐
3 passport ☐
4 printer ☐
5 garage key ☐

A dining room
B desk drawer
C children's bedroom
D garage
E kitchen cupboard
F fridge
G bathroom shelf

Exam Close-up

Identifying the two incorrect options
- Make sure you understand the question.
- Remember that speakers talk about many of the options, but only one is right for each question number.
- You will hear the answers in the order of the questions.
- Try to identify the two answers that are not needed.
- Listen out for negative sentences about the options. This will often mean it is not correct for that item.

E 5.3 ▶❙❙ Listen again and check your answers.

Speaking

A

B

Work with a partner and answer these questions.

- What's your favourite place in your home?
- What is the most important thing in your room?
- What does your room say about you?

Work with a partner. Student A looks at picture A and Student B looks at picture B. Take it in turns to describe your pictures. What are the similarities and differences between the rooms?

Match 1–6 with a–f.

1 Our living room is quite small.
2 The living room walls are white.
3 There are a few paintings on the walls.
4 The living room is usually tidy.
5 There is a small sofa and an armchair.
6 The living room is my favourite room!

a They all have boats in them because my dad loves sailing!
b There's not much space for a lot of furniture.
c I like the chair best – it's really comfortable.
d I like it because the TV is there and my Xbox.
e There's a big window, too, so it's very light.
f My parents get annoyed when it's untidy.

Read the *Exam Close-up*. Then read the *Exam Task* and think of what you like and dislike about your bedroom, and any adjectives you can use to describe it.

Now complete the *Exam Task*.

Exam Task

Work with a partner and tell each other about your bedrooms. **Student A** ask **Student B** first. Then change roles and **Student B** asks **Student A**.

STUDENT A Tell me about your bedroom.	STUDENT B Tell me about your bedroom.
What / colour / walls?	What / favourite thing / in bedroom?
How long / had this bedroom?	Ever / put posters or pictures / on walls?
How often / tidy / bedroom?	How much time / spend / bedroom?
Would / like / change anything in	What / best thing about / bedroom?

Exam Close-up

Making your descriptions interesting

- When you talk about a photo or real place, use adjectives to make your description interesting.
- Describe your feelings about it, say what you like or don't like and why.
- When you talk about a favourite place, you can say what you do there.

Useful Expressions

Describing my bedroom
My bedroom room is great because …
I don't really like my bedroom because …
I've got a computer / laptop / printer / TV …
The walls are white and I've got red curtains.

I keep my … on my bookshelves / in my wardrobe.
I really love my posters of …
My room is usually tidy / untidy … because …

Work with a partner. Take turns to describe your dream bedroom or living room to your partner. Explain what would be in it and why.

- Do you think someone's room tells us about their personality? Why? / Why not?
- 'If my parents want my bedroom to be tidy, *they* should tidy it.' Do you agree? Why? / Why not?

Ideas Focus

Writing: a note

Learning Focus

Explaining why

- Sometimes when we communicate, we need to explain why we have or have not done something.
- To answer a question (e.g. *Why didn't you do your homework?*) we can use the following words and phrases:

  because + subject + verb: *Because I was ill.*

  because of + noun: *Because of illness.*

  that's why + subject + verb: *I was ill, that's why I didn't do it.*

  that's because + subject + verb: *That's because I was ill.*

- You need to understand these phrases and know how to use them, e.g. are they followed by a noun or verb?

People barbecuing despite the heavy rain

A Look at the dialogues. Circle the correct answer.

1 **A:** I haven't got any clean socks Mum!

B: Well, darling … that's why / that's because you didn't do the laundry.

2 **A:** What did you do?

B: Ah, sorry … I dropped your phone. That's why / That's because it's broken.

3 **A:** Why didn't you go to the disco?

B: Because / Because of no one told me about it!

4 **A:** Why did you cancel the barbecue at your house?

B: Because / Because of the rain, it wasn't possible to cook outside.

B Look at the sentences below and circle the correct words to complete the rules.

It was raining. **That's why** we used my umbrella at the barbecue.

We used my umbrella at the barbecue. **That's because** it was raining.

Because of the rain, we used my umbrella at the barbecue.

We used my umbrella at the barbecue **because** it was raining.

1 *That's why* explains a cause / result.

2 *That's because* explains a cause / result.

3 *Because of* explains a cause / result.

4 *Because* explains a cause / result.

C Read the to-do list left by Liam's mum and a schedule of his day. There is a problem. What is it?

Saturday schedule

9 o'clock	football practice
11 o'clock	buy present for Penny
1 o'clock	coffee with Matt
5 o'clock	Jack's house
7 o'clock	disco

Liam, here's what I'd like you to do today while I'm in London.

In the morning
- tidy your room
- do the laundry
- hang out the washing

In the afternoon
- clean the bathroom
- vacuum the carpets

In the evening
- walk the dog

Thanks!
Mum xxx

D Liam used the note and the schedule to leave a note for his mum. Read the note and answer the questions.

Hi Mum,

Because I had a very busy day, I couldn't do everything on your list.

I tidied my room at 8, but I had football practice at 9. That's why I didn't do the laundry or hang out the washing.

I didn't clean the bathroom or vacuum the carpets. That's because I was at Jack's house at 5.

I really wanted to walk Maximus, but because of the disco at 7, I couldn't.

Liam ☺

1 In his note, did Liam write about all of the things his mum asked him to do?

2 Did Liam explain why he couldn't do some of the jobs?

3 Which words or phrases did he use to explain why he didn't do them?

Read this note from your mum. You did some jobs, but not all of them. Write a note to your mum to explain.

I'm out all day. Please do the following:

1 Tidy your room. ✔

2 Put your dirty clothes in the washing machine and switch it on! ✔

3 Buy some milk and bread at the shop. ✘ *had no money*

4 Do your maths homework. ✘ *need your help*

5 Cook dinner for you and your brother. Pizzas in the freezer, salad in the fridge. ✔

6 Make your lunch for school on Monday. ✘ *no time – had to go to tennis lesson*

Exam Task

Read the text message and the email. Fill in the information in Tony's notes.

> Please take out the rubbish and get some milk. Also, take Jane to Cathy's house for a party. It starts at 3 o'clock and finishes at 6. If you can't, ask Uncle Tom.

◄ ► email

From: Dave
To: Tony
Subject: Liverpool vs Arsenal

Match starts at 3:45 p.m.
Let's meet at 3 o'clock at your house and we'll go from there.

F Read the *Exam Close-up*. Then read the *Exam Task* and underline similar pieces of information.

G Now complete the *Exam Task*. Remember to check your spelling.

Useful Expressions

Making excuses

I would like to, but ...
I can't, I'm afraid.
I'm sorry, but ...
I can't, because ...

I have to ...
I couldn't ... because ...
I didn't ... because ...

Exam Close-up

Checking your spelling

- Be careful when you transfer information from the two texts.
- Don't be confused by information that is similar, for example, a number of different times, prices or dates.
- Check your answers by looking back at the texts. Do they give the correct information? What about your spelling? Is it correct?

Mum, I took out **(1)** _____, and I went to the supermarket and bought some **(2)** _____. I would like to, but I can't take Jane to the party at Cathy's house **(3)** _____ the football match. It starts at **(4)** _____, but I have to be there earlier. I've asked **(5)** _____ and he's coming here to take her.

5 The Horse Nomads of Mongolia

Mongol

Before you watch

A What part of the world do the photos below show?
Match the descriptions with the pictures.

1 Mongolian ger from the outside. ☐
2 Monglian ger from the inside. ☐
3 Mongolian boy with his horse. ☐
4 Mongolian wooden ox cart. ☐

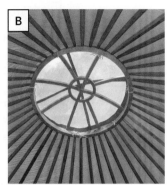

While you watch

B Watch the video and decide if these statements are **T** (True) or **F** (False).

1 Horse nomads have an ancient way of life. ☐
2 The nomad family pack up their camp in less than an hour. ☐
3 The ox carts are made of wood and metal. ☐
4 The nomad's tent symbolises the world. ☐
5 Muktali's horse won at the summer races. ☐
6 Muktali went to hospital when he broke his leg. ☐

After you watch

C Complete the summary of the video below using these words.

centre   life   luck   nature   place   summer   race   trucks

The nomads on the Mongolian steppes are preparing for the summer horse races.
Everything has its **(1)** _____ on the ox cart. Nomads move every few
weeks in spring and **(2)** _____. Their ox carts don't need gasoline and can
reach places that **(3)** _____ can't go. Nomads are deeply
connected to **(4)** _____, and their ger symbolises the universe. At the
(5) _____ of each ger is a rope, which represents the path through
(6) _____ and its twists and turns show that **(7)** _____
will always change. Muktali took first place in the horse **(8)** _____ but that
night he broke his leg when he fell off his new motorbike.

Ideas Focus

- Would you like to move every month? Why? / Why not?
- Do you think the nomads in the video would like to live the way you do? Why? / Why not?

6 The Place to Be

Reading:	multiple-matching, using context to understand signs
Vocabulary:	town- & country-related words, phrasal verbs, buildings & giving directions
Grammar:	demonstratives, articles
Listening:	gap fill (monologue), listening for days, times & numbers
Speaking:	asking & answering questions, understanding what people say, giving directions, checking understanding
Writing:	a formal email, thinking about sequence, using formal language, describing a route

The Batumi Technological
University Tower in Adjara,
Georgia

69

Reading

A **Look at the signs. Where might you see them? Discuss with a partner and match them to the places.**

1 library
2 school
3 car park
4 hospital
5 old building
6 swimming pool

B **Look at the signs in A again and answer the questions. Which sign tells you …?**

1 why you must not make a noise: ☐
2 to wash (2 signs): ☐ ☐
3 how much you have to pay to do something: ☐
4 where you are: ☐
5 what to do with something after you have used it: ☐

C **Find these words/phrases in the signs and underline them.**

return   clean   entering   display   in progress

D **Replace the words/phrases in bold with a word/phrase from C with the same meaning.**

1 Please (**give back**) _____ the tennis rackets after you have used them.
2 (**Wash**) _____ your hands before preparing food.
3 Take off all jewellery (rings, necklaces) before (**getting into**) _____ the hot tub.
4 Please (**show**) _____ your identity card at reception.
5 Please do not enter – a ghost tour of the castle is (**happening now**) _____.

E **Read the story about a tour of a castle. What does Lisa hear?**

The Ghost of Count Wolfgang Vlax

Lisa was visiting Vlax Castle with her mother. They listened to the tour guide talk about the history of the castle. 'The Vlax family is one of the oldest in Germany. They built the castle in 1348.'

The visitors were in the huge banquet hall. There were paintings of the Vlax family on the walls. Lisa thought they all had crazy eyes and faces. Then she noticed a closed door at the far end of the room. A sign on it said 'No Entry!'. 'That looks interesting,' thought Lisa.

She went towards the door very quietly and slowly opened it. The guide continued to talk about the castle. 'Since the 1500s,' the guide said, 'there have been many reports of a ghost. People say it is the ghost of Count Wolfgang Vlax, who was a very violent man and killed many people.' Lisa entered a small, dark room. The room felt spooky and she didn't like it. Suddenly, she heard someone laughing, but there was no one in there. It didn't sound friendly at all. She tried to open the door, but it was locked! Oh, no! What was happening?

Outside, the guide was still talking. 'People say that the ghost laughs, and many who have heard this laughter say it is evil.' Lisa started shouting and banging on the door, but no one heard her. She had to find a way out of that room by herself.

Word Focus

tour guide: person who shows you somewhere and tells you about it

banquet hall: a very large dining room in a castle or a palace

locked: when something can only be opened with the correct key

shouting: speaking very loudly

banging: hitting something very hard more than once

Read the story again and choose the correct answers.

1. Vlax castle is over 650 years old / under 600 years old / 348 years old.
2. Lisa thought the Vlax family looked nice / bad / mad.
3. Visitors were allowed / were taken / weren't allowed through the door Lisa went through.
4. Lisa felt happy / friendly / scared in the room.
5. Lisa could / could not / didn't want to get out of the room.

Read the *Exam Close-up*. Then read the *Exam Task* and decide where you might see the signs.

Now complete the *Exam Task*.

Exam Task

Which notice (**A–H**) says this (**1–5**)?

1. You must not walk here.
2. If there is a problem, leave the building from this door.
3. This place will give you information.
4. You must not take a photo with a flash.
5. You cannot come into the building here.

A No photographs allowed

B Please use other door

C No flash allowed

D Emergency exit

E Ask about Guided Tours here

F Children under 12 must be with an adult.

G Next guided tour: 11 a.m.

H Caution! Floor is wet!

Find and underline these adjectives in the story. Then complete the sentences with the correct words.

crazy	interesting	violent	evil	spooky

1. It was dark and windy on the hill. It was really _____.
2. I love history so I find all these old castles very _____.
3. The Queen was mean to everyone – she was _____.
4. The King loved fighting – he was very _____.
5. The Prince talked to himself. They say he was _____.

- Do you believe in ghosts? Why? / Why not?
- Would you be scared in a haunted house? Why? / Why not?

Ideas Focus

Vocabulary

A Write the correct places in a town next to the sentences.

cinema   corner shop   disco   factory   petrol station
pharmacy   shopping centre   sports
centre   stadium   theatre

1   The tank is nearly empty. Let's stop here and <u>fill up</u>.

   _____

2   I want to <u>take up</u> volleyball. Can I join a team?

   _____

3   I've <u>run out of</u> milk. Can I buy some here?

   _____

4   The tickets <u>sold out</u> quickly. Thousands of fans were there.

   _____

5   I'm enjoying this play. I'm glad they <u>put</u> it <u>on</u>.

   _____

6   I need to buy trainers and a T-shirt. Let's <u>look for</u> them here.

   _____

7   The workers stopped because the machines <u>broke down</u>.

   _____

8   I love dancing It's a great way to <u>work out</u>.

   _____

9   I've <u>come down with</u> the flu and I need some medicine.

   _____

10   I'm really <u>looking forward to</u> this film.

   _____

B Work with a partner. Look at the phrasal verbs that are underlined in A. Can you guess what they mean?

C Match the phrasal verbs with their meanings. Were your answers in B correct?

1	break down	a	be excited about something in the future
2	come down with	b	do exercise
3	fill up	c	begin a new hobby or sport
4	look for	d	become sick with something
5	look forward to	e	have no more of something left
6	put on	f	make full to the top
7	run out of	g	present a play
8	sell out	h	sell all that you have of something
9	take up	i	stop working (car, machine)
10	work out	j	try to find something

D Read what Ben and Daniel say about where they live. Who lives in the city and who lives in the countryside? Do they like where they live?

"There's too much traffic, so it's always noisy and the air is really polluted. The shopping centre and the cafes are always too crowded. I want to live in the countryside." *Ben*

"There's nothing to do – it's really boring. The nearest house is 5 kms away from us! There are no buses, so my parents have to drive me everywhere. My mum loves it here because it's peaceful and my dad finds it relaxing, but I don't like it – I want to live in the city." *Daniel*

E Read what they say again and underline the adjectives from below. Then match them to their definitions. Can you think of more adjectives to talk about the city and the countryside?

noisy   polluted   crowded   boring
peaceful   relaxing

1   makes you feel happy and comfortable:

   _____

2   not interesting or exciting:

   _____

3   loud and busy: _____

4   quiet: _____

5   full of people: _____

6   dirty air, often from cars and other traffic:

   _____

Read the texts and decide which service they are about.

> bank   fire station   hospital   library   museum
> police station   post office   university

1 _____
You go there or you call the people who work there when you need help. This is also where they take you if you do something bad or wrong.

2 _____
A lot of people prefer to use the internet these days, but this place is also full of information on many different subjects.

3 _____
The people who work there have a very dangerous job. They save people's lives and try to save their homes, too.

4 _____
Many people go there every day from Monday to Friday. Most of them are 18–22 years old and they want to gain knowledge.

5 _____
Some people go into a building to use this service. Others use a machine that is outside in a wall. They often go shopping after they visit this place.

6 _____
This place is full of beautiful and interesting items that are important for people who want to learn about art and history.

7 _____
Lots of people use email now, but we still need to send and receive letters. We also go to this place to buy stamps and pay bills.

8 _____
This is where you go if you have a problem with your health, or if you want to visit someone who is staying there because they aren't well.

G **Look at the texts in F again. Underline the key words that helped you to choose your answers.**

H **Circle the correct words.**

1 I was looking for the post office, but I walked into / past the bank by mistake.
2 We rode our bikes over / through the park and breathed in the fresh air.
3 James ran along / under the street quickly because he was late for school.
4 Did you see that? Elsa walked into / past me and didn't say hello!
5 They rowed the boats across / under the bridge and continued down the river.
6 Farmer Brown's horse jumped over / through the gate and ran away.
7 Joe ran across / along the street because he saw his friend on the other side.

Complete the directions with the words.

> cross   follow   get off   get on   go   take   get to   turn

How to get from Paddington Station to the Tower of London

By bus: **(1)** _____ bus number 205 and **(2)** _____ it at bus stop H. To find the bus stop, come out of Paddington Station and **(3)** _____ the road. You can buy tickets on the bus. It takes about 50 minutes to get there. Then **(4)** _____ the bus at St Botolph Street. It's a 15 minute walk from there, so take this map and **(5)** _____ it. Cross the street and **(6)** _____ right onto Aldgate High Street, then turn left onto Jewry Street. Then **(7)** _____ straight on until you **(8)** _____ the river Thames. Turn right, then take the first left and you'll arrive at the Tower of London.

The Tower of London sits on the River Thames in England

A contrast of modern and ol
buildings sit together in the
centre of Moscow, Russia

Grammar

Demonstratives

A Read the sentences below. Underline the words *this*, *that*, *these* and *those*.

  a This tall building is a bank and that glass building is a hotel.

  b These flats are modern, but those houses are old.

  c This traffic is terrible! These roads are always busy.

  d That pollution we saw on the video about Beijing was really bad.

B Match the sentences in A with the uses below.

  1 We use *these* for a plural noun near us and *those* for a plural noun that is far away. ☐

  2 We use *this* for a singular noun near us and *that* for a singular noun that is far away. ☐

  3 We use *that* for an uncountable noun that is far away. ☐

  4 We use *this* for an uncountable noun near us and *these* for a plural noun near us. ☐

C Complete the rule with *this*, *that*, *these* or *those*.

To talk about something near us, we use _____ + singular or uncountable noun and _____ + a plural noun.

To talk about something far away from us, we use _____ + singular or uncountable noun and _____ + plural noun.

▶ Grammar Focus pp. 165 & 166 (6.1)

D Complete the dialogues with *this*, *that*, *these* or *those*.

  1 A: Does _____ lift go to the 12ᵗʰ floor?

    B: _____ lifts are for staff only. _____ lifts over there are for visitors.

  2 A: _____ road is very quiet, there's no traffic today.

    B: Yes, but _____ roundabout ahead looks busy.

  3 A: Do you want to sit in _____ café? We can sit here, _____ chairs are free.

    B: _____ table is near the kitchen and it's very noisy. Let's try _____ café opposite.

  4 A: Does the bus for the centre stop at _____ bus stop?

    B: No, it stops at _____ bus stop over there.

E Rewrite the incorrect sentences in your notebook.

  1 'Can you see those street number on the building opposite?'

    'No, it's too far away! That house here is number 24, and we know the office is in that street.'

  2 'Does that bus go to the centre, driver?'

    'No, you want this bus on the other side of the road.'

  3 'Can you bring me these keys from the hall downstairs?'

    'Are this keys yours? You left them in the bathroom!'

  4 'These information about bus times is really useful!'

    'Yes that phone app has all the timetables, look!'

F Complete the text with *this*, *that*, *these* or *those*.

Athens City Tour

"Welcome to (**1**) _____ bus tour of Athens! (**2**) _____ city is famous for its ancient sites, but it's worth visiting the modern buildings, too. (**3**) _____ building up the hill is the Greek Parliament. (**4**) _____ road that we're driving along now passes two important sites. The first one is here. (**5**) _____ ancient gate is called Hadrian's Arch, and it was built in the second century. In (**6**) _____ times it stood across the ancient road from the centre of Athens to the temple over there. (**7**) _____ temple is the Temple of Olympian Zeus. When it was complete, it had 104 columns, but only 16 of (**8**) _____ columns are still standing today. (**9**) _____ part of the city that we are entering now is called Plaka. (**10**) _____ area is great for sightseeing. (**11**) _____ building right in front of you is the Acropolis Museum. Some of (**12**) _____ streets around here are closed to traffic."

Articles

G Read the sentences. Circle the indefinite articles and <u>underline</u> the definite articles.

1 (A) town needs (a) park, but there isn't (a) park in <u>the</u> town.
2 Is there a river in London?
3 The river in London is called the Thames.
4 There's an old bridge across the river.
5 Traffic is terrible in the mornings.
6 The traffic in London moves slowly.

H Look at the sentences in G and complete these sentences with *a/an*, *an*, *the* or *no article*.

1 We use _____ before a vowel sound.
2 We use _____ when we haven't talked about something before.
3 We use _____ in questions to find out if something exists.
4 We use _____ when we have already talked about the noun before.
5 We use _____ for rivers.
6 We use _____ for cities and countries.
7 We use _____ for countable, singular nouns.

I Read the sentences and underline the articles (*a*, *an*, *the*). Then answer the questions.

1 A house should be warm and comfortable.
2 The house was cold and spooky.
a Which sentence talks about one house (a specific house)? ☐
b Which sentence talks about all houses (houses in general)? ☐

Be careful
We use *the* with instruments, seas, oceans, rivers, deserts, mountain ranges.
He plays the piano. / We flew over the Alps.
We use no article with cities, islands, lakes, mountains, most countries, a person's name, school subjects, games and sport, days, months, meals.
I live in Germany. / Joseph is really friendly. / I had pizza for dinner.

> ⟳ Grammar Focus p. 166 (6.2 to 6.3)

J Complete the text with *a, an, the* or – (no article).

Sailor rescued after 80 days

In January 2012, **(1)** _____ Swedish sailor spent 80 days alone in **(2)** _____ yacht after **(3)** _____ storm damaged part of **(4)** _____ yacht. 66-year-old Swedish yachtsman, Stig Lundvall was lucky. **(5)** _____ Greek ship saw his signal for help and brought him to **(6)** _____ Cape Town, in **(7)** _____ South Africa. **(8)** _____ sailor was on **(9)** _____ voyage from Falmouth in **(10)** _____ Britain to **(11)** _____ Australia when **(12)** _____ weather got worse.**(13)** _____ radio on **(14)** _____ yacht was not working, and **(15)** _____ water and food on the yacht was not enough for him to survive. He collected **(16)** _____ rain in **(17)** _____ bucket and ate **(18)** _____ food slowly. When **(19)** _____ big Greek ship saw him and stopped, it was **(20)** _____ amazing feeling.

K Complete the sentences with *a, an, the* or – (no article).

1 We went to _____ Kenya on safari.
2 We visited _____ Nepal.
3 We flew to _____ Paris.
4 We drove through _____ Arizona.
5 We sailed around _____ Mediterranean.
6 We went skiing in _____ Alps for _____ first time.
a We camped in _____ Himalayas in _____ small tent.
b We had _____ accident in _____ village of Chamonix.
c We stopped at _____ Sicily and _____ Sardinia.
d We went to _____ Eiffel Tower and down _____ Seine.
e We took _____ photos of _____ wildlife that we saw.
f We visited _____ Grand Canyon and took _____ helicopter.

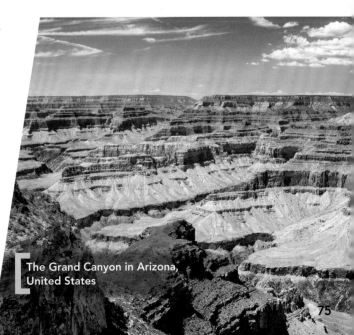
The Grand Canyon in Arizona, United States

L Now match 1–6 with a–f.

Listening

A Match 1–9 with a–i.

1	every day	a	weekly
2	weekday	b	monthly
3	weekend	c	Saturday and Sunday
4	every month	d	eight thirty
5	half an hour	e	thirty minutes
6	every week	f	Monday to Friday
7	a quarter to midday	g	a hundred years
8	a century	h	eleven forty-five a.m.
9	half past eight	i	daily

B Look at the pictures. What kind of museum would you find them in?

C Match the pictures A–F with the words below.

1 marbles

2 dolls' house

3 robot

4 tricycle

5 doll

6 teddy

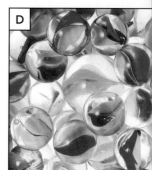

D 6.1 ▶ Listen to four people describing something in the pictures in B. Write the items from C that they are talking about.

1 _____

2 _____

3 _____

4 _____

E 6.2 ▶ Read the *Exam Close-up*. Then read the *Exam Task* carefully. Now listen and complete the *Exam Task*.

Exam Task

You will hear some information about a museum. Listen and complete each question. You will hear the information twice.

Museum of Childhood

Opening hours:	from 10.00 a.m. to (1) _____ p.m. daily
'Explore' event:	between 11.15 and 11.45 at (2) _____
Dolls' houses:	from the last (3) _____ years.
'Small Stories' exhibition:	from December 13th until (4) _____ next year
For children's parties, phone Alison Fielding:	telephone number (5) _____

Exam Close-up

Listening for days, times & numbers

- Look at the gaps and decide what kind of information you need to listen for.
- The missing information will often be days, times or numbers.
- You can write numbers as *3* or *three*, but you must spell the words correctly.
- In English, we say phone numbers 'oh, two, oh etc.', not 'oh, twenty'.
- You can write times like this: *5.45*, or like this: *5:45*.

F 6.3 ▶ Listen again and check your answers.

Speaking

A Tick the places that you find in your town. Then compare your answers with a partner.

1	sports centre	☐	5 bank	☐
2	swimming pool	☐	6 park	☐
3	shopping centre	☐	7 bus station	☐
4	school	☐	8 car park	☐

B Work with a partner. Match 1–5 with a–e to complete the dialogue.

Sam: Is there a bus station in the city centre?

Jo: 1 _____

Sam: Where do I get off?

Jo: 2 _____

Sam: Where is the nearest underground station?

Jo: 3 _____

Sam: Where do I buy tickets?

Jo: 4 _____

Sam: Can I get one at the station?

Jo: 5 _____

Sam: Thanks.

a Yes, or you can buy one from the shop on the corner.

b You go to Victoria. From there it's a short walk to the bus station.

c You can't buy tickets. You have to buy a card called an Oyster Card.

d Go down this road. Turn right at the traffic lights and the underground is on your left.

e No, it's not in the centre. You have to take the underground to get there.

C Look at the photo at the top of the page and the *Exam Close-up*. What do you think the two people are saying to each other?

D Now work in pairs to complete the *Exam Task*. Use the *Useful Expressions* to help you.

Useful Expressions

Asking for directions
Where is the …? / I'm looking for …
Is there a bank near here?
Where is it exactly?

Giving directions
It's at the end of the road.
It's opposite / next to / behind the school.
It's at the crossroads.
Go straight on.
Go / Turn right / left (at the traffic lights / at the roundabout).
Take the first (turning on your) right / left.

Checking understanding
Did you say 'turn right'?
I'm sorry. I didn't understand.
Could you repeat that, please?
I'm not sure what you mean.

Exam Close-up

Understanding what people say

- If you don't understand something, ask the other person to repeat it. You can say, '*Could you repeat that, please?*', or '*I'm sorry, I didn't understand*'. Remember, it's better to do this than answer without understanding.

- If directions are not clear, check with the other person. Say, '*Do you mean …?*' or repeat the directions, '*So I go right at the bank?*'

- If you think you understand, but are not sure, you can say, '*I'm not sure what you mean.*'

Exam Task

1 **Student A:** Look at your map on page 178. Some information is missing. Use these prompts and ask **Student B** questions to get directions and find the places.

- bank?
- Post office?
- café?
- museum?
- from museum to Post office?

2 **Student B:** Look at your map on page 179. Some information is missing. Use these prompts and ask **Student A** questions to get directions and find the places.

- hospital?
- school?
- restaurant?
- swimming pool?
- from hospital to swimming pool?

- When you're lost in a new city, do you prefer to use a map, your phone, or to ask someone directions?
- 'Young people can't use maps or compasses and they don't look around to try and remember a route.' Do you agree? If so, is this bad? Why? / Why not?

Ideas Focus

Writing: a formal email

Learning Focus

Thinking about sequence

- When you explain how to do something or how to go somewhere, you need to put all the steps in the correct order so that the information you give is clear.

- You can do this by using words that show the sequence of the actions, such as *after*, *then*, *next*, etc.

- These words usually go at the start of a sentence and are followed by certain structures:

before / after + subject + verb (without *to*): *Before you get to the bus stop, …*

before / after + -ing: *After crossing the road, …*

before / after + noun: *Before the museum, turn left.*

first + imperative: *First go straight on.*

first + subject + verb: *First, you take bus number 14.*

then / next / after that + imperative: *Next, turn right.*

then / next / after that + subject + verb: *After that, you take the first right.*

eventually / finally + subject + verb: *Eventually you will see the river.*

A Tick the sentences that are correct. Rewrite the sentences that are incorrect in your notebook.

1 First, taking the city train and get off at Richmond station. ☐
2 Before you get on the bus, make sure it's the number 32 to Oxford. ☐
3 After you to leave the station, turn left and walk along Bond Street. ☐
4 Next, walking about 200 metres until you get to a bridge. ☐
5 Then you should cross the street to the other side. ☐
6 Eventually, the road ends and you will see a gate. ☐

B Match the questions with the answers.

1 How far is it to the beach?   a Not really.
2 Is it far to the beach?   b You could take the bus.
3 How can I get to the beach from the station?   c It's quite close.

C Read the email and then answer the questions.

◄ ► email

From: Danny McKay
To: Winstone Hotel

Dear Sir / Madam

I have booked a family room at the Winstone Hotel for this weekend. We're coming by train. How can we get from the train station to the hotel? Is it possible to walk? If so, could you give me some directions?

I look forward to hearing from you.

Kind regards
Danny McKay

1 What information does Danny ask for?
2 Does Danny know the person he is writing to?
3 What phrases does he use to start and end his email?

Read the example email and circle the words that show sequence.

◄ ► | email

Dear Mr McKay

Thanks for your email. It isn't far from the train station to the hotel. After you leave the station, turn left and walk along Carlton Street. Then, take the first right and go straight ahead. Eventually, you'll see the hotel on your right.

We look forward to seeing you at the weekend.

Best regards
Jane Anderson
Hotel Administrator

Read the email again and answer these questions.

1 Underline the phrases Jane uses to show direction.
2 What greeting does Jane use?
3 What sentence does she end with?
4 What sign-off does she use?

Work with a partner. Choose a place in your town that you both know. This is your start point. Read the *Useful Expressions*, then ask and answer questions about how you can get to different places from your start point.

Now read the *Exam Close-up* and complete the *Exam Task*.

Exam Task

Read the email from Joseph Cook.

From: Joseph Cook
To: Bodmin Youth Hostel

Dear Sir / Madam

I am staying at your Youth Hostel next week with my class of 15 students. We are coming by train. Is the Youth Hostel far from the station? How can we get from the station to the Youth Hostel? Also, can we have breakfast at the Hostel?

I look forward to hearing from you.

Kind regards
Joseph Cook
Headteacher

Write an email to Joseph Cook and answer the questions.
Write 40–60 words.

Useful Expressions

Sequencing
first
before
after / then / next /
  after that / afterwards
eventually / finally

Asking for directions
How can I get to …
  from …?
Can you tell me how to
  get to …?

Describing a route
It's not far.
It's quite close.
It's a long way to walk.

Giving directions
Turn left / right.
Take the second left /
  right.
Go straight on.
Go / walk past the
  bank.
Keep going for another
  100 metres.
It'll be on your left /
  right.

Formal email greetings
Dear Sir / Madam
Dear Mrs Smith

Formal email sign-offs
Kind regards
Best regards

Exam Close-up

Using formal language
• If the email you are asked to reply to is formal, then you will also need to write using a formal style.
• Use formal greetings and sign-offs.
• If you don't know who you are writing to, start a formal email with *Dear Sir / Madam*.

The famous 199 steps leading from the town up to the Abbey in Whitby, England

6 One of a Kind

Bahrain

Before you watch

A Look at the photo and read the sentence. Label the photo with the words in red.

A sailor uses the power of the wind in the sails to sail his yacht.

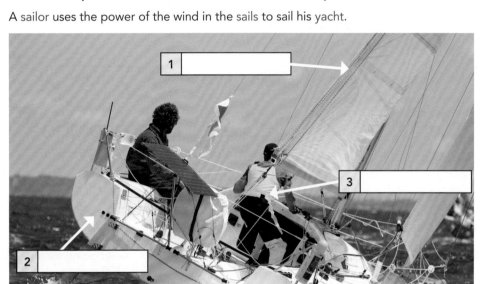

While you watch

B Watch the video and circle the words you hear.

1 Shaun Killa from South America / Africa has designed a green skyscraper. ☐
2 Shaun used his experience as a(n) architect / sailor to find the design. ☐
3 He wanted to design a skyscraper that used the air / wind to make its power. ☐
4 He used his love of sailing to inspire his one of a kind design / building. ☐
5 The shape is like two tall / high sails. ☐
6 The unique design required a special dream / team. ☐

After you watch

C Complete the summary of the video below using these words.

enough   find   first   make   special   true   use   windy

When architect Shaun Killa (1) _____ came to Bahrain, there was a very strong wind blowing. In this (2) _____ capital, on the edge of the Persian Gulf, Shaun's dream was to (3) _____ the power of the wind to make electricity in a one of a kind green skyscraper. He used his experience as a sailor to (4) _____ the right design for his (5) _____ building. His building looks like two tall sails. The wind passes between them, and if there is (6) _____ wind, it moves three turbines which (7) _____ electricity for the building. Two engineers from Denmark worked with Shaun and together they made Shaun's dream come (8) _____.

Ideas Focus

- Would you like to live or work in a building like this? Why? / Why not?
- Do you think cities should have more green buildings? Why? / Why not

Review 3

Vocabulary

A **Circle the correct words.**

1   My cottage / flat / villa is on the third floor of this building.
2   I need to wash my hands; where's the bedroom / hallway / bathroom, please?
3   Please put your dirty clothes in the washing machine / lawnmower / tumble dryer.
4   Be careful! The cooker / shower / fridge is hot – don't burn your hand.
5   We eat at the armchair / dining table / coffee table when my grandparents visit us.
6   It's cold tonight. I need to put another blanket / curtain / rug on my bed.
7   Let's sit on the barbecue / poster / sofa and watch TV tonight.
8   Please put your bicycles in the shed / chest of drawers / wardrobe.
9   It's dark in here and I can't see well; please switch on the blinds / curtains / lamp.
10 That's a very nice mat / painting / duvet on the wall. Where is it from?

B **Complete the sentences with the phrasal verbs in the correct form.**

fill up	look for	look forward to	put away	put up	run out of	take up	work out

1   Your room is very messy! Why don't you _____ your clothes?
2   This room needs some colour; let's _____ a few posters on the wall.
3   Can you _____ the water bottle and put it in the fridge, please?
4   I'm _____ my glasses, but I can't find them. Are they in here?
5   Nina and Tom _____ every day; Nina jogs and Tom goes to a gym.
6   I want to _____ a new hobby, but I don't know what to do.
7   Are you _____ going to London for your university studies?
8   Don't worry if you _____ paint; we can go and buy some more.

C **Complete the words in the sentences.**

1   There are some beautiful old paintings and furniture in the m _ _ _ _ _.
2   Can you go to the c _ _ _ _ _ shop and get some milk, please?
3   What are you going to study at u _ _ _ _ _ _ _ _ _?
4   I'm going to the p _ _ _ office to buy stamps and send a letter.
5   I like studying at the l _ _ _ _ _ _ because it's quiet in there.
6   The shopping c _ _ _ _ _ is always crowded on Saturday morning.
7   When I broke my leg, I had to stay in h _ _ _ _ _ _ _ for a week.
8   They found the thief and took him to the p _ _ _ _ _ station.

D **Circle the correct words.**

1   Look to the left and to the right before you across / cross the street.
2   When I got on / in the bus, I saw my friend so I sat next to him.
3   Just follow / walk the map and you will find the museum easily.
4   A group of joggers ran along / through the park.
5   Walk to the corner and then go ahead / straight on.
6   My dog jumped over / past the gate and ran to the park.
7   We drove through / under the bridge and then turned right.
8   Where do we get of / off the bus? Is it at the next stop?

Grammar

A **Complete the sentences with the words.**

| already | ever | just | never | still | yet | for | since |

1 I've _____ finished painting the house! I'm so tired now!

2 We've known Tom and his family _____ about six years.

3 She _____ hasn't been to the new museum in the city centre.

4 The Smiths have _____ sold their old house and bought a new one.

5 It's strange, but I've _____ been to the Acropolis, and I live in Athens!

6 That restaurant is quite famous and it's been here _____ 1910.

7 Have you _____ sailed in the Aegean? If you haven't, I think you should.

8 It's a big house and I don't think they've finished painting it _____.

B **Correct the mistakes in the sentences.**

1 That's not hers house.

2 I think this pen is my.

3 Is you're new flat nice?

4 Yes, the Ferrari is ours car.

5 I think Jack is in him room.

6 Do you like theirs house?

7 My cats name is Lulu.

8 That's Les new car over there.

9 Where are the childrens toys?

10 This is my grandparents house.

11 The sofa's in this shop are expensive.

12 The hospitals' car park is small.

C **Complete the sentences with *a*, *an*, *the* or – if no article is necessary.**

1 There's _____ new restaurant that I want to try. Everyone says _____ food is really good.

2 When you visit _____ Egypt, don't forget to take a cruise on _____ Nile river.

3 I watched _____ interesting documentary about _____ Rome and how it became powerful.

4 Many people go climbing in _____ Himalayas, but not all of them try to climb _____ Mount Everest.

5 I'm so excited! In _____ July, we're going to fly to _____ United States for our holiday!

6 Let's take _____ holiday and go to _____ Africa next year; it'll be a lot of fun!

7 _____ car Max bought is _____ Mercedes and he's telling everyone about it!

8 Kelly is very sporty; she plays _____ tennis every weekend and basketball on _____ Thursdays.

7 Time Out!

Reading:	multiple-choice & matching, looking for connections (pronouns)
Vocabulary:	hobby-related words, multiple-choice cloze, using prepositions
Grammar:	conditionals: zero & first, gerunds & infinitives, open cloze, looking at the whole text
Listening:	matching, listening for clues
Speaking:	prompt card activity, answering in complete sentences, giving detailed information
Writing:	an advert, making suggestions & persuading, understanding who & what, suggesting & persuading

A participant attempts the course in the Red Bull Soapbox Race in Taipei, Taiwan

Reading

A Match the free-time activities to pictures 1–6.

circus skills   baking   robotics club   singing
gardening club   origami

B Which of the activities in A have you tried? Which would you like to try in the future? Why? Discuss with a partner.

C Read these adverts for clubs. Which one is the most expensive?

Word Focus

to be into something: to really love something

to juggle: to throw balls in the air and catch them

unicycle: a bicycle with only one wheel

tightrope: a long rope, high above ground that people walk on

to practise: to do something often to become good at it

skills: the ability to do something well

confidence: feeling good about yourself

to perform: to do something for others to watch and enjoy

A

ROBOTICS CLUB

Do you like solving problems?
Would you like to build and program your own robot?
If so, come to robotics club!

Tuesdays,
6.00 p.m.–7.30 p.m.,
Science room 2,
£5 per session.

This is what people say about it:

"Some people think I'm boring because I'm into robotics. They think we just play with robots – but actually we make the robots ourselves. It's great fun!"
—David

"I'm working on a new robot. He's called Derek and I want to program him to do my homework!"
—Jessica

B

CIRCUS SKILLS WORKSHOP

Have you watched people juggling on YouTube?
Would you like to try it yourself?
We can teach you to juggle, ride a unicycle and to walk the tightrope.
Come along to learn and practise new skills!

Read what people say about the workshop:

"I can juggle really well. The most important part of juggling is throwing, not catching. It looks difficult, but if you practise hard, you'll be able to juggle too! I practise for two hours every day!"
—James

"I love walking the tightrope. You have to keep your head up – don't look down. And keep your feet straight. Come to the workshop and try it!"
—Katie

Wednesdays, 5.00 p.m.–6.30 p.m,
Sports Hall, £10 per session

C

SINGING CLUB

Do you love singing?
Do you want to make new friends and build your confidence?
Come to Singing club and learn how to sing in a group.
Professional singer, Janice Perkins leads the club.

We perform six shows every year!

Here's what our singers say about the club:

"We learn all kinds of songs. Pop songs, classical songs, and songs from musicals, like Cats and Les Miserables. It's great fun and I've made loads of new friends."
—Tom

"My singing voice has improved so much since I joined the club! Janice is a fantastic teacher. I love performing our shows."
—Anna

Saturdays, 9.00 a.m. – 11.00 a.m
School Hall, it's free!

Read adverts A–C again and decide which club each person should try.

1 "I love sports and I have a strong arms." ☐
2 "I can program computers and I love Science." ☐
3 "I have lots of free time to practise a new hobby." ☐
4 "It's my dream to be a famous pop star." ☐
5 "I don't want to do my own homework." ☐
6 "I love all the famous West End musicals." ☐

Read the *Exam Close-up*. Then read the *Exam Task* and look for names and pronouns.

Now complete the *Exam Task*.

Exam Close-up

Looking for connections (pronouns)

- Read the conversations quickly for general understanding.
- Look for any names and pronouns (e.g. *I, he, them, ours*, etc.).
- Then look for pronouns that match in the options (e.g. *Mary = she, the book = it*, etc.). This will help you to choose the correct answer.

Exam Task

Part 1

Complete the five conversations. Choose the answer **A**, **B** or **C**.

1 Where did you get those juggling balls?
   A I bought it online.
   B My sister gave them to me.
   C I didn't have any money.

2 Why didn't you go to robotics club yesterday?
   A I was helping Jo with her homework.
   B It was great fun!
   C Of course you can.

3 Shall we sing a song from *The Lion King*?
   A It's beautiful.
   B Yes, we did.
   C That's a great idea.

4 Is that red unicycle yours?
   A I love it.
   B I don't like mine.
   C Yes, it's mine.

5 There were too many people at singing club, so I couldn't go.
   A I'd like to.
   B That's a shame.
   C I'm not sure.

Part 2

Complete the telephone conversation between two friends. What does Gary say to Mark? Choose from **A–H**.

Mark: Are you ready to go the circus skills workshop this evening?
Gary: (6) ___
Mark: Me too. I forgot to tell you, Nick's coming.
Gary: (7) ___
Mark: Actually, he's done it before.
Gary: (8) ___
Mark: I don't think so.
Gary: (9) ___
Mark: Because he's not very good at juggling, or riding a unicycle!
Gary: (10) ___
Mark: His brother told me, but don't say anything!

   A Why didn't you tell me?
   B That's good. He can give us some advice.
   C How do you know? Have you seen him trying?
   D Of course I am. I can't wait!
   E Does he do it very often?
   F Really? Why do you say that?
   G I didn't know he was interested in it.
   H I don't believe it.

3 Complete the sentences to make verb + noun collocations. Look at the adverts to check your answers.

solve   make   build   join   program   practise

1 Carl is very shy. He needs to _____ his **confidence**.
2 To be really good at baking, you have to _____ the **skills** you learnt at baking club when you get home.
3 If you like reading and you want to _____ new **friends**, you should try Book Club.
4 I love Maths and I like to _____ **problems**. I want to be an engineer when I leave school.
5 If you're bored after school, you should _____ **a club**.
6 I want to _____ **a robot** to tidy my bedroom for me.

- Which hobbies are most popular with teenagers in your country? Why?
- Which free-time activities are best for teenagers, which for adults, and which for old people? Why?

Ideas Focus

Vocabulary

A Which two things might you need for each hobby? Complete the table with the correct words.

tent paint guitar camera brushes controller
selfie stick instrument video game sleeping bag

Hobby	Equipment
1 camping	
2 art	
3 gaming	
4 photography	
5 music	

B Complete the dialogues with words from A.

1 **A:** You play the _____ really well.
   B: Thanks. It's my favourite _____.

2 **A:** Oh, no! It's really cold and I forgot to bring my
      _____.
   B: It's OK. I brought two. They're in my
      _____.

3 **A:** I'd like a photo of us in front of the Eiffel Tower. Have
      you got the _____?
   B: Yes, here it is. Put it on the _____ and I'll
      hold it.

4 **A:** Have you got enough blue _____ for
      the sky?
   B: Yes, but I need to buy more _____.
      These ones are really old now.

5 **A:** Wow! This is the best _____ I've ever
      played!
   B: Where's the other _____? I want to play
      too!

C Complete the sentences with the words.

creative boring exciting
relaxing unusual active

1 I like baking. I'm a _____ person
   and like making things.

2 I enjoy being _____. I spend a
   lot of time playing sports and team games.

3 Walking on a really high tightrope is so
   _____! There's nothing else
   like it.

4 I don't understand why my dad
   loves gardening. I think it's really
   _____.

5 I love going to the beach. It's very
   _____ to lie on the sand and do
   nothing.

6 Robotics is an _____ hobby – I
   don't know anyone else who does it.

D Match the sentences with the pictures.

1 I live in Scotland so we often go **hiking** in the
   Highlands. ☐

2 I'm always worried, so I do **yoga** to help me relax. ☐

3 We live near the sea and I love to go **sailing**. ☐

4 I love playing **chess** and I can even win against my
   uncle now! ☐

5 We do **athletics** at school and I really enjoy running. ☐

6 I always play **table tennis** at After-school club. ☐

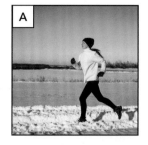

A

B

C

D

E

F

Match the activities in bold in D with these verbs.

go _____ _____

do _____ _____

play _____ _____

Circle the correct words in these conversations.

1 What do you like to do in / on your free time?

2 I'm a big fan in / of chess.

3 How about / What say about going to the theatre tonight?

4 I'm not crazy about / for the theatre. I prefer the cinema.

5 What are you interested about / in?

6 I spend a lot of time on / with sailing.

7 What do you usually do at / for the weekend?

8 I'm involved in / to a youth club so I go there.

9 What sort of hobbies do you do / have?

10 I'm really into / onto sport and keeping fit.

11 I love football. Are you keen in / on it, too?

12 I love soap operas. I can't / don't stop watching them!

Exam Close-up

Using prepositions

- For the multiple-choice task, you are often tested on prepositions (*in, on, at,* etc.).
- Read the text and underline any words before or after the gaps that need a preposition (e.g. *interested in*).
- Think of which preposition could go in the gap.
- Then look at the answer choices and choose the best preposition.

G Read the *Exam Close-up*. Then read the *Exam Task* and underline any words before or after the gaps that need a preposition.

H Now complete the *Exam Task*.

Exam Task

Read the article about two teenage hikers. Choose the best word (**A**, **B** or **C**) for each space.

Hiking teens lucky to be alive!

When teenagers Kyndall Jack and Nicholas Cendoya decided to go hiking (**1**) _____ the forest near Los Angeles, they didn't plan to get lost (**2**) _____ five days. They were hiking (**3**) _____ near the city they could see the tall buildings and hear the traffic, but the forest was so thick they couldn't find a road that was just 150m (**4**) _____. When they realized they were lost, they called 911, but their phone stopped (**5**) _____ before police could find where they were. They only had a (**6**) _____ water and soon it was all gone. Police used dogs to help search (**7**) _____ them. (**8**) _____ Kyndall and Nicholas were taken straight to hospital. They were tired and thirsty, but knew they were lucky to be alive!

	A	B	C
1	at	in	up
2	for	since	about
3	too	enough	so
4	away	far	short
5	to work	worked	working
6	little	few	lot
7	after	around	for
8	Both	Each	They

- Do you prefer to spend your free time doing something active, relaxing, exciting or creative? Why?
- "If you don't have a hobby, you're boring!" Do you agree? Why? / Why not?

Ideas Focus

7 Time Out!

Grammar

Conditionals: Zero & First

A Underline all the verbs in these zero conditional sentences.

   a If you have a smart phone, you don't need a camera.
   b If you buy this book, you get a free CD.

B Look at the sentences in A again and choose the correct words to complete the rules.

   1 We form the zero conditional with *If* + present simple + present perfect / present simple.
   2 When the sentence starts with *If* we use a question mark / comma in the middle of the sentence.
   3 We use the zero conditional to talk about facts / future possibilities.
   4 In zero conditional sentences, we can replace *if* with how / when.

C Underline all the verbs in these first conditional sentences.

   a If you go camping, you'll need a tent.
   b If you practise hard, you'll be a good guitar player.
   c You'll find juggling difficult if you don't have strong arms.

D Look at the sentences in C again and choose true (T) or false (F).

   1 We form the first conditional with *If* + past simple + *will* + infinitive. ☐
   2 We use the first conditional to talk about something that is likely to happen in the future. ☐
   3 You still need a comma when *if* is <u>not</u> at the start of a conditional sentence. ☐
   4 In first conditionals we can replace *will* with *can, may, might* or *could*. ☐

▶ Grammar Focus p. 166 (7.1 to 7.2)

E Complete the sentences using the zero conditional and the verbs in brackets.

   1 If you _____ a picture, you _____ paints and paper. (paint, need)
   2 If Dad _____ chess, he usually _____. (play, win)
   3 If they _____ a word, they _____ their dictionary. (not understand, use)
   4 If my sister _____, everyone _____ the room. (sing, leave)
   5 John _____ if he _____ online games. (not sleep, play)
   6 I _____ some yoga if I _____ worried and stressed. (do, feel)

F Read a–e and complete the sentences 1–5 using the first conditional.

   a The winner of the game is the person who finishes first.
   b Join this club and learn to paint and draw!
   c Answer this question correctly and win €5000!
   d 'Read this book and laugh out loud!
   e BBQ tomoz if weather gr8.

   1 If you _____ first, you _____ the game.
   2 If you _____ this club, you _____ to paint and draw.
   3 If you this _____ question correctly, you _____ €5000!
   4 If you _____ this book, you _____.
   5 They _____ a barbecue tomorrow if the weather _____ great.

G Match 1–6 with a–f.

   1 Daddy, will you buy me an ice cream
   2 You'll feel better in the morning
   3 If she finds this stamp.
   4 If you talk in the class,
   5 If he likes skateboarding,
   6 They make a snack

   a if you go to bed early.
   b if I'm good?
   c he'll love snowboarding.
   d if they feel hungry.
   e she'll complete her collection.
   f the teacher will send you out.

Gerunds

H Read the sentences about John and underline all the verb + *-ing* forms.

1 John isn't interested in studying.
2 He goes swimming twice a week.
3 He loves hiking.
4 Singing is his least favourite activity.

I These *-ing* forms are examples of gerunds. Look at the sentences in H again and choose the correct words to complete the rules.

a Gerunds act as nouns / adjectives in a sentence.
b Gerunds can come after a verb or a preposition / pronoun.
c A gerund can / cannot be the subject of a sentence.

Infinitives

J Read the sentences and underline the infinitives with *to*.

a Jo doesn't want to go on holiday with her parents.
b She's happy to stay at home and hang out with her friends.
c Jason isn't old enough to drive, so he usually walks to college.
d Today he's going shopping to buy a bike.

K Match the sentences in J with the uses below.

1 an infinitive to show purpose ☐
2 an infinitive following an adjective ☐
3 an infinitive after *too* or *enough* ☐
4 an infinitive after a verb ☐

L Read the sentences and underline all the infinitive verbs without *to*.

a I love skateboarding! I would rather spend my day at the skate park than at school!
b Why don't you try skateboarding? You can get fit and it might help you to make some new friends.
c But if you want to come to the skate park, you had better practise first – all the kids there are brilliant skateboarders!

M Match the sentences in L with the rules below.

1 Use an infinitive without *to* after *had better* to show something is the correct thing to do. ☐
2 Use an infinitive without *to* after a modal verb. ☐
3 Use an infinitive without *to* after *would rather* to show preference. ☐

▶ Grammar Focus pp. 166 & 167 (7.3 to 7.4)

N Complete the half dialogues with the correct form of the verbs.

1 The team hope _____. (win)
2 Do you like _____ horror films? (watch)
3 We should _____ to the museum. (go)
4 Could we _____ a room in that hotel? (book)
5 I'm worried about _____ the exam. (take)
6 Is it worth _____ the new shopping centre? (visit)

a I'm sure you are clever enough _____. (pass)
b I'd rather _____ a comedy. (see)
c Yes, it's great, I went _____ there today. (shop)
d They had better _____! (not lose)
e _____ tickets for that exhibition is difficult. (get)
f No, it's too expensive _____ there. (stay)

O Now match 1–6 with a–f.

P Read the *Exam Close-up* and then complete the *Exam Task*.

Exam Task

Complete the text about hobbies. Write **ONE** word for each space.

A hobby makes you happy!

If you are bored of (**1**) _____ television every night, it's worth (**2**) _____ a new hobby. If you (**3**) _____ sporty, you could (**4**) _____ a gymnastics club or start learning to play a ball game. If you do a sport, you (**5**) _____ become fitter and make new friends. If you are (**6**) _____ interested (**7**) _____ sports, perhaps you would rather (**8**) _____ something creative, like art or woodwork. It's (**9**) _____ trying a new hobby because there are lots of activities you can enjoy! Don't be afraid (**10**) _____ try something new! You might find you have a talent!

Exam Close-up

Looking at the whole text
• Always read the whole text through first to get the general idea.
• Look out for negative words that may be missing; they can change the meaning of a sentence.
• Make sure you use the right forms in conditional clauses.
• Check if you need a gerund or infinitive.

Listening

A Match the hobbies in the pictures (A–F) with the words (1–6) below.

1 board game / quiz ☐
2 traditional dancing ☐
3 making jewellery ☐
4 photography ☐
5 playing the drums ☐
6 origami ☐

B Work with a partner and discuss this question. Which hobbies from A could you try if you are …

1 sociable? ☐ ☐
2 musical? ☐
3 competitive? ☐
4 creative? ☐ ☐ ☐

C 🔊 7.1 Listen to the conversations. In each one, do the two people have the same opinion (S) or a different opinion (D)?

Conversation 1: ___
Conversation 2: ___
Conversation 3: ___
Conversation 4: ___
Conversation 5: ___
Conversation 6: ___

D 🔊 7.1 Decide if these phrases are used to show that you think someone is right (R) or wrong (W). Then listen again and tick [✓] the ones you hear.

1 actually ___ ☐
2 that's true ___ ☐
3 but ___ ☐
4 in actual fact ___ ☐
5 absolutely ___ ☐
6 you're right ___ ☐

Exam Close-up

Listening for clues

- Conversations in the listening tasks often include discussion of what's true and what isn't.
- Listen for words like *absolutely, that's true, you're right*. They show that the speaker thinks what the other person says is true.
- Listen for words and phrases like *actually, in fact, but, in actual fact*. They show that the speaker is going to correct the other person.
- Noticing these clues in the conversation will help you choose the correct answers.

E Read the *Exam Close-up* and then read the *Exam Task*. Does it ask about hobbies in the past or in the present?

F 🔊 7.2 Now listen and complete the *Exam Task*. Remember to listen for clues to help you decide what is correct and what isn't.

Exam Task

Listen to Mark and his mother talking about themselves and people they know. Which hobby does each person have? For questions **1–5**, write a letter **A–G** next to each person.

You will hear the conversation twice.

1 John ☐
2 Pat ☐
3 Mark ☐
4 Mum ☐
5 Sandra ☐

A playing football
B playing the guitar
C playing the drums
D playing the piano
E photography
F making jewellery
G painting

G 🔊 7.3 Listen again and check your answers.

Speaking

A Read sentences 1–4. Then match the words in bold to definitions a–d.

1 I'm always scared before I walk onto the **stage**.
2 The biggest **audience** our band has played to was 200 people.
3 I love **performing** – I like to show everyone what I can do.
4 My sister has a real **talent** for music – she can play the violin and piano, and she can sing!

a Singing, dancing, acting, playing music, etc. in front of a lot of people.
b A natural ability to be really good at something.
c The place in a theatre where the actors / dancers / singers are.
d The group of people who come to one place to watch something.

B Look at the pictures. Work with a partner and answer these questions.

- What do the people in the pictures enjoy doing?
- What do these activities have in common?
- Do you enjoy performing?
- Have you ever been on the stage?

C Read the *Exam Close-up*. Then work with a partner and decide who is Student A and who is Student B. Read your information in the *Exam Task* and think how you will form complete sentences.

D Now work in pairs to complete the *Exam Task*. Use the *Useful Expressions* to help you.

Useful Expressions

Giving detailed information
The competitions starts at 8 p.m. / 8.30 a.m.
The exhibition starts on the 1st of May / 4th January.
It finishes on the 15th April / 20th June.
The website address is …
You can enter if you are aged between … and …
You can win a laptop / iPod / guitar.

Exam Close-up

Answering in complete sentences
- There will be a lot of information on your card, so read it carefully before you begin.
- When your partner asks you a question, scan your card quickly for the correct information.
- Give your answer in a full sentence. Don't just read out the information.

Exam Task

1 **Student A:** Look at the information about a Talent Competition. Answer B's questions.
Student B: Turn to page 179. Ask **Student A** questions about the Talent competition.

Talent competition

at Greenhill School on 30th June
For ages 13–18
Show us your talent and win a prize!
Ist Prize = Win an iPad!
visit www.greenhill_talent@edu.com for more information

2 **Student B:** Look at the information about a Photography exhibition.
Student A: Turn to page 178. Ask **Student B** questions about the Photography exhibition.

Photography exhibition

Enter your photos in the summer exhibition at the city library
from June 30th – July 30th.
Open from 9 a.m. – 9 p.m. daily
Photos by children aged 10 – 18 only.
You could win a camera!
For more information, visit www.ports.library.com

- Do you enjoy being on stage? Why? / Why not?
- 'Talent is more important than practice if you want to be good at something.' Do you agree? Why? / Why not?

Ideas Focus

Writing: an advert

Learning Focus

Making suggestions & Persuading

- There are different structures you can use to make suggestions.
- Some are followed by the infinitive form (*to do = Would you like to do* some singing?), others by a noun or a gerund (*doing = How about doing some singing?*). Other structures are followed by a pronoun and the infinitive without *to* (*… we do = How about we do some yoga?*).
- We can use imperatives (the infinitive form without *to*) to persuade others to do something. We usually add a reason, e.g. *Come to tennis club! You can make new friends and get fit!*
- Use *do not* or *don't* before the imperative for the negative, e.g. *Don't waste your time on gaming! Get outside and join our running club!*

A Read the email and the advert. Then answer the questions. Write Andy, Max or Sam.

FREE LESSONS!
Learn how to be a
DJ!
We will teach you how to mix and play songs. Be the most popular person at parties!
Come along every Saturday 3-5
TRAX STUDIO
Ask for Sam

email

From: Andy
To: Max

Hi there,

How are things?

I've got a great idea. What do you think about taking DJ lessons? Would you be interested in trying it? My cousin Sam is the teacher! Maybe you could ask Dave, too. Anyway, if you're interested, let me know.

Bye for now,

Andy

1. Who wrote the email? _____
2. Who received the email? _____
3. Who is spoken about in the email? _____

4. Who makes a suggestion? _____
5. Who is offering something to other people? _____

B Look at the suggestions and circle the correct words.

1. Join / To join Swimming Club and get fit!
2. Would you be interested in do / doing it?
3. What about to take / taking art lessons?

4. How about we start / starting stamp collecting?
5. Would you like to learn / learn about robotics?
6. Aren't / Don't be lazy! Try something new!

C Read the information and then complete each gap in the advert with one word.

- Drama club
- Thursdays 3.30 p.m. for 2 hours
- 10 weeks = £80

Drama club
Are you bored after school? Can you sing, dance or act?
Don't **(1)** _____ shy!
How about **(2)** _____ to Drama club?
It's every Thursday after school from 3.30 p.m. till **(3)** _____.
Only £ **(4)** _____ per week!
Be brave and **(5)** _____ something new!

Read these notes about a new activity in your town and write an advert for it. Use the phrases in the *Useful Expressions* to help you.

- **Activity:** skateboarding
- **Where:** new skateboarding park
- **Reasons to try:** healthy, fresh air, fun, free

Read the *Exam Close-up*. Then do the *Exam Task* below. Remember to underline the important information.

Exam Task

Read Julie's email and Rob's notes. Fill in the information on Rob's advert.

◀ ▶ | email

From: Julie
To: Rob

Hi Rob

I'm planning a free Talent Night. Why don't we meet this evening to talk about where we could do it and when? You're good at art so you can make the advert.

Speak soon
Julie

TALENT NIGHT

On Saturday 14th December
At Wheelers Hill Youth Club
Starts at 6.30 p.m. Two and a half hours.
Drinks for sale but no food – people should bring snacks.
Contact Julie for more info.

Useful Expressions

Suggesting
Why don't we …?
How about we …?
What about + -ing …
Would you like to …?
Would you be interested
  in + -ing …

Persuading
Come to …
Try something new!
Don't be lazy / shy / boring!
Be brave / strong / active!

Talent Night

Why **(1)** _____ you show the world your talent!

Don't be shy! **(2)** _____ to Talent Night at

Wheelers Hill Youth Club!

Starts at 6.30 p.m.

Finishes **(3)** _____.

Drinks for sale, but please bring some **(4)** _____.

For more information: **(5)** _____

Young girls training at a special school for circus performers in Shoreditch, London

7 Mechanical Lizard Car

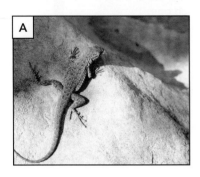

A

B

C

Before you watch

A Which of these can get around the desert more easily?
Match the words with the pictures.

1 desert rat ☐
2 off road vehicle ☐
3 desert lizard ☐

While you watch

B Watch the video and decide if these statements are T (True) or F (False).

1 Before Cam built his machine, he made a model of it. ☐
2 Cam uses nature to get ideas for his machines. ☐
3 Cam wants his car to be like a lizard. ☐
4 John has driven Cam's machine before. ☐
5 John can drive Cam's machine anywhere. ☐
6 John and Cam are not having fun. ☐

After you watch

C Complete the summary of the video below using these words.

careful   hand   hills   idea   lizard   machine   see   top

Cam wanted to make a(n) **(1)** _____ that could go anywhere in
the desert, like the animals that live there, so his **(2)** _____ was
to make a mechanical **(3)** _____. First he made a small model
that he could hold in his **(4)** _____. His machine can go up and
down **(5)** _____. Cam tells John how to operate it. John drives
up a steep hill and when he gets to the **(6)** _____, he stops
because Cam never drives anywhere that he can't **(7)** _____.
John goes down the hill with help from Cam. He has to be very
(8) _____ because he doesn't want to have an accident.
Both of them have a great time with Cam's mechanical lizard.

Ideas Focus

- Would you like to drive a machine like the mechanical lizard? Why? / Why not?
- Do you think Cam's machine could become popular? Why? / Why not?
- Would you like to travel through a desert? Why? / Why not?

8 Personal Best

Reading:	matching, looking for words with similar meanings
Vocabulary:	sport-related words, collocations, phrasal verbs
Grammar:	modals for advice, permission, ability, intention, necessity & obligation
Listening:	gap-fill (monologue), listening for numbers & dates
Speaking:	asking about likes, asking for advice, giving advice & responding to advice
Writing:	a blog, using the correct tense, using appropriate vocabulary, positive emotions & negative emotions

A team of people whitewater rafting down Six Mile Creek. Chugach National Forest, Alaska

Reading

A Match these signs with the correct sports.

1 Tennis ☐ 3 Formula 1 ☐ 5 Football ☐
2 Athletics ☐ 4 Volleyball ☐ 6 Ice Hockey ☐

A
The Grand Prix Circuit
- ▣ General public admission area
- ▣ Limited spaces left
- ▣ Sold out
- ▣ VIP area
- ▣ Employees only
- ☐ Paddock and pits

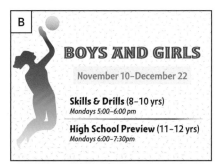

B
BOYS AND GIRLS
November 10–December 22

Skills & Drills (8–10 yrs)
Mondays 5:00–6:00 pm

High School Preview (11–12 yrs)
Mondays 6:00–7:30pm

C
TICKET
BARCLAYS PREMIERSHIP
CHELSEA V NEWCASTLE UNITED

Saturday, 19 NOV
Kick off time: 3:00 PM

EAST UPPER STAND

GATE: 1	IMPAIRED VIEW
ROW: 31	
SEAT: 0159	£47.00

D

13:05	MEN'S LONG JUMP
13:12	WOMEN'S 150M
13:22	WOMEN'S 200M HURDLES
13:32	MEN'S 200M HURDLES
13:44	MEN'S 100M
13:57	WOMEN'S 100M
14:06	MEN'S T44 100M
14:10	WOMEN'S LONG JUMP

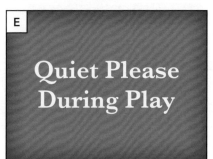

E
Quiet Please During Play

F

HELMET	£70
FACE PROTECTION	£76
HOCKEY SKATES	£190
GLOVES	£40
SHOULDER PADS	£72
SHIN GUARDS	£40
ELBOW PADS	£35
TOTAL	**£523**

B Which sport in A is your favourite? Why? Tell your partner.

C Work with a partner and answer the questions. Then quickly read both brochures to check your answers.

1 Who brought cricket to Jamaica?
2 Which country did baseball originally come from?

Word Focus

colony: a country or area under the control of another country

independent: an independent country is not ruled or governed by another country

authorities: people or an organisation with power and control

bullfighting: a traditional entertainment in Spain where a person fights and sometimes kills a bull

JAMAICA
relax, unwind, and enjoy some cricket!

Are you looking for beautiful beaches, friendly people and amazing music and culture? Then come to Jamaica!

And if you love sport, don't forget that Jamaica is also famous for cricket. The island's great weather means that cricket lovers can play and watch this sport all year!

The Brits brought cricket to Jamaica when it was a British colony. When Jamaica became independent our people continued to play cricket at a high level. If you want to know more about the history of cricket in Jamaica, visit the Sports museum in Kingston.

And if you want to see the best Jamaican players, remember that in international cricket we don't take part as 'Jamaica'. We form a team with Barbados and other small islands, and are called the West Indies. The West Indies is one of the best teams in the world. Buy a ticket to see the West Indies play during your holiday!

Read the text again then decide which sentences are true (T) and which are false (F).

1 Jamaica doesn't have its own national cricket team. ☐
2 Jamaicans taught the British how to play cricket. ☐
3 The West Indies is a country in the Caribbean. ☐
4 Two university students showed baseball to the Cubans. ☐
5 c150 years ago, Spain was in control of Cuba. ☐
6 The Spanish in Cuba loved baseball. ☐

Complete the sentences with *back, for, in, of* and *to*.

1 What do you think _____ when I say 'Hawaii'?
2 Brazil is famous _____ its national football team.
3 I have never taken part _____ a marathon, but I want to.
4 The stadium is very close _____ the train station.
5 My uncle went to the Olympics and he brought _____ a present for me.

Exam Close-up

Looking for words with similar meanings

- The sentences often contain key words that are similar to the key words in the notices.
- Look for such synonyms (e.g. *exit / way out, cannot use / closed, no talking / quiet*) and underline them.

F Read the *Exam Close-up*. Then look at the *Exam Task* and underline any words with similar meanings.

G Now complete the *Exam Task*.

Exam Task

Which notice (**A–H**) says this (**1–5**)?

1 Do this if you need help.
2 Keep your things safe in here.
3 You cannot use this at the moment.
4 The time for your class will change.
5 This is a special offer for new members.

A

SAUNA CLOSED DUE TO REPAIRS

B

NOTICE
Make sure your things are secure from thieves!
Use the lockers provided.

C
New aerobics timetable starts from March 23rd.

D
Did you find a pair of black swimming goggles? Please call me: 07364 577283

E

CHANGING ROOM
No food or drinks allowed

F

Join Now, Pay Later
This month only

G

IMPORTANT
SHOES MUST BE WORN AT ALL TIMES IN THE GYM

H

NOTICE
HELP
Push button for assistance

CUBA

the perfect combination of history, culture, beaches and baseball!

If you ever get tired of the wonderful beaches, and fascinating culture here in Cuba, come to the exhibition on baseball to find out why this sport became a symbol of freedom for Cubans. How did it all start? Well, in the 1860s, two Cuban brothers returned home from a university in the USA. They brought the baseball back with them and it quickly became popular.

Soon after this, Cuba and Spain had a war because the Cubans wanted to be independent from Spain. The Spanish authorities tried to stop the sport. This is because the Cubans began to prefer baseball to bullfighting, which was the traditional Spanish sport. Cubans did not want anyone to tell them what to do. So, baseball became a symbol of freedom.

Find out more at the exhibition. Starts tomorrow and runs for two months!

- Is there a sport that you don't like? Why don't you like it?
- 'Everyone should be a sports fan. It's fun and it brings people together.' Do you agree? Why? / Why not?

Ideas Focus

Vocabulary

A Match the sports to the pictures.

| basketball cricket football table tennis tennis volleyball |

1
_____

3
_____

5
_____

2
_____

4
_____

6
_____

B Match a sport from A with the words.

1 net + racket + court = _____

2 goal + ball + pitch = _____

3 basket + ball + court = _____

4 net + ball + court = _____

5 bat + ball + pitch = _____

6 bat + ball + net = _____

C Complete the table.

Verb	Noun (person)	Noun (sport)
dive	diver	(1)
cycle	(2)	cycling
-	gymnast	(3)
-	(4)	athletics
swim	swimmer	(5)
sail	(6)	sailing

D Complete the sentences with words from C.

1 My grandfather was a _____ and he travelled all over the world on ships.

2 You should not _____ from rocks into the sea because you might hit your head.

3 In my _____ class at school, I have learned to stand on my hands.

4 Is Usain Bolt the best _____ in the world?

5 There was an accident during the race and three _____ fell off their bikes.

6 _____ at the beach got out of the water quickly when the shark appeared!

E Complete the sentences with the correct form of *do* or *go*.

1 Last summer, I _____ swimming every day and I really enjoyed it.

2 I'm _____ cycling in the park later. Do you want to come with me?

3 Olga was _____ gymnastics when she fell and hurt her leg badly.

4 My cousins are so lucky. They _____ diving in the Bahamas every year.

5 I really hate _____ athletics outdoors in the winter when it's raining!

6 If we have the money, we will _____ sailing in the Aegean this summer.

F Complete these sentences with the correct people.

| fan opponent referee manager goalkeeper |

1 The _____ blew the whistle to start the game.

2 The _____ stopped the ball from going into the goal.

3 James is my strongest _____ at tennis – he almost always wins!

4 I'm a big _____ of Chelsea and I go to all their matches.

5 The team lost all their games so they fired the _____ .

Circle the correct words.

The Special Ks

Novak Djokovic, Rafal Nadal, Roger Federer and Andy Murray. These are the tennis players who have been the best in the world for the last ten to fifteen years. They have (**1**) taken / won the big tournaments such as Wimbledon, the Australian Open, French Open and US Open. But they can't be champions forever. New talent is coming!

Meet Nick Kyrgios and Thanasi Kokkinakis. They're both from Australia and they're known as the Special Ks. They started (**2**) doing / playing tennis when they were very young, and now is their turn to be number one. But they have to (**3**) prepare / train very hard before that can happen. There are many things that the best players can do. Firstly, they can (**4**) hit / kick the ball with a lot of strength and make it difficult for their opponent to return it. Secondly, they can (**5**) keep going / keep doing and not get tired. Sometimes, a tennis match can go / hold on for 4 or 5 hours, so they must (**7**) feel / stay healthy and strong. Finally, the best players think like champions. They never (**8**) come up / give up and they fight until the end.

Remember their names – these guys will be the champions of the future.

Look at the pictures and complete the sentences with the words in the correct form.

| bounce | lose | miss | score | serve | throw |

1 He's going to _____ the ball.

2 Look! The ball is _____.

3 The team has _____ a goal!

4 Germany _____ the match.

5 Oh, no! He _____ the penalty!

6 She's going to _____ the ball.

Work with a partner. Write the verbs next to the correct group of nouns.

| win | score | race | coach | beat |

1 _____ a horse, a car, a motorbike
2 _____ another team, an opponent
3 _____ a goal, a point
4 _____ a race, a game, a match, a tournament
5 _____ a team, an athlete

Match the phrasal verbs in bold with their meanings.

1 It's so hot in the sauna. I'm going to **pass out**!
2 You should always **warm up** before you play a sport.
3 I **work out** three times a week at my local gym.
4 I need more time to study, so I have to **drop out** of the football team.
5 Darren runs really fast and I can never **catch up**.

a move fast enough to be equal to someone else
b exercise your body to keep fit
c become unconscious for a short time, like you are sleeping
d leave a class or a group that you were going to
e prepare for a sport by doing some gentle exercise

- Do you think top athletes should make a lot of money? Why? / Why not?
- Do you think all students should do sport at school? Why? / Why not?

Ideas Focus

8 Personal Best

Grammar

Modals (1)

A Read the sentences below and underline the modal verbs.

a Mark is a good swimmer; he could swim before he could walk.

b You can use my old racket if yours is broken.

c Can I borrow your bike, Mum?

d You can't borrow my bike, I will need it later.

e Shall I drive us to the swimming pool?

f Should we join the tennis club?

g We should learn to play before we join.

h I shall score a goal next time.

B Look again at the sentences in A. What form of the verb follows a modal? Which modal verb can we replace with *may*?

C Which sentence in A uses a modal verb to … ?

1 refuse permission (say no) ☐

2 give advice ☐

3 ask for permission ☐

4 say what someone was able to / was not able to do in the past ☐

5 ask for advice ☐

6 offer to do something ☐

7 give permission ☐

8 express a strong intention ☐

Asturias Motocross Championship in Valdesoto, Spain

D Read the questions with modal verbs. Which three questions have a similar meaning? What do they mean?

a Shall I check your bike?

b Should I check your bike?

c May I check your bike?

d Can I check your bike?

e Could I check your bike?

E At a motocross competition, which questions in D might a friend ask and which questions might a member of staff ask?

F Match a–e in D with answers 1–3. You can use some of the answers more than once.

1 Oh yes, please. I think there's a problem with the brakes.

2 No, I should check it and fix it myself.

3 Of course you can. You'll see that it's fine.

▶ Grammar Focus p. 167 (8.1 to 8.6)

G Make these sentences negative.

1 Motorcyclists should wear trainers.

2 He can play basketball.

3 They may jump into the pool.

4 I shall lose again!

5 She could run fast when she was young.

H Use the words in brackets and write a sentence in your notebooks giving advice with *should*.

1 Sam broke his ankle on the volleyball court. (hospital)

2 Sue wants to learn to ski. (lessons)

3 George's football boots are too small. (new boots)

4 John wants to enter a marathon. (run every day)

5 Andy doesn't like his tennis coach. (new coach)

I Rewrite the sentences with a modal verb.

1 Is it OK if I go fishing?

2 Please run faster!

3 It's a good idea to bring your swimsuit.

4 It's impossible for them to snowboard without snow

5 Do you want us to go to the sports centre?

6 Bring me a drink of water, please!

7 I don't have permission to play rugby.

8 It's a bad idea to swim in this water, children.

Modals (2)

J Read the sentences and underline the modal verbs.

1 You have to wear a helmet when you go climbing.
2 You must wear a lifejacket when you go sailing.
3 You mustn't ride a bike without a helmet.
4 You needn't put lights on your bike if you don't ride in the dark.
5 You don't have to run in the stadium, you can run on the road.

K Which modals in J are used to . . . ?

a say that it is a rule to do something (obligation) ☐ ☐
b say that it is not necessary to do something, (but you can if you want) ☐ ☐
c say that something is not allowed / forbidden ☐

A female climber abseiling down a rock face in the French Alps

L Complete the rule with the correct modals.

> mustn't   needn't   have to   must   don't have to

We use _____ and _____ to express obligation. We use _____ to say that something is not allowed (negative obligation), but to show there is no obligation or necessity we use _____ or _____.

➲ Grammar Focus pp. 167 & 168 (8.7 to 8.11)

JUNIOR PARK RUN

Do you like running? Or do you enjoy running races against your friends?
Come to Green Park 2km Junior Park Run every Saturday at 10 a.m!

- Junior Park Run is for children aged between 4–14 only.
- All runners need a parent / adult at the race to watch them.
- No bikes or scooters.
- No dogs allowed in the race.
- No need to bring water – we have a water station half-way.
- Entry is free!

Call 0788 926481 for more information.

M Complete the rules for Junior Park Run using *must, mustn't* and *don't have to*.

1 You _____ be aged between 4 and 14 to race.
2 You _____ use bikes or scooters in the race.
3 You_____ to bring water – there is a drink station at 1km.
4 Dogs _____ join the race.
5 You _____ come with an adult.
6 You _____ pay to do Junior Park Run.

N Complete the dialogues with *must, mustn't, don't have to, have to.*

1 **A:** Should I buy a tennis racket?
  B: You _____ buy a new one, you can borrow mine.
2 **A:** _____ I _____ wear boots for my riding lesson?
  B: Yes, you _____ wear riding boots.
3 **A:** Athletes _____ practise every day.
  B: That's right, everybody _____ rest sometimes.

4 **A:** Can I go to an exercise class at the sports centre?
  B: You _____ become a member first.
5 **A:** You _____ run around the swimming pool – it's dangerous!
  B: OK, sorry.
6 **A:** If you're under 14, you _____ bring an adult with you to the football match – it's a rule.
  B: OK – I'll ask my grandad to come with me.

Listening

A Look at these numbers. Practise saying them with a partner.

1	13	30	13th	30th
2	14	40	14th	40th
3	15	50	15th	50th
4	16	60	16th	60th
5	17	70	17th	70th
6	18	80	18th	80th
7	19	90	19th	90th
8	1st	21st	31st	
9	2nd	22nd	32nd	
10	3rd	23rd	33rd	

B `8.1` Listen and circle the numbers that you hear in A.

C `8.2` Look at the pairs of numbers. Listen and underline the part of each word that is stressed.

1	forty	fourteen
2	a hundred	a thousand
3	second	twenty-second
4	eighty	eighteen
5	seven	seventeen
6	sixteen	sixty

Exam Close-up

Listening for numbers & dates

- Be careful with the numbers like *fifteen* and *fifty*, which sound similar.
- Make sure your answer is logical, for example, *50th January* cannot be correct.
- Remember dates are pronounced *(twenty-)first, (twenty-)second, (twenty-)third, (twenty-) fourth,* etc.

D Work with a partner. Say a word from C. Can your partner tell you which word it is?

E Read the *Exam Close-up.* Then read the *Exam Task* and think about what kind of information is missing.

F `8.3` Now complete the *Exam Task.*

Exam Task

You will hear a man on the radio talking about a new sports club. Listen and complete each question. You will hear the information twice.

Watersports

Summer courses for children (**1**) 11- _____ years old.

Learn to sail, surf or (**2**) _____

Courses from June 13th until (**3**) _____

Prices from (**4**) _____ for three weeks.

Discount of (**5**) _____ for 2nd child.

G `8.4` Listen again and check your answers.

Speaking

A Which of these sports do you like best and least? Number them from 1 (best) to 8 (least).

table tennis	☐	running	☐
basketball	☐	swimming	☐
football	☐	zumba	☐
tennis	☐	yoga	☐

B Compare your answers with a partner.

C Complete the five conversations. Circle the correct answer, A, B or C.

1 I'd like to try a new sport.
   A Why don't you learn table tennis?
   B Shall I learn table tennis?
   C Do you start table tennis?

2 Does it cost a lot?
   A It isn't.
   B It isn't expensive.
   C You mustn't pay very much.

3 What should I wear?
   A You should buy a bat.
   B You needn't buy a table.
   C You needn't buy special clothes.

4 Where can I learn?
   A You must take lessons.
   B You should ask at the sports centre.
   C You have to play after school.

5 Could you teach me?
   A Yes, you may.
   B I'm afraid I can't play.
   C I'm not playing.

Exam Close-up

Making & responding to suggestions
- When you give advice use *should* and *could* <u>not</u> *must*.
- Remember you are making suggestions and giving advice, not giving orders, so give your advice in a friendly way.
- When you respond to advice, say if you think it is useful.
- If you don't accept the advice give a reason and be polite.

D Read the *Exam Close-up*. Then look at the *Exam Task* and think about the language you will use to ask questions and give / respond to advice.

E Work with a partner and complete the *Exam Task*. Use the *Useful Expressions* to help you.

Useful Expressions

Asking about likes
Do you like doing sport inside or outside?
Do you prefer doing sport alone or in a team?
Do you enjoy running?

Giving advice
Why don't you …?
You should …

You needn't / don't have to …
You could try …
You have to …

Responding to advice
That's a good idea.
I don't think that's a good idea because …
Or perhaps I could …

Exam Task

Your partner wants to start a new sport. Ask questions using the prompts. Listen then give advice and suggest a sport from the photos that your partner should try.

- alone or in a team?
- inside in outside?
- with a ball?
- with a racket?
- with music?
- to get fitter or to be stronger?

 Working out in the Gym

 Football

 Table Tennis

 Aerobics

 Basketball

 Running

Now change roles and repeat.

Ideas Focus

- Do you think everybody should do exercise? Why? / Why not?
- Do you think winning is important? Why? / Why not?

Writing: a blog

> ### Learning Focus
>
> **Using the correct tense**
> - When you describe an event that happened in the past, make sure you use the correct tenses.
> - Use the past simple to talk about a series of actions that happened one after the other, or for an action that began and ended in the past. Use the past continuous for actions that lasted longer.

A Read the blog and circle the correct tense.

Stan's Sports blog

Thursday 15th November

Yesterday I was at Capital Stadium and the atmosphere was electric! **(1)** I waited / was waiting for the start of the men's 100 metre race. It was so exciting to be there! Everyone there **(2)** looked forward to / was looking forward to a great race.

Smith **(3)** didn't start / wasn't starting well, but he quickly **(4)** caught / was catching the other runners. He was impressive and everyone was truly amazed! He **(5)** finished / was finishing first and **(6)** won / was winning easily!

B Read the sentence. Underline the adverb and circle the adjective.

The gymnast performed brilliantly. Her movements were incredible!

C Look back at the sentence in B. Then complete these rules with *adverb* or *adjective*.

1 We use an _____ to describe nouns.

2 We use an _____ to say more about verbs.

3 We often form an _____ by adding -*ly* to an _____.

D Look at the blog in A again. Write the adjectives and adverbs used to make the blog more interesting.

1 Adjectives: _____ _____
   _____ _____

2 Adverbs: _____ _____
   _____ _____

E Complete the blog post with the adjectives and the adverbs below.

    fast   close   slowly   amazing   suddenly   unbelievable

I saw an **(1)** _____ race last week. It was the best of the competition! The swimmers were all swimming **(2)** _____ to win, but only one could become the champion.

It was very **(3)** _____ because the swimmers were together in a line. But the American, Jack Johnson, was last and he was going **(4)** _____. Then **(5)** _____, he began to pass the others. It was **(6)** _____! I didn't think he could do it, but he did! Johnson touched first and won!

When you describe an event, you can also say how you feel about it. Look at the underlined words and phrases in the text. Which ones show positive emotions and which show negative emotions?

Last year I went to the Champions League final. My team, Arsenal, was playing against Barcelona and I was <u>thrilled</u>. It was <u>a dream come true</u> for me. The game started well and we scored a goal. I <u>couldn't stop cheering</u>! I was <u>confident</u> we could win. But then, it was <u>a disaster</u>! Barcelona quickly scored two goals. I was really <u>worried</u>. My team tried hard to score again, but they couldn't. Barcelona won and I was really <u>upset</u>.

Positive: _____

Negative: _____

3 Write a blog about the last Sports Day at your school OR a sports event you went to. Use the *Useful Expressions*. Remember to use the correct tenses, adjectives and adverbs, and say how you felt during the event.

4 Read the *Exam Close-up*. Then do the *Exam Task below*. Remember to use appropriate vocabulary.

Useful Expressions

Positive emotions	Negative emotions
thrilled	sad
excited	worried
confident	upset
looking forward to	disappointed
a dream come true	a disaster
couldn't stop shouting / cheering	

Exam Task

Read the text message from your friend, Emily.

● ○ ○	Email Message	↗
From: Emily		
To:		
Which sport did you see at the Olympic Games? Who won? Was it exciting? Text me! Emily xxx		

Write a text message to Emily and answer the questions. Write 35–45 words.

Exam Close-up

Using appropriate vocabulary

- When you describe an event, you have to use the right kind of vocabulary.
- Use adjectives and adverbs to make your description more interesting.
- Use positive and negative adjectives and phrases to show how you were feeling.

The opening ceremony at the Winter Olympics Turin, Italy

Before you watch

A Label the picture with these words.

helmet   pedal   tyre
unicycle   wheel

1

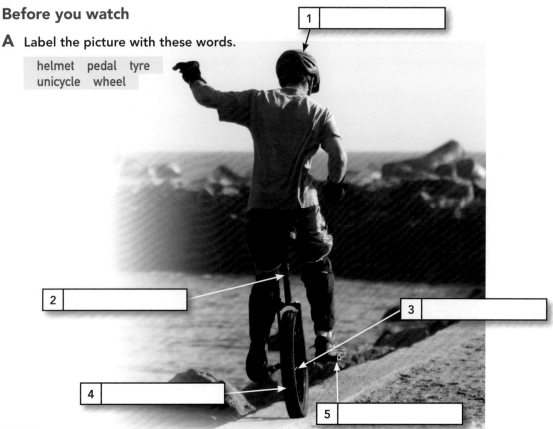

2

3

4

5

While you watch

B Watch the video and circle the words you hear.

1 What is it like to ride down a hill / mountain on a bicycle?

2 Now imagine doing it on one wheel / tyre.

3 The family ride unicycles which have special / thick tyres.

4 Every spring / summer they ride down Utah's ski slopes.

5 These one-wheelers may be safer / faster than traditional mountain bikes.

6 The sport requires the same skill / strength and endurance as mountain biking.

After you watch

C Complete the summary of the video below using these words.

bikes   crazy   pedals   perfect   popular   skill   strength   whole

Riding down mountains on one wheel is a sport called mountain unicycling, or muni for short. It started in the 1990s, and it is getting more **(1)** _____ every day. For muni, people ride special unicycles with thick tyres with rubber knobs and high grip **(2)** _____. In summer, Utah's ski slopes are **(3)** _____ for the fans of off-road unicycling. It looks **(4)** _____ and unstable but one-wheelers may be safer than traditional mountain **(5)** _____ because you can only ride as fast as you can pedal. Mountain unicycling needs the same **(6)** _____ and endurance as mountain biking, but it exercises the **(7)** _____ body. Mountain unicyclists must also have a lot of **(8)** _____ and concentration. When they are bored with the slopes, some even jump off the ski towers!

Ideas Focus

- Do you like outdoor sports that get you close to nature? Why? / Why not?
- Is it a good idea for a family to do the same sport together? Why? / Why not?

Review 4 Units 7 & 8

Vocabulary

A **Complete the words in the sentences.**

1 I enjoy camping and I love sleeping in a t _ _ t in the countryside.

2 The only instrument I can play well is the electric g _ _ _ _ r.

3 Without a c _ _ _ _ _ _ _ _ r, I can't play any video games.

4 Carla loves sport – she can play v _ _ _ _ _ _ _ l and tennis.

5 Last week I bought a tennis r _ _ _ _ t and started tennis lessons.

6 Get your bike. Let's go c _ _ _ _ _ g in the park.

7 Oh, no! The r _ _ _ _ _ e gave him a red card! Boo!

8 Is Usain Bolt the best a _ _ _ _ _ e in the world?

9 My phone has a c _ _ _ _ a that takes really nice photos.

10 To hit the ball, you should hold the b _ t like this.

B **Circle the correct words.**

1 This selfie stick / video game / sleeping bag isn't very comfortable!

2 Jane made this beautiful vase; she's very boring / creative / relaxing.

3 It's good to be active / exciting / unusual and to exercise regularly.

4 We do / go / play athletics at school every Friday afternoon.

5 What do you like to do at / for / in your free time, Mandy?

6 When you play tennis, you must hit the ball over the court / net / pitch.

7 He hurt his leg and dropped out / passed out / worked out of the race.

8 When the weather is good, we usually do / go / play sailing.

9 Shall we have a picnic by the sea at / in / of the weekend?

10 Gregory is in / into / to chess and has become a very good player.

C **Complete the sentences with the words in the correct form.**

beat	coach	dive	lose	score	spend	stay	throw	train	win

1 Max _____ all of his free time playing video games.

2 He's a great player because he _____ very hard every day.

3 I can't believe it! Arsenal _____ Manchester United, 3-0!

4 He picked up the ball and _____ it for his dog to catch.

5 Bob _____ a junior football team and he has taught them a lot about the game.

6 Oh, I didn't see the goal! Who _____ it? Was it Ronaldo?

7 I think our team will _____ the game because we're better.

8 You shouldn't _____ into the water from the rocks; it's dangerous.

9 If you eat good food and play sport, you will _____ healthy.

10 Emma is upset because she _____ her match in the tennis tournament.

D **Complete the sentences with the words.**

about	in	of	on	on	on	up	up

1 Let's warm _____ for a few minutes before we start jogging, OK?

2 The tennis match that I watched went _____ for five hours!

3 Jack is a real fan _____ football; he follows his team everywhere!

4 Are you involved _____ any activities after school?

5 How _____ going swimming this weekend if the weather is warm?

6 Do you spend a lot of time _____ your hobbies?

7 Come on, Susie! Don't give _____ now! You can win this race.

8 I'm not keen _____ sport; I prefer to read when I have free time.

Grammar

A Circle the correct words.

1 If you want to meet people, join / will join a youth club.

2 You can do a lot of activities if you go / will go to a summer camp.

3 We won't have / don't have our picnic if it rains.

4 If I go away, I always take / will take my laptop with me.

5 I will send / send you an email every day if I go to Greece.

6 If you need / will need any help, just ask Sally.

7 If we don't hurry, we miss / will miss the match!

8 Remember / You will remember to buy cheese if you go to the supermarket.

B Complete the dialogues with the words in the correct form.

1 **A:** What does Paul want _____ (do) after he finishes school?

   B: He's thinking about _____ (become) a football player.

2 **A:** You mustn't _____ (eat) so much junk food, Billy!

   B: OK. I promise _____ (not have) any more junk food, Mum.

3 **A:** Imagine _____ (be) the best athlete in the world! It would be fantastic!

   B: I think there would a lot of pressure _____ (win) all the time.

4 **A:** Kelly has decided _____ (not come) with us to the beach.

   B: Oh, no! I was really looking forward to _____ (go) with her.

5 **A:** We should _____ (buy) our concert tickets soon.

   B: OK. I don't mind _____ (get) them tomorrow after school.

6 **A:** I can't stand _____ (watch) reality TV shows.

   B: Really? You seemed _____ (enjoy) *The Bachelor* last year!

C Choose the correct answer, *a*, *b* or *c*.

1 Did you know that Tanya _____ ride a horse when she was only five?

   a must   **b** can   **c** could

2 The school _____ buy new equipment for the gym; it's all old now.

   a should   **b** shall   **c** can

3 You _____ swim here; the water isn't clean and you will get sick.

   a needn't   **b** mustn't   **c** don't have to

4 It's a great party, but we _____ leave now because it's very late.

   a could   **b** may   **c** have to

5 _____ I make a healthy salad and some fish for lunch today?

   a Shall   **b** Must   **c** Need

6 You _____ use my cricket bat; I don't need it this week.

   a have to   **b** can   **c** shall

7 We have enough orange juice; you _____ buy any more.

   a needn't   **b** couldn't   **c** can't

8 '_____ I help you?' 'Yes, please. I'd like to buy a bike.'

   a Should   **b** Must   **c** Can

9 Take a Break

Reading:	right, wrong, doesn't say, checking for enough information
Vocabulary:	holiday-related words, word completion, looking for clues
Grammar:	open cloze, choosing the correct word type, relative pronouns, adverbs
Listening:	multiple choice (pictures), getting ready to listen
Speaking:	asking & answering questions, getting information about places, asking about & describing a holiday
Writing:	a social media post, making your writing flow, using correct punctuation, greetings, saying where you are, arriving, talking about activities

Unique accommodation found in the west coast rainforest of Vancouver Island, Canada

Reading

A Do the quiz with a partner to find out what kind of holiday would be best for each of you. Do you agree with the quiz?

1 Where would you like to stay when you're on holiday?

   a A large hotel on the coast.
   b A tent or caravan.
   c A hotel in the centre of a town/city.
   d A chalet or cottage.

2 What activities would you like to do?

   a Sunbathing, swimming in the sea, reading a book.
   b Going for walks and bike rides.
   c Visiting museums, art galleries, shops and cafés.
   d Doing sport and being active outside.

3 What would the weather be like?

   a Hot, sunny weather.
   b Dry, warm weather.
   c Any kind of weather is OK.
   d Dry, cold and sunny weather.

4 Where (and what) would you like to eat?

   a Eating at the same hotel for all meals.
   b Cooking easy meals on a BBQ.
   c Trying lots of different restaurants.
   d Big meals, freshly cooked – eating out OR cooking in.

Q&A

You answered mostly a

An all-inclusive holiday near the beach is the best option for you. How about a week in Barbados?

You answered mostly b

A camping holiday would be good for you. What about a week camping in the Dordogne, France?

You answered mostly c

A city break is the best holiday for you. How about a long weekend in Istanbul?

You answered mostly d

A skiing holiday would be great for you. How about a week of skiing in Austria, staying in a traditional chalet?

B Quickly read the blogs about two people's summers. Then choose the correct title for each blog and write it in.

Where History Meets Geography

The Land of the Midnight Sun

Tim, 14

1 _____

I wasn't looking forward to coming here. I mean, who wants to go to Iceland for their summer holiday? But I'm glad that I did. I love it! It's a <u>unique</u> place – I've never seen anywhere like it!

Did you know that they have daylight for 24 hours in the summer? It's <u>weird</u> to go to sleep when the sun is shining!

During our holiday, we've seen volcanoes, waterfalls, mountains, lakes and glaciers. The landscape is <u>awesome</u>. It looks like something out of Star Trek. I also saw the Northern Lights; it was an incredible experience!

It's about 10°C which is <u>typical</u> for summer here! It doesn't matter because we go swimming in the hot springs. Yesterday we went to one called the Blue Lagoon. The water was a beautiful blue colour and very warm.

I'll tell you about the food next time. You won't believe what they eat!

The Northern Lights, also known as Aurora Borealis, in Reykjavik, Iceland

Read the *Exam Close-up*. Then read the short text below. Choose the correct words to answer the questions.

When I think of summer holidays, I think of beaches and swimming. But some British people prefer camping and hiking in the countryside. I know that the countryside is very pretty in the summer, but it's not my idea of a holiday. I want to dive into the sea, put my sunglasses on, sunbathe and eat ice cream!

Ellie, 14

1 Ellie enjoys being at the seaside.
Right / Wrong / Doesn't say

2 Ellie prefers holidays in the countryside.
Right / Wrong / Doesn't say

3 Ellie doesn't like camping or hiking.
Right / Wrong / Doesn't say

Now complete the *Exam Task*. Remember to check there is enough information about a specific question before choosing your answer.

Look at the underlined words in Tim's blog. Read them in context and then match them to the group that has a similar meaning.

1 impressive, wonderful, fantastic _____
2 different, uncommon, unusual _____
3 average, common, normal _____
4 odd, strange, unnatural _____

Checking for enough information
- Sometimes, there is not enough information in the text to answer a question.
- Look at the text carefully to make sure it doesn't say anything about a specific question. If it doesn't, choose 'Doesn't say' as your answer.

Exam Task

Read the holiday blogs written by two teenagers. Are sentences 1–8 'Right' **(A)** or 'Wrong **(B)**? If there is not enough information to answer 'Right' **(A)** or 'Wrong' **(B)**, choose 'Doesn't say' **(C)**.

1 Tim wanted to visit Iceland very much. ☐
2 He watched Star Trek in Iceland. ☐
3 In Iceland, it's too cold to go swimming. ☐
4 Tim will write another entry for his blog. ☐
5 Grace enjoys the sunsets on Santorini. ☐
6 All of the beaches have red or black sand. ☐
7 You can see far when you are on the cliffs. ☐
8 Akrotiri is a place that many tourists visit. ☐

Word Focus

Northern Lights: natural red or green light in the sky

hot spring: a small lake or natural pool with hot water that comes from underground

erupt: when fire and rocks explode out of a volcano

ash: the soft black powder that is left after something has burned

Grace, 13

2 _____

I'm writing this from my hotel on Santorini. It's got a swimming pool and I sit by the pool to watch the sunset every day. The colour of the sky is magical then.

Perissa beach in Santorini, Greece

There's lots to see and do here. I've been to beaches with black sand and red sand. About 3,500 years ago a volcano erupted and left a big hole in the island. That's why there are high cliffs. If you are on a cliff, you can see more islands in the distance.

Yesterday I visited Akrotiri, a town which was covered by ash when the volcano erupted. You can see the streets and the houses that people lived in. There are also shops and workshops where they worked. There's a roof to protect it from the sun and rain.

I love it here and I want to stay forever!

- Would you prefer to visit a place where lots of tourists go or a place where very few tourists go? Why?
- Which is better – one long holiday or a few short ones every year? Why?

Ideas Focus

Vocabulary

A Complete the country fact files with the name of the continent.

> Asia   Africa   Europe   Oceania   North America   South America

1 _____
Country: Portugal
Population: 10.5 million
It's a popular tourist destination

2 _____
Country: South Africa
Population: 53 million
World famous safari parks

3 _____
Country: Peru
Population: 30.5 million
Ancient home of the Incas

4 _____
Country: Canada
Population: 35.2 million
There are beautiful landscapes

5 _____
Country: Australia
Population: 23.2 million
Another world under the water

6 _____
Country: South Korea
Population: 50.2 million
A high tech place with history

B Look at the places in A. Discuss with a partner where you want to go.

C Where can you stay when you go on holiday? Write the name of the place next to each sentence.

> bed and breakfast   campsite   caravan park   hotel   villa   youth hostel

1 It was very basic and cheap. There were six beds in each room and one bathroom for all of the rooms on the same floor. _____

2 We parked under some trees and connected to the electricity. Then we cooked our lunch in the little kitchen and ate it outside. _____

3 We had our own room, but we shared the bathroom. The breakfast was very basic – just toast, an egg and tea or coffee. _____

4 It was uncomfortable to sleep at night and I was worried the rain might come through the tent. _____

5 There were three bedrooms, two bathrooms and a huge kitchen. We spent lots of time by the pool and we ate outside on the patio. _____

6 My room was on the fourth floor. It had a comfortable bed, a bathroom, a small fridge and a TV.
_____

D Match the two halves of the sentences.

1 There's a *tourist*
2 A very nice *tour*
3 Our local *travel*
4 Hooray! It's a *long*
5 We stayed at a *holiday*

a *weekend* next week, and there's no school on Monday.
b *guide* showed us all of the important the sights.
c *resort* on the Spanish island of Majorca, and it was very nice.
d *information* centre in the town, and we can get maps there.
e *agent* recommended this hotel and booked it for us.

Complete the sentences with the words.

amusement park   city break   day trip
excursion   guided tour

1 If it's a nice day this Saturday, we might go on a
_____ to the countryside and have a picnic
there.

2 The best thing about a _____ is that you visit
the most important sights and someone explains everything
to you.

3 Let's spend Sunday at the _____ near the
beach; we can have fun on the rides and buy lunch there too.

4 A _____ is a good idea if you only have a few
days to spend and you're interested in visiting museums,
shopping and going to restaurants.

5 Unfortunately, our school _____ to a country
farm was cancelled because it was raining.

Circle the correct words in the dialogues.

1 A: Can you help me to pack / make my suitcase?
  B: Sure, but are you really going to take all of those
     clothes with you?

2 A: I'm really excited about our holiday!
  B: Me too. I've never lived / stayed at a luxury
     hotel before!

3 A: What shall we do after dinner?
  B: Let's wander / wonder around the streets of
     the Old Town.

4 A: When my exams finish, I'm going / taking
     a holiday.
  B: Where are you going to go?

5 A: I can't wait to see / look the sights in Paris.
  B: You'll love it. It's the most amazing city
     on earth.

6 A: I want to go on / go to a short trip this weekend.
  B: I heard it's going to rain.

7 A: If you do / go sightseeing in Rome, don't
     forget the Colosseum.
  B: Of course we'll visit it! I'll send you a postcard!

8 A: Did you make / take a lot of photos in Portugal?
  B: Yes, lots of them! I'll show you.

G Read the *Exam Close-up*. Without knowing
the first letter or number of letters, can you
use clues in the descriptions to guess the
words for 1–5?

1 It's the hot time of the year.
2 It's an activity where you sleep outside.
3 You pay to stay here on your holiday.
4 This place has water all around it.
5 There is fresh air and grass here.

H Now complete the *Exam Task*. Remember to
look for clues in the descriptions.

Exam Close-up

Looking for clues

- Look for clues in the descriptions. They are
  key words that give you an idea about the word
  you need to write.
- A clue will tell you if you need to think of a
  person, an object, an activity, etc.
- You will also be given the first letter of the word
  and you will see the number of letters you need
  to write.

Exam Task

Read the descriptions of some words about holidays. What is the word for each one? The first letter is already there.
There is **ONE** space for each other letter in the word.

1 This has a picture on it and you send it to your friends   p _ _ _ _ _ _ _
2 This is a person who visits a place for a holiday.   t _ _ _ _ _ _
3 You show this when you arrive in another country.   p _ _ _ _ _ _ _
4 You do this in the sea on a special board.   s _ _ _ _ _ _
5 You wear these on your face when it's sunny.   s _ _ _ _ _ _ _ _ _

- Imagine you could go anywhere in the world. Where
  would you go? Why?
- Do you use your English when you are on holiday? Why? /
  Why not?

Ideas Focus

Grammar

Relative Pronouns

A Read the sentences below and underline the pronouns. The first one is done for you.

  a This is the guide. <u>He</u> showed us the forest.

  b This is the guide who showed us the forest.

  c This is the guide that showed us the forest.

  d This is the giant tortoise. It lives in the Galapagos Islands.

  e This is the giant tortoise which lives in the Galapagos Islands.

  f This is the giant tortoise that lives in the Galapagos Islands.

B Look at the pronouns that you underlined in A and answer the questions.

  1 Which of the pronouns are personal pronouns?

  2 Which are relative pronouns?

  3 Which two relative pronouns can we use when we are talking about a person?

  4 Which two relative pronouns can we use when we are talking about a thing / an animal?

C Complete the rule.

In a relative clause, a relative pronoun replaces a _____ pronoun. When the relative pronoun is the subject of the verb in the relative clause, we use _____ or *that* to talk about people and _____ or *that* to talk about things.

D Underline the pronouns in these sentences.

  1 **a** This is the guide. We met him on holiday.

     b This is the guide who we met on holiday.

     c This is the guide that we met on holiday.

     d This is the guide we met on holiday.

  2 **a** This is the giant tortoise. I saw it on holiday.

     b This is the giant tortoise which I saw on holiday.

     c This is the giant tortoise that I saw on holiday.

     d This is the giant tortoise I saw on holiday.

E Look at the pronouns that you underlined in D and answer the questions.

  1 Are the pronouns the subject or the object of the past simple verbs *met* and *saw*?

  2 In which sentences could you replace the relative pronoun with *whom*?

  3 In which sentences are there no pronouns?

F Complete the rule.

When the relative pronoun refers to the _____ of the relative clause, we use *whom*, *who* or *that* to refer to people and _____ or *that* to refer to things. We can also leave out relative pronouns when they are the _____ of the verb.

> **Be careful**
> A relative pronoun replaces another pronoun. You can't
> ● say: 'This is the guide who he showed us the forest', as *who* and *he* refer to the same person.

▶ Grammar Focus p.168 (9.1)

G Cross out the pronouns that are incorrect or unnecessary.

  1 These are the photos that we took on holiday.

  2 We want a hotel which it is near the beach.

  3 This photo shows the friends who we met on holiday.

  4 The tourist who he lost his passport was upset.

  5 The room that it has a balcony is ours.

  6 The person that they took my suitcase thought it was theirs.

I Imagine you've just had a holiday in Spain. Take turns to tell your partner about the holiday by finishing sentences 1–4. Use relative pronouns where necessary.

  1 This is the tram …

  2 This is the villa …

  3 That's the meal …

  4 That's the man …

H Complete the sentences with relative pronouns where necessary.

  1 This is a rare bird _____ lives in the forest.

  2 The plane _____ we caught stopped in Dubai.

  3 That's the taxi driver _____ drove us to the airport.

  4 Max and Brad are the boys _____ we met on the train.

  5 Is this the suitcase _____ you lost?

  6 This website is useful for people _____ travel a lot.

Adverbs

J **Read the sentences and circle the adjectives. Now underline the adverbs.**

1 a Maria is a careful driver.
   b Maria drives carefully.
2 a It is easy for George to make friends.
   b George makes friends easily.
3 a The traffic was very slow.
   b The traffic moved slowly.
4 a The taxi journey was fast.
   b The taxi driver drove fast.
5 a The barman made a good coffee.
   b The barman made coffee well.

K **Complete these rules.**

1 Adjectives describe nouns, but adverbs describe _____.
2 To form an adverb, we add _____ to the adjective.
3 If the adjective ends with –y, it changes to _____ and we add –ly.
4 Some adverbs are irregular and have the _____ form as adjectives.
5 The adjective *good* changes to _____ to become an adverb.
6 With the verb *be*, we use _____, not adverbs.

▷ Grammar Focus p. 168 (9.2)

L **Write the correct adverbs for each adjective.**

beautiful _____   loud _____
fast _____   good _____
happy _____   healthy _____

M **Complete the sentences with a word from L.**

1 The cars go _____ through the empty streets.
2 The sun shone _____ on the sea.
3 The square was full of men talking _____.
4 The children played _____ in the street.
5 The food was fresh so we ate very _____ in Asia.
6 I played tennis _____ on holiday and beat my dad!

N **Match verbs 1–6 with adverbs a–f.**

1 ask   a sweetly
2 prepare   b politely
3 shout   c angrily
4 sleep   d hungrily
5 smile   e deeply
6 eat   f carefully

O **Read the *Exam Close-up*. Then look at the *Exam Task*. Can you see any adverbs, adjectives and relative pronouns in the answer options?**

P **Now complete the *Exam Task*.**

Exam Close-up

Choosing the correct word type
- When the options look similar, identify the type of word you need.
- Do you need an adjective or an adverb?
- If it's an adverb, is it regular or irregular?
- If you need a relative pronoun check what it refers to and choose your answer carefully.

Exam Task

Read the postcard to a family from the grandparents. Choose the best word (**A**, **B** or **C**) for each space.

Dear family,

We're having a (**1**) ____ time on our trip. This is a picture of the mountain (**2**) ____ we climbed yesterday. The guide (**3**) ____ showed us the way is called Raj and he speaks English very (**4**) ____. We arrived late at our hotel, but they welcomed us (**5**) ____. They prepared a (**6**) ____ meal very which we ate (**7**) ____! We were in such a (**8**) ____ sleep the first night that we woke up late and missed breakfast!

Love,

Granny and Grandpa

1	A wonderful	B wonderfully	C well	
2	A who	B whom	C that	
3	A —	B which	C who	
4	A good	B well	C slow	

5	A warm	B warmly	C nice	
6	A beauty	B beautiful	C beautifully	
7	A hungry	B angrily	C hungrily	
8	A deeply	B deep	C depthly	

Listening

A Look carefully at the pictures. What can you see in each picture?

A  B  C

A  B  C

A 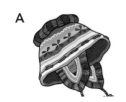 B  C

B Work with a partner and talk about each set of three photos. What are the similarities / differences between the three photos in each set?

C 9.1 ▶️ Now listen and circle the correct picture, A, B or C.

1 Where are they going to stay?
2 What is the weather like today?
3 What do they buy in the shop?

D Read the *Exam Close-up*. Then read the *Exam Task* below and study the pictures carefully. Where do you think the conversations might take place?

E 9.2 ▶️ Now complete the *Exam Task*.

Exam Close-up

Getting ready to listen
- Study the pictures carefully to identify differences and similarities.
- Decide where the conversation might happen.
- Remember that conversations are usually predictable and talk about common situations.
- The conversations are between two people, usually a male and female, so it's easy to follow who says what.

Exam Task

You will hear five short conversations. You will hear each conversation twice. There is one question for each conversation. For each question, choose the right answer (**A**, **B** or **C**).

1 Which is the woman's luggage?

A   B   C

2 What time will their flight leave?

A  B   C

3 Which country are they visiting?

A  B   C

4 What activity are they doing this morning?

A  B   C

5 Which person is the tour guide?

A  B   C

F 9.3 ▶️ Now listen again and check your answers.

Speaking

Match the words with their opposites.

1	ancient		a	boring
2	empty		b	beautiful
3	exciting		c	quiet
4	expensive		d	cheap
5	noisy		e	modern
6	ugly		f	crowded

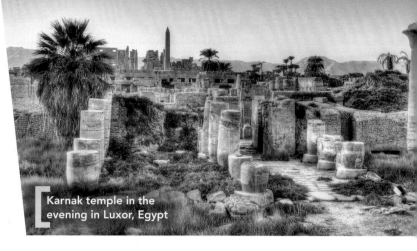

Karnak temple in the evening in Luxor, Egypt

Choose the correct answer to complete the conversations.

1 Where did you go?
  A I went to Egypt.
  B I goed to Egypt.
  C I went Egypt.

2 What was the weather like?
  A I liked it.
  B It was warm and sunny.
  C The weather bad.

3 What activities did you do?
  A I did swimming and sunbathed.
  B I went swimming and sunbathed.
  C I went swimming and did sunbathed.

4 How long did you stay there?
  A We stayed since two weeks.
  B We stayed in two weeks.
  C We stayed for two weeks.

5 Did you enjoy the holiday?
  A No, I didn't.
  B No, I not.
  C No, I didn't enjoy.

6 Why didn't you enjoy the holiday?
  A I get sunburn and feel ill.
  B I got sunburn and felt ill.
  C I was sunburn and felt ill.

Work with a partner and practise the conversations in B.

Read the *Exam Close-up* and the *Exam Task*. Think about some holidays you have had. Which was the best and which was the worst?

Now work in pairs to complete the *Exam Task*. Use the *Useful Expressions* to help you.

Exam Task

Work with a partner. Find out about a holiday your partner had. **Student A** asks **Student B** about his / her favourite holiday. Then **Student B** asks **Student A** about his / her worst holiday.

Favourite holiday
- Where / favourite holiday?
- Stay in hotel / cottage / caravan?
- What activities / there?
- What food / there?
- Why / like it there?

Worst holiday
- Where / worst holiday?
- Who / go with?
- Weather?
- What activities / there?
- Why / didn't / like it?

Useful Expressions

Asking about a holiday
Where did you go?
Where did you stay?
What was the weather like?
What activities did you do?
Did you enjoy the holiday?

Describing a holiday
We went to a place called Trapani.

It was in the countryside / near the beach / in the city.
It was a really modern / noisy / busy city.
It was really quiet and boring.
It was amazing!

Exam Close-up

Giving information about places
- When you talk about a place, remember to use adjectives.
- Answer questions with complete sentences, not just one word.
- Say what you think about a place – give your opinion and explain why.

- 'If you enjoyed a holiday you should go back to the same place every year.' Do you agree? Why? / Why not?
- Would you like a holiday in a big city? Why? / Why not?
- Do tourists visit your hometown? Why? / Why not?

Ideas Focus

Writing: a social media post

Zermatt Valley and Matterhorn Peak at dawn in Switzerland

Learning Focus

Making your writing flow

• When you write a paragraph, the sentences in it must connect smoothly and be easy to read.

• One way to do this is to avoid repetition in your writing. Try to think of other ways to express some words you have already written. This will make your writing more interesting and enjoyable for the reader.

A Look at the two social media posts. Which one is easier and more enjoyable to read? Why?

connect   Q   ⚙ Post

Hey, guys! I'm in Switzerland! I arrived in Switzerland yesterday. I'm going to do a lot of things today. I'm going to go skiing first! After skiing, I think I'll go hiking. More news later. Bye!

connect   Q   ⚙ Post

Hey, guys! I'm in Switzerland! I arrived here yesterday. I'm going to do a lot of things today and the first is skiing! After that, I think I'll go hiking. More news later. Bye!

B Underline the words and phrases in A that the writer has used to avoid repetition.

C Read the post below and think of ways to avoid repetition.

Hi, all. Here I am in Lisbon. Lisbon is a beautiful city. I arrived a few days ago. When I arrived, the weather was cold, but it's warm and sunny today. Because it's sunny, I'm going to go sightseeing. Bye for now!

D Rewrite the post with the words and phrases below. Are any the same as your ideas in C?

so   it's   got here

Hi, all. Here I am in Lisbon. (**1**) _____ a beautiful city. I arrived a few days ago. When I (**2**) _____, the weather was cold, but it's warm and sunny today (**3**) _____ I'm going to go sightseeing. Bye for now!

Vintage yellow trams run through the city in Lisbon, Portugal

Think of an interesting place you have been to or would like to visit. Complete some notes about it.

Where: _____

_____

Weather: _____

_____

Sights: _____

_____

Activities: _____

_____

Read the *Exam Close-up* and the punctuation rules. Then find and correct the mistakes in sentences 1–6.

Exam Close-up

Using correct punctuation
- When you write, you must use correct punctuation such as capital letters, commas, full stops, question marks and apostrophes.
- Check these carefully because you will lose marks for silly mistakes.

1 Romes Angelas favourite city and shes visited it a few times.
2 if you go to Paris youll fall in love with it.
3 I didnt visit my grandparents village in spain last year.
4 You and helen should see the great wall of china.
5 Theyre late and the planes ready to leave
6 On the greek islands all of the tourists favourite activity is swimming.

Useful Expressions

Greetings
Hi, guys!
Hi, all!
Hey, everyone!

Saying where you are
Here I am in …
I'm in …

Arriving
I got here …
I arrived …

Talking about activities
I'm going to …
I think I'll …
I'm planning to …
I'm looking forward to …

Now complete the *Exam Task*. You can use your notes in E for ideas. Remember to check your punctuation and use the *Useful Expressions* to help you.

Exam Task

Read the social media post from your friend, Nick.

connect 👤 💬 🌐   Q _____

_____ ⚙ **Post**

Hi! Tell us about your holiday. Where are you? When did you arrive? What are you going to do there?

Write a post for your social media page and answer the questions. Write 25–35 words.

The Travelling Photographer

Rajasthan, India

Before you watch

A **Look at the photos. Work with a partner and discuss these questions.**

• Which photo do you like best? Why?
• Do you think pictures of people or places are more interesting?
• What can you learn about a place from pictures of its people?

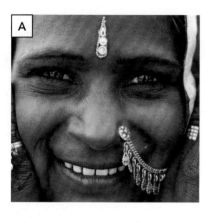

While you watch

B **Watch the video and decide if these statements are T (True) or F (False).**

1 Steve's first job was working on a newspaper. ☐
2 Steve wanted to travel and see the world. ☐
3 He has been working for *National Geographic* for 13 years. ☐
4 Rajasthan is south of Mumbai. ☐
5 Steve says he feels very comfortable in Rajasthan. ☐
6 Steve is quite a shy person. ☐

After you watch

C **Complete the summary of the video below using these words.**

> colour   face   interested   music   people   photographer   places   village

Steve McCurry has been working as a *National Geographic* **(1)** _____ for about thirty years. India is one of his favourite **(2)** _____ because it is full of culture and **(3)** _____. He travels to a **(4)** _____ in Rajasthan and photographs the people there. For Steve, Rajasthan is like another planet; the landscape, **(5)** _____, food and religion are all strange and wonderful. The **(6)** _____ are gentle and friendly. He is shy at first when he meets entertainers like snake charmers and fortune tellers, but then he relaxes and feels happy and **(7)** _____ in these people. When he takes their photos, he says that it is the **(8)** _____, not just the eyes that tell their stories.

Ideas Focus

• Do you think Steve's job as a photographer is interesting? Why? / Why not?
• How can faces tell stories?

10 Road Trip!

Reading:	matching, looking for words with similar meanings
Vocabulary:	travel- & transport-related words, phrasal verbs, collocations
Grammar:	the passive voice: present simple & past simple
Listening:	gap-fill (dialogue), predicting the answers before listening
Speaking:	prompt card activity, asking for & giving travel information
Writing:	an invitation, using modals, responding correctly to questions

The bottom of the funicular railway in Saltburn-by-the-Sea in North Yorkshire, England

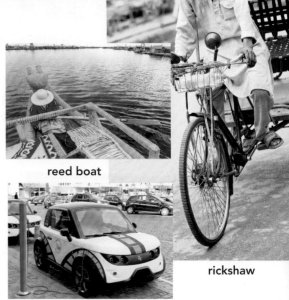

Reading

A People use some unusual forms of transport. Look at the photos and answer the questions.

rickshaw   reed boat   electric car

1 Which one needs a battery? _____

2 Which one can make your legs tired? _____

3 Which one can exercise your arms? _____

reed boat

rickshaw

electric car

B Work with a partner and discuss the questions.

1 Have you tried one of the forms of transport in A? What was it like?

2 If not, which one would you like to try and why?

3 Do you see people using rickshaws, boats or electric cars in your town? Why? / Why not?

C Look at the pictures of basket boats. What do you think they are made from? Quickly read the article and check your ideas.

Word Focus

gear: equipment

floating market: a market on boats that float on the water

waterproof: not allowing water to go through

Basket Boats

Meet Minh. He's 15 and he's from Vietnam. Minh's got two brothers – Sang and Thao. You can see them in this photo. Minh is the boy on the left.

Minh is a student, but when he isn't at school he **gives his father a hand**. His father is a fisherman who uses a **traditional** Vietnamese basket boat to catch fish. Minh's father has two basket boats: a one-man boat that he can use when he is **on his own**, and a bigger boat that can carry several men, their fishing gear and the fish they catch as well. Minh pushes the boat into the sea and uses paddles to move the boat over the water. When he finds a good spot for fishing, he throws a net into the water and waits for the fish. Then, with his father, they pull the net into the boat and **remove** the fish from the net.

Then it's time to sell the fish. Minh's mum does this at the floating market. She sells the fish, as well as fruit and vegetables from their garden, on her boat. It's also a basket boat, but it isn't round – it's long and looks like a normal boat.

They are called basket boats because they look like baskets, but also because they are made with the same material as baskets – bamboo. After the boats are made, they are painted with something to make them waterproof. Basket boats are very **popular** in Vietnam because they have many advantages. Firstly, they are cheap to make because bamboo is found everywhere in Vietnam. Secondly, bamboo is very strong. If it is hit by a big wave, the boat will not break.

Minh's grandfather is teaching him how to make a basket boat. Minh isn't interested in becoming a fisherman, but if he **changes his mind**, he'll know what to do!

D Read the text again and circle the correct words.

1 Minh's father goes fishing alone all the time / sometimes.
2 Minh takes / doesn't take the fish to the floating market.
3 Minh's mother grows / doesn't grow fruit and vegetables at home.

4 Basket boats are made in different shapes / one shape only.
5 The boats are painted to make them pretty / stop water entering them.
6 It's very easy / difficult to find bamboo in Vietnam.

E Look carefully at these sentences from the text. Find a sentence in a–c that has the same meaning.

1 … when he isn't at school he gives his father a hand.
  a His father helps at Minh's school.
  b In his free time, Minh helps his father.
  c Minh can't go to school because he has to help his father.

2 When he finds a good spot for fishing, he throws the net into the water and waits for the fish.
  a He sees fish, he throws the net in, he waits for the fish to go into the net.
  b He throws the net in, he looks for fish, he moves to another place.
  c The net is always in the water, he waits for fish to go into the net.

3 Minh isn't interested in becoming a fisherman …
  a Minh thinks fishing is boring.
  b Minh doesn't want his future job to be fishing.
  c Minh would like to work with another fisherman.

Exam Close-up

Looking for words with similar meanings
- The sentences often contain key words that are similar to key words in the notices.
- Look for such words (e.g. *put back / return, right / correct*) and underline them. This will help you to choose the correct notices.

F Read the *Exam Close-up*. Then read the *Exam Task* and look for and underline similar words.

G Now complete the *Exam Task*.

Exam Task

Which notice (**A–H**) says this (**1–5**)?

1 Your train will leave from here.
2 Be careful where you stand.
3 Wait in this line to get a ticket.
4 You must take two different trains.
5 You must wait longer for your train.

A — Smith Street exit will be closed next week.

B — There will be extra services on New Year's Eve.

C — Please QUEUE here for tickets OR USE THE MACHINES

D — WARNING! This lift is out of order.

E — WAIT BEHIND THE YELLOW LINE

F — NOTICE
Clayton passengers please note: Change train at Caulfield station

G — NOTICE
The Wickham train will depart from Platform 3.

H — NOTICE
The 10:15 train has been delayed.

H Look at the words and phrases in bold from the text. Match them with their meanings.

1 This box is heavy. Can you **give me a hand**, please?
2 A gondola is a **traditional** Venetian rowing boat.
3 I never use buses or trains at night if I am **on my own**.
4 The most **popular** form of transport in London is the Underground.
5 Maybe Mum will **change her mind** and drive us to the concert.
6 Don't forget to **remove** your luggage from the overhead lockers.

  a old fashioned
  b alone
  c help
  d make a new decision
  e well-used
  f take out

- 'All new cars should be electric cars.' Do you agree? Why? / Why not?
- Which do you think is the most dangerous to travel in? A basket boat, a helicopter, or a motorbike? Why?

Ideas Focus

Vocabulary

A Complete the sentences with these words.

| plane   coach   ferry   helicopter   motorbike   taxi |

1 When the _____ arrived at my place, I wasn't ready and the driver had to wait.

2 Sometimes when there is a traffic report on the news, the reporter is in a _____ and can see any problems from above.

3 I don't like flying, so I often travel by _____. The drivers are good, it's very comfortable and I can see the countryside.

4 You must always wear a helmet to protect your head when you ride or travel on a _____.

5 It's always really exciting when the _____ leaves the ground and flies higher and higher.

6 Last year I travelled around the Greek islands by _____. It was really nice to sit on the deck and enjoy the fresh air.

B Write the correct words under the pictures.

| lorry   platform   captain   petrol   van   timetable |

1

3

5

2

4

6

C Write the correct name of the place next to the group of words that are connected to it.

| airport   bus stop   motorway   petrol station   port   train station |

1 cars + lorries + road = _____

2 platform + timetable + announcement = _____

3 passport + flight + pilot = _____

4 wait + rain + ticket = _____

5 ships + sail + captain = _____

6 snacks + magazines + petrol = _____

D Circle the correct words in the dialogues.

1 **A:** Has your son got his driving diploma / licence yet?
   B: No, he didn't pass the test.

2 **A:** Do you know a good engineer / mechanic?
   B: Why? Is there a problem with your car?

3 **A:** Run fast or we'll lose / miss the bus!
   B: Forget it. The bus has left.

4 **A:** Which exit at this all around / roundabout?
   B: The first exit, I think.

5 **A:** How long is the journey / road from Paris to Nice?
   B: It's about six hours if you take the train.

A French high-speed train, known as a TGV Duplex, passing near Sens, France

Ed is using a ticket machine to buy a train ticket. Look at his ticket and use the correct words to complete his description.

fare   child   first   cash   destination   adult   standard   return

At the ticket machine

"The machine said 'select your (1) _____', so I chose Severn Tunnel. It asked me if I wanted a single or a (2) _____ ticket. After that I chose (3) _____ class because it's cheaper than (4) _____ class. I'm over 21, so I had to click on (5) _____ not (6) _____. Then the machine told me the (7) _____. It was £9.20. I didn't have any (8) _____, so I paid by card."

F Complete the phrasal verbs with *off, up, into, on* or *out*.

1 I **got** _____ the train at Newbury station. It was packed! There were no free seats so I had to stand.
2 I called mum and asked her to come and **pick me** _____ from the station.
3 The traffic was really bad so I **got** _____ the bus at the library and walked the rest of the way to school.
4 We left the restaurant and **got** _____ the first taxi we saw.
5 I was taking a lot of luggage, so dad **dropped me** _____ at the train station.
6 My grandad is very old now and I had to help him **get** _____ of our car.
7 Rob just **drove** _____ and left me there without saying goodbye properly!

G Circle the correct words in the dialogues.

1 **A:** When did you learn how to drive / ride a car?
   B: My dad taught me a few years ago.
2 **A:** If the pilot is out here, who is driving / flying the plane?
   B: Don't worry. There's a co-pilot.
3 **A:** I drove / rode a motorbike last week.
   B: Really? Where did you do that?
4 **A:** My grandfather was a captain.
   B: Did he sail / move many ships?
5 **A:** I think we're going to be late for the match.
   B: Let's call / shout a taxi instead of taking the train.
6 **A:** I can't drive you to school tomorrow, Alex.
   B: It's OK, Mum. I can catch / go the bus.

• Do you like using public transport in your area? Why? / Why not?
• Will you learn to drive? Why? / Why not?

Ideas Focus

Grammar

The Passive Voice: Present Simple

A Read the two sentences and look at the verbs in bold. Which sentence uses the passive voice and which use the active voice?

a My mum **packs** my suitcase.

b My suitcase **is packed** by my mum.

B Look at the sentences in A again and answer the questions.

1 What is the object in sentence a? _____

2 What is the subject in sentence a? _____

3 What is the subject in sentence b? _____

4 Who is the agent (who does the action) in sentence b? _____

5 Which word do we use to mention this person? _____

C Read the four sentences and look at the verbs in bold. Then answer the questions below.

a Bad weather **delays** flights.

b Flights **are delayed** by bad weather.

c The flight **is delayed** by bad weather.

d The flight **is delayed**.

1 Which sentences are passive? _____

2 Which verb do we use before the past participle to make a passive? _____

3 What is the agent in sentences b and c? _____

4 What is more important in sentence b and c, the action or the agent? _____

5 Which sentence does not mention the agent? _____

D Now complete the rules with the words below.

> active *be* by focus on past

- We use the passive voice to _____ the action or event, or when we don't mention who or what did the action.

- For the present simple tense, we form the passive with the verb _____ in the present simple and the _____ participle of the main verb.

- The object of the _____ sentence becomes the subject of the passive sentence. We use _____ when we want to mention the agent.

> ▷ Grammar Focus p. 168 (10.1 to 10.2)

E Complete the second sentences with the passive voice. Use the word *by* if necessary.

1 Passengers leave hundreds of umbrellas on trains every month.

Hundreds of umbrellas _____ on trains every month.

2 Robots make cars in this factory.

Cars _____ robots in this factory.

3 The police often stop lorries at the port.

Lorries _____ police at the port.

4 This machine checks your passport.

Your passport _____ this machine.

5 Do they sell snacks at the station?

_____ at the station?

6 The train manager checks tickets on the train.

Tickets _____ on the train.

F Complete the sentences with the correct passive form of the verbs in brackets.

1 These trains _____ (make) in Korea.

2 Your ticket _____ (not always check) on the train.

3 How many passports _____ (steal) every year?

4 This new car _____ (drive) by a computer.

5 What kind of meal _____ (serve) on the flight?

6 Change _____ (not give) by this ticket machine.

The Passive Voice: Past Simple

G Read the sentences and underline all the verbs.

> **John:** Where was this photo taken?
> **Anna:** This photo was taken in India.

H Look at the sentences again. Work with a partner and answer these questions.

1 What is more important to John? The place in the photo or the photographer?
2 If he wanted to know about the photographer, what question would he ask?

I Look at the sentences in G again and complete the rule.

We form the passive of the past simple with the past simple of the verb _____
+ _____ participle.

➲ Grammar Focus p. 168 (10.3)

Complete the sentences with the past simple passive form of the verbs in brackets.

1 My camera _____ (steal) on my trip.
2 Our passports _____ (check) at the airport.
3 My luggage _____ (lose) by the airline.
4 Diamonds _____ (find) in the passenger's bag.
5 Passengers _____ (not tell) about delays.
6 My flight _____ (book) online.
7 Why _____ the station _____ (close) yesterday?
8 A new road _____ (build) last year.

K Match 1–6 with a–f.

1 Did you pay for your ticket?
2 Did you lose your passport?
3 Where did you get that hat?
4 Who left their bike here?
5 Where did they find your sunglasses?
6 Where did they send your ticket?

a It was parked here by a tourist.
b No, the trip was paid for by my dad.
c It was sent to my email address.
d No, it was stolen from my bag.
e It was given to me on a trip.
f They were found at the station.

Complete the text with the correct form of the passive of the verbs in brackets.

The most dangerous road?

In every country, roads (1) _____ (need) to connect places. In Bolivia, a mountainous country, highlands and lowlands (2) _____ (connect) by the Yungas Road. This narrow mountain road (3) _____ (sometimes call) 'The Road of Death', because hundreds of people (4) _____ (kill) on it every year. It (5) _____ (build) in the 1930s. Then, for the first time, the route (6) _____ (change) from a path for animals and people on foot to a road for cars. It follows the edge of the mountain and accidents are quite common. Sometimes accidents (7) _____ (cause) by the terrible weather. The local people believe that passengers (8) _____ (protect) by those who have died, but many lives (9) _____ (lose) even today. The Yungas Road (10) _____ (use) by many different vehicles, from trucks to mountain bikes. For travellers who are not easily scared, it offers adventure and amazing views.

The Yungas Road in Bolivia, South America

127

Listening

A Look at the expressions below. Circle the ones that are clock times.

1 ten and a half / half past ten
2 five past eight / eight and five
3 ten minutes to ten / nine and fifty
4 quarter to six / quarter before six
5 a quarter past three / three and a quarter
6 twelve noon / twelve afternoon

City tour boats sail on the River Thames, near Tower Bridge, in London, England

B Write the correct clock time from A under each clock.

1
_____

3
_____

5
_____

2
_____

4
_____

6
_____

C 10.1 ▶ Now listen and write the times.

1 Bus arrives at: _____
2 Train leaves at: _____
3 Boat returns at: _____

4 Plane takes off at: _____
5 Tour ends at: _____

D Read the *Exam Close-up* and look at the gaps in the *Exam Task*. Work with a partner and discuss what might go in each gap.

E 10.2 ▶ Now listen and complete the *Exam Task*.

Exam Task

You will hear a man asking a woman about a river cruise. Listen and complete each question.

You will hear the conversation twice.

Thames River Cruises
Place: Westminster Pier

Circular cruise lasts: (**1**) _____ minutes

Red Rover ticket allows stops at: (**2**) _____ Eye, Tower Bridge and Greenwich

Boats leave every: (**3**) _____ minutes

Next boat leaves at: (**4**) _____

Cost of Red Rover ticket: Adult £18, Child (**5**) £ _____

Exam Close-up

Predicting the answers before listening
- Before you listen, think about the kind of information that is missing (number, time, price, etc.).
- Think about the questions the speakers might ask during the conversation.
- Write your answers clearly. If you make a mistake, cross it out. Never write two answers for one question!

F 10.3 ▶ Now listen again and check your answers.

Speaking

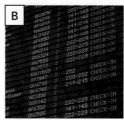

A Work with a partner and discuss which questions and answers match each picture.

1 A: Where does it depart from?
   B: It departs from gate D34.
2 A: Which platform do I need?
   B: The train leaves from platform 1.
3 A: Where do we buy a ticket?
   B: There's a machine over there.
4 A: How far is it to Koblenz?
   B: It's 112 kms away – we'll be there soon.
5 A: When does the flight to Hong Kong leave?
   B: It leaves at ten past three in the afternoon.
6 A: Where are the next services? We need more petrol.
   B: I don't know. It doesn't say on the sign.

B Complete the questions with the words below.

| fare ferry gate line platform port stop ticket |

1 What time does the _____ leave?
2 Which _____ does the train depart from?
3 Which _____ does flight EZ509 go from?
4 How much is the taxi _____ to the airport?
5 Can I buy a _____ online?
6 Can I take this metro _____ to the city centre?
7 Which _____ do I get off at for the mall?
8 Which _____ does the ferry for Mykonos leave from?

C Read the *Exam Close-up*. Now work in pairs to complete the *Exam Task*. Use the *Useful Expressions* to help you.

Useful Expressions

Asking for travel information
What time does the bus leave?
Where does it leave from?
Which stop do I need?
How far is … from … ?
How long does it take to get from … to …?
How much is the fare for a … ticket?
Which metro line do I need for the airport?

Giving travel information
The airport is 30km away.
The port is 5km from the town centre.
Trains run every half hour.
It leaves from gate 22.
It departs at 8 a.m.
The taxi fare is €20.

Exam Close-up

Asking for & giving travel information
• Make sure you know how to ask about times, prices and distances. Use *wh-* questions: *when, what time, where, which*, as well as *how* questions.
• Make sure you know how to say website addresses. For example, www. airporttaxi.com/metro-airport is '*www **dot** airport taxi* **(one word)** *dot com* **slash** *metro* **dash** *airport*'.
• If you don't understand something, ask your partner to tell you again.

Exam Task

GETTING TO THE ISLAND

From the airport, take the metro.
The trains depart **every half hour** from 06.35 until _____.
The fare is €_____ for a single and **€14** for a return.
You can buy a ticket from a machine at the station.
Get off at Monastiraki.
The trip takes about _____ minutes.
At Monastiraki, you take the **green** line to _____.
This part of the trip takes about **30** minutes.
The ferry to Santorini leaves at _____ on **Wednesdays** and the fare is € _____.

To book tickets online go to: **www.pireaus.travel/santorini**

1 **Student A:** Look at the information on the left about a trip. Ask Student B questions to fill in the gaps.
   Student B: Go to page 179 to answer Student A's questions.

2 **Student B:** Look at the information on page 179 about a trip. Ask Student A questions to fill in the gaps.
   Student A: Use your information on this page to answer Student B's questions.

• 'It's easier to travel by car than by public transport in my city.' Do you agree with this? Why? / Why not?
• Do you enjoy flying? Why? / Why not?

Ideas Focus

Writing: an invitation

The Midsumm
Night Festival
Svalbard, Nor

Learning Focus

Using modals

* When you invite someone or respond to an invitation, you often need to use modal verbs.
* We use modal verbs to invite, to ask permission, to politely accept or decline invitations, to ask for advice and to make offers.

Look at the examples below:

Could / May / Can I bring a friend to your party? (polite permission)

Shall I help you with the decorations? (offer)

Would you like to go out with me? (invitation)

I *would* love to come! (accepting an invitation)

Should I bring anything to the party? (asking for advice)

I'm sorry, but I *can't* make it. (declining an invitation)

A Look at the invitation and the email. Who is having the party and who has been invited?

SPLISH SPLASH!

Join us for a

BEACH PARTY
on SUNDAY

14th July at
2 p.m. until 7 p.m. at
MANDY'S
BEACH HOUSE
take train or bus to
Bayside Beach

Reply to

Mandy   or   Brad
9569 0344   0431 673455
sandymandy@bmail.com
bradman@iconnect.com

B Underline the modal verbs in Kate's reply.

Email Message

From: Kate
To: sandymandy@bmail.com
Subject: Beach party

Hi, Mandy

Thanks for inviting me to your party. I'd love to come! Could I bring my cousin, too? She's visiting us from the USA and I don't want to leave her at home. Should I take the train or a bus? Which is better?

Let me know!

Love,
Kate

C Tick ✔ the things that Kate does in her reply.

a accepts the invitation	✔
b makes an offer	☐
c expresses a possibility	☐
d asks for permission	☐
e makes a suggestion	☐
f asks for advice	☐

D Complete this reply to the invitation. Use the modal verbs below.

have to   might   can't

Email Message

From: Todd
To: bradman@iconnect.com
Subject: Beach party

Hey Brad,

Thanks for inviting me to your party. Unfortunately, I
(1) _____ make it. We're painting our house that day and I
(2) _____ help my parents.

I **(3)** _____ be free after 7 o'clock if we finish early. Maybe we can meet up then.

Bye for now,
Todd

Write your own party invitation like the one in A. Then swap with a partner. Reply to their invitation. Use Plan A or Plan B below and the *Useful Expressions*.

Plan A

Accept the invitation.

Ask for permission to do something.

Ask for advice.

Plan B

Decline the invitation.

Explain the reason why.

Express the possibility of meeting.

Read the *Exam Close-up*. Then match questions 1–7 with answers a–g.

1   Will you go to the party?
2   Could you lend me your CDs?
3   May I bring a friend with me?
4   Shall I help you with the decorations?
5   Would you like to go to the cinema with me?
6   Do I have to bring anything?
7   Should I get a DJ for the party?

a   Yes, you need to take food with you.
b   Yes, please; that would be really helpful.
c   I might, but I'm not sure yet.
d   You could, but it might be expensive.
e   I'm afraid not – there isn't enough room.
f   I'd love to do that, thanks.
g   Yes, of course I can, no problem.

Now complete the *Exam Task*. Remember to respond correctly to the questions.

Exam Close-up

Responding correctly to questions

- Make sure that you understand a question before you begin to respond.
- If a question includes a modal verb, read it carefully and make sure you understand the function of the modal verb (e.g. asking advice, inviting, etc.). This will help you to write a correct response.

Exam Task

Read the text message from your friend, Bob.

> Hi,
> Would you like to come to a music festival? It's at 7 on Saturday. You can bring your sister. Do you think she might be interested? Also, can I borrow your wellies? Let me know!

Sent 12:45

Write a text message to Bob and answer the questions. Write 25–35 words.

10 Travelling in India

India

Before you watch

A Label the pictures with these words.

> carriage   passenger   rush hour   station   steam train   track

1

2

3

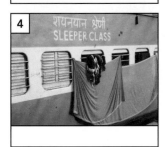
4

5

6

While you watch

B Watch the video and circle the words you hear.

1   The best / fastest way to travel in India is by train. ☐
2   The British built the railways in the eighteenth / nineteenth century. ☐
3   Today, the Indian railways travel along 38,000 miles of track / road. ☐
4   Many of the stations / trains have impressive names. ☐
5   India's railways are the country's / world's largest employer. ☐
6   For passengers / travellers Indian railways are their own adventure. ☐

After you watch

C Complete the summary of the video below using these words.

> adventure   carriage   cities   food   hour   passengers   staff   station

It is always rush **(1)** _____ at the Victoria terminus in Mumbai. Since the first steam train in 1853, trains in India have always been popular and today over four billion **(2)** _____ a year travel on India's railway. With one and a half million people on its **(3)** _____ the Indian railway is the world's biggest employer. Most of the passengers on the railway come from big **(4)** _____ but even those people who live in villages can reach a **(5)** _____ if they walk for up to a day! At the stations there are people who sell **(6)** _____ and others who carry bags or entertain the crowds. In a second class **(7)** _____ travellers from different backgrounds from all over India find ways to pass the time. They talk, play games and tell stories on their own Indian **(8)** _____.

Ideas Focus

• Would you like to travel like this? Why? / Why not?
• How would you spend a long train journey?
• Would you talk to other passengers? Why? / Why not?

Vocabulary

A **Complete the sentences with the words in the correct form.**

| catch | drive | go | go on | miss | pack | ride | sail | stay | see | take | wander |

1 When my sister _____ a suitcase, she puts her clothes in neatly.
2 We usually go camping, but this year we are going to _____ in a hotel.
3 The day was nice, so we bought ice creams and _____ through the park.
4 If I'm lucky and I win the lottery, I will _____ a holiday with all my friends.
5 I wanted to _____ the sights of Berlin, but it was raining so I didn't.
6 My class is _____ a trip to France and we're all really excited about it.
7 Look! There's the bus! If we run, we might _____ it, but we have to hurry!
8 My brother Joe is 18 years old, so he's old enough to _____ a car.
9 The ancient Greeks _____ their ships to many places in the Mediterranean.
10 Dave doesn't want a car because he prefers to _____ his motorbike.
11 I woke up late and _____ the train so I had to get a taxi to work.
12 Where do you want to _____ sightseeing first in New York?

B **Complete the words in the sentences.**

1 It's very hard to sleep when you travel on a p _ _ _ e.
2 We saw two dolphins while we were sailing on the f _ _ _ y.
3 The p _ _ _ _ _ _ m was full of people waiting for the train.
4 Look at the t _ _ _ _ _ _ _ e. The next bus is in 10 minutes.
5 After I arrived at the a _ _ _ _ _ t, I had to wait ages for my suitcases.
6 I don't think I look like the photo in my p _ _ _ _ _ _ t.
7 Is the museum free or do I have to buy a t _ _ _ _ t?
8 The f _ _ _ _ t to Tokyo was very long, but it was comfortable.
9 We drove from Paris to Athens, which was a long j _ _ _ _ _ y.
10 We were going to Egypt; our d _ _ _ _ _ _ _ _ _ n was Cairo.
11 The bus f _ _ e is one euro for adults and fifty cents for children.
12 It was a busy day at the p _ _ t because many ships were arriving.

C **Circle the correct words.**

1 I was really happy because we had a big / long weekend and went back to school on Tuesday.
2 We got into / got on the taxi and asked the driver to take us to our hotel.
3 When we were in Paris, we went on a day visit / trip to the countryside.
4 Mum dropped me off / picked me up from the station and we went home.
5 When did your sister get her driving diploma / licence?
6 When we got out / got off the plane in Singapore, it was really hot outside.
7 Our tour / travel guide in Madrid was very nice and answered all of our questions.
8 Could you please tell me how much a first / return ticket to London costs?
9 I'll meet you at the bus stand / stop outside the supermarket at one o'clock.
10 I don't think it costs a lot of money to stay at a bed / sleep and breakfast.
11 Why don't we find out about some guide / guided tours of the city?
12 When my cousin travelled around Europe, he stayed at youth / young hostels.

Grammar

A Complete each sentence with a relative pronoun. If no pronoun is needed, write –.

1 Is that the girl _____ won a trip to Disneyland?

2 The amusement park _____ we went to was really fun!

3 There is a train station _____ is near my house.

4 My friend Mario is the boy _____ goes to Italy every year.

5 Are these the tickets _____ you bought for the museum?

6 The city _____ we have chosen to visit is Copenhagen.

7 Are you the person _____ writes the teen travel blog?

8 China, Japan and Vietnam are all countries _____ are in Asia.

B Some of the sentences contain mistakes. Find them and correct them.

1 The ferry sailed very slow and it stopped at many islands.

2 My brother is learning to drive and dad says he drives good.

3 The taxi driver shouted angry at a man on a motorbike.

4 They decorated the new hotel in the city centre beautiful.

5 Why are you driving so fast? Slow down!

6 The hotel receptionist answered our questions very polite.

7 Harry worked hard so that he could have the money for a holiday.

8 Stupid, I pushed the wrong button and got the wrong ticket.

C Rewrite the sentences. Use the present simple passive voice.

1 They sell train tickets over there.

_____

2 They don't serve breakfast after 9 o'clock.

_____

3 Every day, the traffic delays drivers.

_____

4 They ask me many questions.

_____

5 Where do they make these cars?

_____

6 The driver checks the tickets.

_____

7 What language do they speak in Austria?

_____

8 They don't drive the coaches every day.

_____

D Choose the correct answer, *a* or *b*.

1 Did you know that London _____ the Romans?
  a was named Londinium by   b named Londinium from

2 The Pyramids of Cairo _____ by the Persians!
  a weren't building   b weren't built

3 Tea _____ for the first time in China.
  a has drunk   b was drunk

4 The Parthenon of Athens _____ in bright colours.
  a was painted   b painted

5 When _____? How many years ago did it happen?
  a did Machu Picchu destroy   b was Machu Picchu destroyed

6 They say that America _____ by Christopher Columbus.
  a was discovered   b has discovered

Reading:	multiple-choice & matching, understanding questions
Vocabulary:	weather-related words, open cloze, deciding what kind of word is missing
Grammar:	comparative adjectives & adverbs, superlative adjectives & adverbs, open cloze, writing the correct word
Listening:	gap-fill (monologue), listening for numbers, adjectives & common words
Speaking:	asking & answering questions about the weather, expressing differences & similarities
Writing:	a postcard, using a variety of tenses, planning your answer, talking about present, past & future activities

A local farmer stranded on his tractor after flooding in Gloucestershire, England

Reading

A Look at the pictures and match them with the words.

rain   snow   sunshine   wind

B Quickly read the emails. Which pictures below show the problems Natalie and Zach had?

C Find these words in Zach's email and underline them. Do we use them to talk about good things or bad things? Match them with their meanings.

1	buried	a	impossible to leave a place
2	collapsed	b	covered completely by something
3	injured	c	hurt a part of the body
4	trapped	d	fell and broke into pieces

Email Message

From: Natalie
To: Zach

Hi Zach!

I just had to email and tell you about our day at the beach. It was a disaster! You should be happy that you didn't come too.

It was lovely when we first arrived, but not long after that, everything changed. Dark clouds began to move closer towards us, and we started to worry about rain. But that's not what happened. In fact, I think what happened was worse. The sand started flying everywhere. It was in my hair and up my nose. It stung my eyes and I couldn't keep them open.

Somehow, we managed to get back to the car and we left as quickly as possible! It was definitely not the day out I was hoping for!

Have you ever had such bad weather at the beach?

Natalie
X

Email Message

From: Zach
To: Natalie

Hi Natalie

Your day at the beach sounds terrible! I've never had bad weather on the beach but your email did remind me about the worst weather I've ever known.

It was the time when me and my family were trapped in our house and couldn't open the door because of snow. Some streets, like ours, were covered. No one could come or go. Driving was impossible and some cars were buried. My uncle and his family had bigger problems, though. The roof of their house collapsed and they were very lucky no one was injured. Many homes in the city, including mine, had no electricity for a few days, so people couldn't cook or use their heaters in the cold weather. It was terrible!

Let's hope we get good weather this weekend! I'd like to go go-karting. Would you like to come too?

Zach
X

Word Focus

disaster: a very bad event

sting: to cause sharp pain, but not for long

somehow: in a way that is not known

heater: a machine that produces heat

Use the words from C to complete the sentences.

1 The old wall _____ because the wind was very strong.
2 The door was locked and we couldn't escape; we were _____!
3 When the bookcase fell on me it _____ my shoulder.
4 I found my phone; it was _____ under all the clothes on my bed.

Write Natalie or Zach next to each question.

1 Who could not leave? _____
2 Who expected something else to happen? _____
3 Who was not able to see? _____
4 Who did not have a warm house? _____

Read the *Exam Close-up*.

Complete the *Exam Task*. Read the questions carefully before you look at the answer options.

Exam Close-up

Understanding questions
- You need to understand questions so that you can find the correct replies.
- Underline the question words. Ask yourself if they are Wh-questions or yes/no questions. Then look at the answer options and choose one that makes sense.

Exam Task

Part 1

Complete the five conversations. Choose **A**, **B**, or **C**.

1 Have you seen the weather forecast for tomorrow?
   A Yes, it's going to be sunny.
   B Yes, you're right.
   C No, it's not mine.

2 The football match was cancelled due to bad weather.
   A That's a good idea.
   B That's a shame.
   C I don't know.

3 Can you come to my house after school?
   A That's wrong.
   B I hope not.
   C I'm afraid I can't.

4 Why didn't you go for a run yesterday?
   A I like going to school.
   B It was too cold and windy.
   C I didn't see you there.

5 Did you hear that thunderstorm last night?
   A Why did it happen?
   B It doesn't matter.
   C It was really loud, wasn't it?

Part 2

Complete the online chat between two friends. What does Natalie say to Zach? Choose the correct answer **A – H**. There are three letters you do not need to use.

Zach: Hi, Natalie. It's Zach.
Natalie: (6) ___
Zach: Why? Has something happened?
Natalie: (7) ___
Zach: Don't tell me you can't come. I was looking forward to it!
Natalie: (8) ___
Zach: Oh, no! Are you sure about that?
Natalie: (9) ___
Zach: So what do you want to do instead?
Natalie: (10) ___
Zach: Yes, I suppose we could do that.

A I was also looking for something.
B Absolutely. I heard it on the news today.
C Hey, I'm glad you contacted me. I wanted to message you.
D You'll never believe what happened!
E Me too! But it's going to rain then.
F Ask me again later.
G Sort of. It's about go-karting on Saturday.
H How about we watch a film at my house?

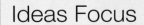

- Do you think hot weather is better than cold weather? Why? / Why not?
- Do you hate winter? Why? / Why not?

Ideas Focus

Vocabulary

A Complete the table.

Noun	Adjective
rain	(1)
cloud	(2)
fog	(3)
ice	(4)
snow	(5)
storm	(6)
sun	(7)
wind	(8)

B Complete the sentences with words from A.

1 It was a warm day and the _____ felt nice on my face.

2 The strong _____ blew away my new umbrella!

3 When the roads are _____ like this, you shouldn't drive.

4 The road was _____ and I couldn't see anything at all.

5 There was a _____ at sea and three boats nearly sank.

6 I didn't want to go out. It was _____ and dull–I couldn't see the sun.

C Match the adjectives with the temperatures they describe.

| hot | cool | cold | warm | boiling | freezing |

1 _____
  35°C or more

2 _____
  28°C – 35°C

3 _____
  15°C – 28°C

4 _____
  10°C – 15°C

5 _____
  0°C – 10°C

6 _____
  0°C or less

D Match the two halves of the questions.

1 What's it	a the weather?
2 How's	b raining?
3 What's	c like outside?
4 Is it	d the weather like?

E Work with a partner. Student A, you went to London last week. Student B, you went to Naples. Look at your weather diaries and ask and answer questions about the weather.

'What was the weather like on Monday?' 'It was sunny.'

Student A

London		
Mon	☀	18°C
Tues	⛅	16°C
Wed	☁	14°C
Thu	🌧	10°C
Fri	〰	8°C
Sat	❄	5°C
Sun	☀	10°C

Student B

Naples		
Mon	☀	28°C
Tues	☀	26°C
Wed	⛅	23°C
Thu	⛈	24°C
Fri	☁	22°C
Sat	🌬	23°C
Sun	☀	24°C

Match the words to the meanings.

1	bush fire	**a**	large amount of water that covers an area
2	flood	**b**	a long period of time where there is no rain
3	lightning	**c**	flash of bright light in the sky
4	thunder	**d**	loud noise during a storm
5	drought	**e**	fire in an area of land that is difficult to control

G Complete the sentences with words from F.

1 Suddenly, I heard the _____, and it was very close to my house.
2 The _____ burnt many trees in the forest and destroyed homes, too.
3 All the plants in the field died during the _____ and we had almost no food.
4 Water covered everything; it was the worst _____ in the history of the town.
5 _____ suddenly hit the building and caused a fire.

H Write the seasons for the UK next to the months. Where are the months for the seasons different?

autumn   summer   winter   spring

1 March, April, May: _____	**2** June, July, August: _____	**3** September, October, November: _____	**4** December, January, February: _____

Complete the sentences with both words.

1 freezing   hot
On New Year's Day, it's usually _____ in Australia, but _____ in the UK.
2 autumn   spring
In October, it's _____ in England, but _____ in Australia.
3 surfing   skiing
In January, Beth goes _____ in Canada and Jack goes _____ in Australia.
4 September   January
In Australia, the school year starts at the end of _____ and in the UK it starts in _____.

K Now complete the Exam Task.

Exam Task

Read Anna's blog. Write **ONE** word for each space.

Hi, everyone

I have to tell you (**1**) _____ the fantastic Rock Blast festival. I (**2**) _____ given two tickets for my birthday and I decided (**3**) _____ take my cousin. We had the (**4**) _____ time of our lives! If you went too, you (**5**) _____ know what I mean!

First (**6**) _____ all, the weather was perfect! There wasn't a cloud in the sky and it was warm. Lots of bands performed, but (**7**) _____ band I liked the most was *Thick As A Brick*.

The place (**8**) _____ they had the festival was beautiful. It (**9**) _____ in a forest! I'm going to make (**10**) _____ that I go again next year!

J Read the Exam Close-up. Then read the Exam Task and look carefully at the words before and after each gap. Can you decide what kind of word should go in each gap?

Exam Close-up

Deciding what kind of word is missing

- The words before and after each gap give you clues about the missing word.
- The gaps often come in the middle of a phrase or a collocation. Read the gapped sentence in your head to help you think of the missing word.
- Sometimes gaps are in the middle of a grammatical structure (e.g. passive voice, conditional, etc.). Think carefully about which word you will use and which tense.
- Other gaps come before nouns. Then you need to decide if you need an adjective, an article (*the*, *a*, etc.), or a superlative, etc.

- What is the weather usually like in your town? Do you like it? Why? / Why not?
- Would you like to live in a very hot country? Why? / Why not?

Ideas Focus

Grammar

Heavy rainfall in the Panama jungle in Central America

Comparative Adjectives

A Read the sentences below. Underline the adjectives and circle the comparative adjectives.

a A mountain road is <u>dangerous</u> in bad weather; it's (more dangerous) than a city street.

b The climate in Africa is warm all year round, and summer is warmer than winter.

c The wet weather continues, and this week is wetter than last week.

d The weather is dry, it's drier than last month.

e The climate in southern Europe is good. Is it better than the climate in northern Europe?

B Which sentence in A has a comparative adjective . . .

1 with a double consonant + -er? ☐

2 where -y changes to -i + -er? ☐

3 with the word *more* + the adjective with no spelling changes? ☐

4 with no spelling changes + -er? ☐

5 which is irregular? ☐

C Complete the rules with the correct words.

1 We form a comparative adverb / adjective by adding -er.

2 If the adjective ends in -y / -e, it changes to -i and we add -er.

3 If the adjective has a short vowel, i.e. *hot*, *thin*, *wet*, *fat*, then we double the first / last consonant and we add -er.

4 For an adjective of more than two syllables we put *more* before / after the adjective.

5 Some adjectives, for example *good* and *bad* have irregular / no comparative forms.

D Read the sentences and answer the questions.

a The temperature by the sea is **not as** high **as** the temperature in the city.

b The snow in the city is **not so** deep **as** the snow on the mountain.

c The winter sun is **as** bright **as** the summer sun.

1 Which sentence shows that two things are the same? ☐

2 Which sentences show that two things are different? ☐ ☐

E Complete the rule.

We can use *as* + adjective + _____ to show that two things are similar. We can use (*not*) *as* / *so* + _____ + *as* to show a person or thing has less of a quality than another.

Comparative Adverbs

F Read the sentences below. Underline the adverbs and circle the comparative adverbs.

a The bus goes slowly; more slowly than the cars.

b The cars go fast. They go faster than the bus.

c The motorbike doesn't go as slowly as the bus.

d The motorbike goes more quickly than the bus.

e The cars behind the bus go as slowly as the bus.

G Which sentence in F ...?

1 means the same as a? ☐

2 means the same as d? ☐

3 shows two things are the same? ☐

4 contains an irregular adverb? ☐

H Choose the correct words to complete the rules.

To form a comparative adverb we use more / than in front of the adverb followed by more / than. Irregular comparative adjective and adverb forms are different / the same: *fast > faster, well > better*. We can also use (*not*) *as* / *so* + adverb + *like* / *as* to show a person or thing has less of a quality than another.

▷ Grammar Focus pp. 168 & 169 (11.1 to 11.2)

I Complete the table.

Adjective	Comparative Adjective	Adverb	Comparative Adverb
slow		slowly	
fast			
easy			
good			
		badly	
strong			

J Use words in I to complete the sentences.

1 The cars travel _____ in fog than in clear weather.

2 The sea wind is _____ than the wind in the city.

3 You can cross the jungle _____ on foot than in a jeep.

4 We often feel _____ on sunny days than on rainy days.

5 Cyclists go _____ with the wind behind them.

6 The weather is improving; it is not as _____ as yesterday.

Superlative Adjectives

K Read the sentences. Circle the superlative forms.

   a The hottest summer was in 1976.
   b A storm is the most frightening weather for dogs.
   c The best weather for tennis is a warm, dry day.
   d The earliest flowers appear in spring.
   e Yesterday was the coldest day of the year.

L Look again at the sentences in K. Which sentence has a superlative adjective that is . . .

   1 formed with the adjective + -*est*? ☐
   2 formed by changing -y to -i + -*est*? ☐
   3 formed with a double consonant + -*est*? ☐
   4 formed by putting *most* before the adjective? ☐
   5 irregular? ☐

M Choose the correct words to complete the rule.

We use the superlative to show that something or someone has the most of a quality. We form the superlative with *the / the most* + adjective + -*est* if the adjective has one or two syllables. For adjectives with more syllables, we use *the / the most* + adjective.

Superlative Adverbs

N Which sentences contain superlative adverbs?

   1 The strongest wind is a hurricane.
   2 The wind blows the most strongly during the winter.
   3 The brightest sunshine is at midday.
   4 The sun shines the most brightly at midday.
   5 The heaviest rain falls during the monsoon season.
   6 The rain falls the most heavily during the monsoon season.
   7 The rain caused the most serious damage in the countryside.
   8 The rain damaged the countryside the most seriously.

O Complete the rule.

We use _____ + _____ + adverb to form a superlative adverb.

▶ **Grammar Focus pp. 168 & 169 (11.1 to 11.2)**

Complete the questions with a superlative adjective.

   1 Which ocean is _____ ? (deep)
   2 Which part of the world has _____ weather? (bad)
   3 Where does _____ rain fall? (heavy)
   4 Which month of the year is _____? (sunny)
   5 Which country has _____ winter? (long)
   6 Which is _____ night of the year? (short)
   7 Which weather conditions are _____? (difficult)
   8 Where is _____ place on earth? (cold)

Read the *Exam Close-up* and then complete the *Exam Task*.

Exam Task

Complete the text about the weather.

Write ONE word for each space.

Extreme Weather

Extreme weather, like heavy rainstorms and heatwaves now happens **(1)** _____ regularly than in the past. Research shows that, as the atmosphere becomes warmer, more water evaporates from the oceans. This hotter and wetter climate causes extreme weather. In the UK, where the rain is often heavy, the **(2)** _____ rain fell in Cumbria in 2009, when 316 mm of rain fell in 24 hours. The climate is getting hotter; 13 of the 14 **(3)** _____ years on record have occurred since 2000. The situation is bad and it will get **(4)** _____. Dry areas will also become **(5)** _____ than in the past because there will not be as much rain **(6)** _____ before. The winds that blow across the Pacific Ocean have become stronger **(7)** _____ they used to be. This made the drought in California worse. It is the **(8)** _____ serious drought to hit California for 1,200 years. Global warming is perhaps **(9)** _____ most dangerous problem that faces the planet, so why aren't we acting more **(10)** _____?

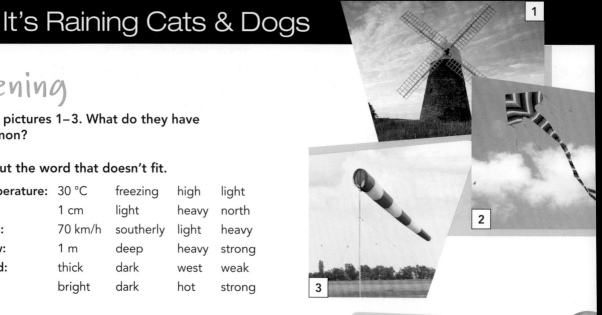

Listening

A Look at pictures 1–3. What do they have in common?

B Cross out the word that doesn't fit.

1	temperature:	30 °C	freezing	high	light
2	rain:	1 cm	light	heavy	north
3	wind:	70 km/h	southerly	light	heavy
4	snow:	1 m	deep	heavy	strong
5	cloud:	thick	dark	west	weak
6	sun:	bright	dark	hot	strong

C Write the words on the compass.

east   north   south   west

D 11.1 ▶❙❙ Listen and circle the correct words.

1 Temperatures will reach 30°C / 13°C in the south.
2 The rain will be heavy in the north / west.
3 The wind will be warm / cool on the coast.
4 The snow was 1 cm / 1 m deep in some places.
5 There will be some snow / rain in the afternoon.
6 Wear sunglasses because the sun is very bright / hot.

E Read the *Exam Close-up* and the *Exam Task.*

F 11.2 ▶❙❙ Now complete the *Exam Task.*

G 11.3 ▶❙❙ Listen again and check your answers.

Exam Close-up

Listening for numbers, adjectives & common words

- For temperatures, we use degrees: we say 'twenty degrees' (20°C) or 'minus five degrees' (–5°C). For distances, we use 'miles' or 'kilometres'.
- Listen for adjectives and any explanations for them. When something is described as 'unusual', we expect to hear why.
- Remember the spelling of common words must be correct, e.g. months, compass points, colours. The speaker only spells unusual words.

Exam Task

You will hear a weather forecast on the radio. Listen and complete each question. You will hear the information twice.

Weather Forecast

Day:	Saturday, 3rd	(1) _____
Temperature:		(2) _____
Unusual rain:	in the	(3) _____
'Blood rain' leaves:		(4) _____
		dust everywhere
The wind blows the dust:		(5) _____
		miles from the Sahara desert

Cars driving through a heavy sandstorm that surrounded the city of Dubai in 2015

Speaking

Work with a partner. Choose one of the pictures and say if you have seen weather like it. Which weather is most usual in your country?

Look at the picture. Work with a partner and answer these questions.

1 Which day was slightly warmer than Friday?
2 Which day was the sunniest?
3 Which day was a bit cooler than Wednesday?
4 When was the worst weather this week?
5 Which was the hottest day?
6 Which day was much colder than Thursday?
7 Which day was a little warmer than Saturday?

Read the *Exam Close-up*. Then read the *Exam Task*. Decide who is A and who is B. Look at your questions and read your forecasts.

D Now work with a partner and complete the *Exam Task*. Use the *Useful Expressions* to help you.

Useful Expressions

Asking questions about the weather
When will there be snow?
Will it rain on Monday?
Which city has the warmest weather?
What will the temperature be in Prague?
Which city has the best weather?

Describing differences
On Saturday, Madrid will be colder than Athens.
There will be more rain in Oslo than in Stockholm.
Miami will be hotter than Chicago.

Describing similarities
London is as sunny as Rome today.
It's cold and wet in Paris and Amsterdam.

Exam Close-up

Expressing differences & similarities
• Take a moment to think about the differences and similarities between the pictures or situations.
• To compare them, use comparative adjectives.
• To talk about small differences, use words like *a bit/ slightly*.
• To talk about big differences, use words like *a lot/ much*.
• To talk about similarities use *both / X is as . . . as Y*.

Exam Task

1 **Student A:** Look at this weather forecast for two cities for Monday and Tuesday. **Student B:** Turn to page 179 and ask questions about **A's** forecasts.

Lisbon, Portugal		Berlin, Germany	
Mon	Rainy 21°C	Mon	Cloudy 22°C
Tues	Sunny 27°C	Tues	Sunny 20°C

2 **Student B:** Look at this weather forecast for two cities for Monday and Tuesday. **Student A:** Turn to page 178 and ask questions about **B's** forecasts.

New York, USA		Los Angeles, USA	
Mon	Sunny 23°C	Mon	Sunny 33°C
Tues	Foggy 19°C	Tues	Stormy 25°C

• Do you think the weather changes how you feel? Why? / Why not?
• Does bad weather mean a bad holiday? Why? / Why not?

Ideas Focus

Writing: a postcard

Learning Focus

Using a variety of tenses

- When you write a postcard, you usually talk about activities done at different times, so you need to use a variety of tenses.

- To talk about what you're doing now, use the present continuous, (e.g. *I'm lying on the beach.*).

- To talk about things you did, use the past simple. If you want to use words such as *just, yet* or *already*, remember to use the present perfect, (e.g. *We've just been to the beach. Yesterday we went to the zoo.*).

- To talk about future activities, use *be going to* or present continuous for more fixed plans, (e.g. *We're going to go on a boat trip tomorrow and I'm going to take lots of photos.*).

A Complete the sentences with the verbs in brackets. Use the time expressions to decide which of the tenses from the *Learning Focus* you will use.

1   We _____ (have) lunch in Hyde Park at the moment.

2   For dinner last night, I _____ (go) to a restaurant by the sea.

3   I think we _____ (visit) the Empire State Building tomorrow.

4   The weather _____ (not be) good for the last two days.

5   We _____ our tour guide at 3 o'clock tomorrow afternoon.

B Read Lucy's postcard to Phoebe. Then circle the following parts of the postcard and label them.

> sign off   ending sentence   address   date   starting sentence
> greeting   stamp

Thursday, 15th Sept

Hi Phoebe

How are you? I'm writing to you from Anchorage in Alaska! I told you I love holidays in cold places!! We arrived on Monday. On Tuesday morning we went to the Anchorage museum, but unfortunately it was raining all afternoon so we couldn't go on the guided coastal walk. Yesterday it was sunny, so we went on a bike ride. It's so beautiful here, but I was exhausted at the end of the day. We've just visited the Alaska zoo. The brown bears were amazing! Tomorrow we're driving south to a town called Whittier where we're going to get on a boat and start our 26-Glacier cruise. I can't wait! I'm going to take loads of photos!

I'll tell you more when we get back.

Love,

Lucy

To: Phoebe Watkins

23 St Peter's Road

Birmingham

B14 2HR

U.K.

C Look at Lucy's postcard again. Underline all the verbs. What tenses does Lucy use?

Look at the notes about a trip to London and write a postcard to your friend. Remember to talk about activities in the past, present and future.

Day	Activities
Monday	1 p.m. arrive in London
Tuesday	10 a.m. shopping 2 p.m. the British Museum
Wednesday	12 p.m. London double-decker bus 2 p.m. Buckingham Palace
Thursday	10 a.m. Big Ben ~~8 p.m. London By Night Walking Tour~~ *Cancelled! Freezing!*
Friday	7 p.m. Football match! Chelsea v Arsenal!
Saturday	9 a.m. airport, fly home

Correct these sentences in your notebooks.

1 Tomorrow we visit the Eiffel Tower.

2 Yesterday we've done a city tour.

3 It is snowing heavily yesterday, so we couldn't go out.

4 We going to visit the art museum tomorrow.

5 We haven't went to the beach yet.

6 I'm write from Mombasa in Kenya.

Read the *Exam Close-up*. Then read the *Exam Task*. Make some notes to help you plan your postcard.

> Where?:
> Doing now?:
> Did?:
> Tomorrow?:

Exam Close-up

Planning your answer

- Before you write, you should think carefully about what you want to say and then take a few minutes to plan your answer.
- Write brief notes about every point you need to cover to make sure you include everything.

Now complete the *Exam Task*. Use the *Useful Expressions* to help you.

Exam Task

Read the task.

Imagine you are on a school trip in another country. Write a postcard to your family and tell them what you are doing, what you have done and what else you're going to do before you return home.

Write your postcard. Write between 40–50 words.

11 Snow on Tigers

Before you watch

A Work with a partner and answer these questions.

- Do you like visiting zoos? Why? / Why not?
- Would you enjoy working in a zoo? Why? / Why not?
- What problems do zoos have in winter?

While you watch

B Watch the video and decide if these statements are T (True) or F (False).

1 Diamond, the tiger is going to have babies soon. ☐
2 Bud and Carrie are expecting a snowstorm. ☐
3 Snow means that there is more work for Bud and Carrie. ☐
4 Bud and Carrie have extra help in winter. ☐
5 Bud says the bad weather this year is normal. ☐
6 Carrie says they have fun in the snow. ☐

After you watch

C Complete the summary of the video below using these words.

> end   future   help   meat   money   new
> snowstorm   summer

At the end of the **(1)** _____ this zoo in Michigan earns less **(2)** _____ because there are fewer visitors. There is some hope for the zoo's **(3)** _____ because the white tiger, which arrived recently, is going to have cubs. The bad news is that a **(4)** _____ is coming. Early snow brings an early **(5)** _____ to the tourist season. It also means that Bud and Carrie have a **(6)** _____ set of chores to do every day. There is no one to **(7)** _____ them deliver 2000 pounds of **(8)** _____ and over 500 gallons of water every day. While other people have fun doing winter sports and playing in the snow, for Bud and Carrie snow simply means a lot of extra work.

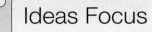 Ideas Focus

- Does the weather ever cause you problems? Why? / Why not?
- Would you like to work outdoors? Why? / Why not?

12 The World Around Us

Reading:	multiple-choice, looking for specific information
Vocabulary:	environment- and animal-related words, phrasal verbs, prepositions
Grammar:	ordering adjectives, adjectives ending in *-ing* and *-ed*
Listening:	multiple choice, preparing to choose the right option
Speaking:	asking & answering questions, formulating questions, *wh-* questions, other questions
Writing:	a report, structuring a report, reading both texts, giving background information, recommending

A rainforest surrounded by mist in the Botanical Gardens in Atlanta, United States

Reading

A Look at the animals in the pictures. What do you think they have in common?

orangutan

panda

sea turtle

polar bear

B Match the adjectives with their meanings.

1	cute	a	attractive or sweet
2	furry	b	unusual
3	funny	c	being angry or violent
4	aggressive	d	frightening
5	strange	e	not now existing
6	scary	f	very big
7	extinct	g	covered with soft hair
8	massive	h	makes you laugh

C Work with a partner. Talk about the animals in A using words from B.

D Read the article and then match each picture with the correct description.

Experiencing the sea   Finding the eggs   Helping them reach the water   Protecting the nest

1

2

3

4

Why I became a volunteer
by Jake Nichols

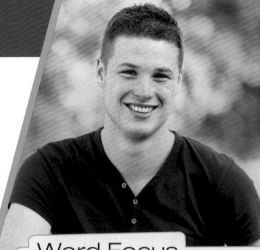

I never used to care about animals or the environment, but when I read that pandas and polar bears could become extinct, I changed my mind.

That's why I decided to help. I love the sea so I joined an organisation in Spain that protects *Caretta caretta*, the loggerhead turtle. They were looking for volunteers, so I flew there in the summer to help.

I learned a lot about the loggerhead turtle. It is disappearing because people build near the sandy beaches where the turtle needs to leave its eggs. Also, baby turtles sometimes need the moonlight to find the sea. But if there is a town near the beach, the lights trick the baby turtles and they never reach the sea. Plus, loggerhead turtles eat plastic rubbish because it looks like fish, and they die. They need clean beaches to survive.

I had an interesting job. Every day, I searched for turtle nests and counted the eggs in them. Then I put cages around the nests to protect them. At night, I checked the beach to make sure that no animals were trying to eat the eggs. I also cleaned the beach and helped baby turtles return to the ocean.

The best day was when some baby turtles walked slowly towards the water. I watched closely, ready to help if one went the wrong way. When the babies entered the water and swam away, I felt like crying, but I was so happy to help them.

Word Focus

environment: the air, water and land where people, animals, and plants live
organisation: a group of people who work together to do something
volunteer: a person who gives their help without pay
moonlight: the light from the moon at night
cage: a space with bars all around it where animals are sometimes kept

Find the words below in the article and underline them. Then use them to replace the words in bold.

> reach   return   search   protect   survive   become extinct

1   If pandas **die out**, I will be
   very sad.   _____

2   Animals need a safe environment
   to **stay alive**.   _____

3   It is important that we **keep** all
   animals **safe**.   _____

4   Some birds **go back** to the same
   place every summer.   _____

5   It's terrible; hunters **look** for lions
   and kill them.   _____

6   How did the baby elephant **get to**
   the river?   _____

Read the *Exam Close-up*. Then read the *Exam Task* and answer these questions.

1   What are the key words in the six
   questions?

2   Underline the part of the reading text that is
   connected to the key words.

3   Do you need to read all of the text to answer
   the question?

Now complete the *Exam Task*.

Exam Close-up

Looking for specific information

- When you are looking for specific information, you do not need to read the whole text.
- Find the key words in each question and look for similar words or information about them in the text.

Exam Task

Read the article about Jake. Choose the best answer (**A**, **B** or **C**) for each question.

1   Jake decided to help
   A   because he loves the sea.
   B   so that he could visit Spain.
   C   after he learnt something.

2   *Caretta caretta* is
   A   an animal.
   B   a Spanish organisation.
   C   the name of a place.

3   Why are sandy beaches important?
   A   People swim there.
   B   Nice buildings are there.
   C   Turtles leave their eggs there.

4   Baby turtles
   A   can get lost.
   B   prefer towns.
   C   stay away from lights.

5   What did Jake do on the beach?
   A   He counted nests.
   B   He protected eggs.
   C   He gave food to other animals.

6   How did Jake feel when the baby turtles left?
   A   helpful but sad
   B   happy and helpful
   C   sad and happy

- 'We should give money to help people, not animals.' Do you agree? Why? / Why not?
- Would you like to become a volunteer to protect animals? Why? / Why not?

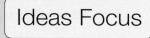

Vocabulary

A Label the pictures with the words.

| desert | lake | mountain | ocean | rainforest | river |

1
_____

2
_____

3
_____

4
_____

5
_____

6
_____

B Complete each sentence with a word from A.

1 People ride camels across the Sahara _____.
2 The tourists sailed down the _____ Nile in a boat.
3 Kilimanjaro is the highest _____ in Africa and has snow on it.
4 Hawaii and Tahiti are tropical islands in the Pacific _____.
5 _____ Como in Italy is surrounded by beautiful buildings.
6 The Amazon _____ has millions of trees and animals.

C Circle the correct phrasal verbs.

Environment fact sheet
- Every year we (**1**) cut down / fall down more than 20,000 km² of rainforest.
- In many places, it hasn't rained for a very long time and rivers have (**2**) dried up / given up.
- The animals that used to live in these places are dying, so their numbers are (**3**) moving down / going down.
- We must save these animals now; we are (**4**) finishing with / running out of time.
- We are (**5**) bringing up / using up all of the planet's trees and clean water.
- It's everyone's problem, so we must all learn how to (**6**) deal with it / fix it up.
- Here's a simple thing you can do at home: (**7**) turn off / switch off the tap while you are brushing your teeth.

D Complete the gaps in the sentences with *at, in, of, on* or *to.*

1 Pandas are _____ risk of disappearing because of the damage _____ their environment.
2 Penguins spend their lives _____ land and _____ water.
3 Fish cannot survive out _____ water. They will live for only a few minutes _____ most.
4 So many animals are _____ danger. Look at all of the species _____ this list.
5 Monkeys live _____ trees and they jump from one to another, but they also walk _____ the ground.

E Choose the correct words.

Gabby's Garden blog

A Monarch butterfly

It's very easy to (**1**) grow / make plants in your garden. Just follow these tips:

First, you have to (**2**) put / plant some seeds. Make sure sunlight can reach this area of the garden – it's not good for plants to be in dark places.

Then you must (**3**) water / wet the seeds, especially if the weather is warm.

In about a week, you will see the first small, green (**4**) leaves / branches coming up through the ground. You don't have to give the plants any special food. All they need is sunlight and water.

Your plants will attract insects and other small creatures:

(**5**) Snails / Butterflies are slow, but they can eat your plants quickly.

(**6**) Flies / Spiders are scary and they could bite you.

(**7**) Bees / Ants can sting you, but they also make delicious honey.

(**8**) Snails / Flies are annoying, especially in the summer if you want to eat outside.

(**9**) Ants / Spiders work hard. If you look closely, you can see them in a line as they carry food across your garden.

(**10**) Bees / Butterflies look very pretty in a garden. Some of them have wonderful colours like blue and orange.

F Match the words to pictures 1–8.

> dog   snake   hamster   cat   guinea pig   rabbit   goldfish   canary

G Complete the sentences with words from F.

1 I want a _____ as a pet, but my dad said no. My sister thinks they're really scary and they eat rats and mice so it wouldn't be easy to get their food.

2 My grandparents have a _____. She's lovely, but they have to take her for a walk twice a day.

3 We have a _____. He lives in a hutch in the garden. His favourite foods are lettuce and cabbage.

4 I have two _____. They live in a cage in our kitchen, but we let them out in the garden when it's sunny.

5 The only pet my parents will allow me to have is a _____. It swims around a tank in our living room. I think it has a really boring life so I want to buy another one to be its friend.

6 My uncle has a _____. He lives in a cage in his garage. He sings a lot and I like feeding him.

7 We have a _____. She's really cute and furry, but she often brings birds and mice back to our house!

8 My brother has a _____ in a cage his bedroom. It smells bad and it's really boring. It doesn't do much, but it has a wheel to exercise in.

- 'Gardening is boring. It's a waste of time.' Do you agree? Why? / Why not?
- What could you do to help the environment? Will you do it? Why? / Why not?

Ideas Focus

Grammar

Ordering Adjectives

A Underline the adjectives in a–d.

a There were horrible, old, plastic fishing nets on the beach.

b I found a broken, wooden, garden chair.

c We saw an old, giant, Chinese panda.

d I put it in a big, orange, rectangular, plastic litter bin.

B Which of the underlined adjectives in A describe these qualities?

nationality ————————————————

general opinion ————————————————

shape ————————————————

age ————————————————

size ————————————————

colour ————————————————

noun as adjective ————————————————

material ————————————————

C Look back at the examples in A. Then read the rules and complete the adjective order with the correct words.

colour   material   specific opinion
shape   nationality   age   size

- Some adjectives give a general opinion and we can use them to describe almost any noun (e.g. *nice, bad, important*).

- Other adjectives give a specific opinion – we can only use them to describe particular kinds of nouns (e.g. food = *tasty*, person / animal = *intelligent*).

- Other adjectives describe facts, not opinions (e.g. *round, German, wooden*).

- When we use more than one adjective before a noun, they usually come in this order:

1 general opinion

2 ————————————————

3 ————————————————

4 ————————————————

5 ————————————————

6 ————————————————

7 ————————————————

8 ————————————————

9 noun as adjective

▷ Grammar Focus p. 169 (12.1)

D Write these adjectives in the correct order.

a blue metal old Chinese square little special lunch box

————————————————

E Think of something you own. Describe it with as many adjectives as possible in your notebooks.

F Look at the pictures and write two or three adjectives in the correct order to describe each one. Use these words or think of your own.

busy   cute   pretty   ugly   scary   polluted
modern   little   massive   round   green   brown

G Work with a partner to describe things in the classroom or in your bags. Your partner must guess what you are describing.

Example:

A: It's a big flat rectangular white thing.

B: The whiteboard.

Adjectives ending -ing and -ed

H Read the sentences and look at the adjectives in bold.

   a The documentary about dolphins is **interesting**.

   b I'm really **interested** in wildlife so let's watch this panda documentary.

> **Be careful**
> Adjectives ending in -ing and -ed form the comparative with more.
> - This trip is **more tiring** than the last trip.
> - The pupils were **more bored** in the classroom than in the playground.

I Look back at the sentences in H and answer the questions.

   1 Which adjective describes the documentary? _____

   2 Which adjective describes the speaker? _____

   3 Which sentence shows what the speaker feels about something? _____

   4 Which sentence shows the effect something has on the speaker? _____

▶ Grammar Focus p. 169 (12.2)

J Write the adjectives for these verbs.

verb	adjective -ing	adjective -ed
amaze		
bore		
excite		
frighten		
interest		
tire		

K Choose the correct adjectives.

1. The frightening / frightened gorillas ran away from the hunters.
2. Seeing a gorilla up close can be very frightening / frightened.
3. After the long walk through the forest, the explorers were tired / tiring.
4. Walking through the thick rainforest is tired / tiring.
5. We need volunteers to clean up the beach; please sign here if you are interesting / interested.
6. This programme about the environment is not very interesting / interested.
7. The view from the top of the mountain is amazed / amazing.
8. I didn't expect the island to be so beautiful, but I was amazed / amazing.
9. The boring / bored children started talking during the Geography lesson.
10. The boring / bored Geography lesson did not interest the children.

L Look at the photos and describe them with adjectives from J.

1

2

3

4

5

6

153

Listening

A Work with a partner. Look at the pictures and describe the similarities and differences.

B Answer these questions about the pictures.

1 Which pictures show safety equipment? ☐ ☐
2 Which picture shows an electric vehicle? ☐
3 Which picture shows heights? ☐

C 🔊12.1 Listen to the dialogues. Which activity from A is discussed in each conversation?

Conversation 1 _____
Conversation 2 _____
Conversation 3 _____

D 🔊12.2 Listen to the first part of a conversation between Sally and Jake about a day in the country. Which activity from A are they going to do?

E Match questions 1–7 with a–g.

a	40 kilos	1	What time does it open?
b	2 hours	2	How long does it take?
c	£20	3	How much does she weigh?
d	9 a.m.	4	How old is your big sister?
e	5 p.m.	5	What time does it close?
f	No	6	Can I wear my own helmet?
g	14	7	How much does it cost?

F Read the *Exam Close-up*. Then look at each question in the *Exam Task* and discuss with a partner what you might hear if option A is correct. Then do the same for B and C.

G 🔊12.3 Complete the *Exam Task*.

Exam Close-up

Preparing to choose the right option

- Imagine what the speakers will say if option A is correct, then do the same for option B and C.
- Try to 'hear' the speakers in your head, before you listen to the conversation.
- Think about the different ways they could talk about times, numbers and rules.
- Check your answers the second time you listen.

Exam Task

Listen to Sally talking to her friend Jake about a day in the country. For each question, choose the right answer (**A**, **B** or **C**). You will hear the conversation twice.

1 Who is afraid of heights?
  A Sally
  B Jake
  C both Sally and Jake

2 What time will they start the 'Segway Safari'?
  A 10.20 a.m.
  B 11.40 a.m.
  C 1.00 p.m.

3 How long does the 'Segway Safari' take?
  A an hour and a twenty minutes
  B an hour
  C twenty minutes

4 What is true about the helmet?
  A you must borrow a helmet
  B you must rent a helmet
  C you must bring a helmet

5 How much must you weigh to go on a 'Segway Safari'?
  A 10 kilos
  B between 40 and 45 kilos
  C 45 kilos or more

H 🔊12.4 Listen again and check your answers.

Speaking

A Match photos A–D with the descriptions 1–4.

1 These are in danger from overfishing. ☐

2 This way of shopping is good for the environment. ☐

3 25% of these important insects have disappeared in Europe since 1985. ☐

4 This is an environmental problem that nearly all of us create every day. ☐

B Work with a partner and discuss what effect the food we eat has on the environment? Think about the following issues.

- waste
- animal welfare
- food miles
- chemicals

C Read the *Exam Close-up* then correct the mistakes in these questions.

1 How much money you spend on food every week?

2 Where you buy most of your food?

3 How much food you do throw in the bin every week?

4 Why people buy more food than they need?

5 What could you to stop wasting food?

6 What should the supermarkets does to stop people wasting food?

D Work with a partner. Take turns to ask and answer the questions in C.

E Now look at the *Exam Task*. Which photos in A do they refer to?

F Now work in pairs to complete the *Exam Task*. Use the *Useful Expressions* to help you.

Useful Expressions

Wh- questions
Where is the ... ?
Where can I buy ...?
Why do people waste so much food?
What can you buy in your local shops?
What is the cost of ...?

Other questions
How much food is wasted ...?
Is there a website ...?

Exam Close-up

Formulating questions

- You will often need to ask your partner *Wh-* questions in the speaking exam.

- Make sure your questions are complete and include all the necessary verbs.

- Remember that you need the auxiliary verb *do* or the verb *be* or a modal when you formulate questions with *Where, What, Why*, e.g. *What is ...? Why do you ...? Where can you ...?*

- Be careful with word order in questions, e.g. *What do you think?* NOT *What you do think?*

Exam Task

1 Student A: Here is some information about food waste.
Student B: Turn to page 179 and ask **A** questions about food waste.

Food Waste

In the UK 7 million tonnes of food and drink goes in the bin every year. This waste costs £60 for the average family per month.

Two reasons we waste food:

1 we prepare too much
2 we don't use food quickly enough

The type of food we waste the most:
fresh fruit and vegetables

To find out more:
www.lovefoodhatewaste.com

2 Student B: Here is some information about a Farmer's Market.
Student A: Turn to page 178 and ask **B** questions about the Farmer's Market.

Farmers' Market

Every Saturday in West Street

Start: 9 a.m.
Finish: 12.30 p.m.
Fresh fruit and vegetables from local farms!
Better quality than the supermarkets!
Help the environment (all fruit and vegetables travel less than 5km)!

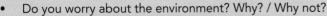

- Do you worry about the environment? Why? / Why not?
- Is your government doing enough to help the environment? Why? / Why not?

Ideas Focus

12 The World Around Us

Writing: a report

Structuring a report
- When you write a report you need to use section headings.
- The sections are usually as follows: Introduction, Background, Findings, Conclusion / Recommendations.
- A report is formal so you need to use full forms and formal language.

A Read the questionnaire, then ask and answer the questions with as many students in your class as possible. Write all the answers in your notebooks.

1 How often do you eat meat?

every day ☐   most days ☐   1–3 times a week ☐

hardly ever ☐   never ☐

2 Which bags do you use at the supermarket?

new plastic bags ☐   my own reusable bags ☐

other (please say what) ☐

3 How often do you throw food in the bin at school / college / work?

every day ☐   most days ☐   1–2 times a week ☐

hardly ever ☐   never ☐

B Read this report and then answer the questions.

Introduction
The purpose of this report is to suggest how all students at our school can change what they do to help the environment. It is based on the results of a questionnaire that I sent to students.

Background
The students all know that many environmental problems are caused by what people eat and how they shop. However, many students don't understand how they can change what they do to help the environment.

Findings
- 72% of students eat meat most days or every day
- 81% of students use new plastic bags at the supermarket
- 59% of students throw food in the bin every school day

Conclusion & recommendations
Students in the school can change what they do to help the environment. I recommend that all students:
- eat less meat – only 1–3 times a week.
- always take their own bags to the supermarket.
- make, buy or choose their own lunches.

1 Are the findings similar to what you found out about your class in A?

2 Do you agree with the recommendations? Why? / Why not?

C Read the report again and match the headings (1–4) with their uses (a–d).

1 Introduction
2 Background
3 Findings
4 Conclusion & recommendations

a says what the writer found out
b gives a reason for writing the report
c suggests what should happen in the future
d explains what is happening now

D Find and underline these words / phrases in the report in B. Then use them to complete the sentences.

however   recommend   is based on
purpose of   (be) caused by

1 Air pollution in cities _____ too much traffic.

2 This report _____ the results of the questionnaire.

3 I _____ that we take our own bags to the supermarket.

4 We know that we should save energy. _____, many of us still waste energy every day.

5 The _____ this report is to suggest how the school can save money.

Ask and answer these questions with as many students in your class as possible. Use the answers and the *Useful Expressions* to write your own short report.

1 Do you leave the tap running when you brush your teeth?

always ☐   sometimes ☐   hardly ever ☐

never ☐

2 How do you travel to school?

car ☐   bus ☐   walk ☐   bike ☐   other ☐

3 How often do you switch off the lights when you leave a room?

always ☐   sometimes ☐   hardly ever ☐

never ☐

Read the *Exam Close-up*. Then compare the two texts in the *Exam Task* and answer the questions.

Which text (the email or the notes) contains information about ...

1 the background?   _____

2 findings?   _____

3 conclusion / recommendations?   _____

4 what the report will be based on?   _____

Now complete the *Exam Task*.

Exam Close-up

Reading both texts

- You need to complete five notes and the information you need will be in one or the other text, not both.
- If you cannot find the information you are looking for in one text, check for it in the other.

Useful Expressions

Giving background information

The purpose of this report is to ...

The results are based on ...

... is caused by ...

Recommending

I suggest that ...

I recommend that ...

I think that ...

It would be a good idea to ...

Exam Task

Read the email and the notes. Fill in the information in Richard's report.

● ● ●	Email Message

Hi Laura

How are you? I'm writing a report on food waste caused by supermarkets in our city at the moment. Did you know that 40% of the food in this country is thrown in the bin? I've sent a questionnaire to all the supermarkets and I'm waiting for the results. When I've written my report, I'll send it to you.
Speak soon

Richard

<u>Information from the questionnaire</u>

30% of fruit and vegetables is wasted

90% of food is thrown away because of 'best before dates' – why? lots of food still safe to eat

10% is thrown away because it's damaged or doesn't look perfect – people will still buy this food if it is cheaper

Introduction
The purpose of this report is to suggest what supermarkets in our city should do to stop food waste. It is based on results from a **(1)** _____ sent to supermarkets in the city.

Background
About **(2)** _____ of food is wasted in the UK. A quarter of this waste is caused by supermarkets. A lot of the food that supermarkets throw away is safe to eat.

Findings
- **(3)** _____ of fruit and vegetables is thrown away.
- 90% of food that is thrown away is past its 'best before' date.
- 10% is damaged or does not look perfect.

Conclusion & recommendations
Supermarkets can change what they do to stop wasting so much food. I recommend that they:
- give food past its 'best before' date (but still safe to eat) to people who need it.
- stop using **(4)** _____ dates on fruit and vegetables.
- sell damaged food or food that does not look good at a lower **(5)** _____ .

12 Mega Green Museum

San Francisco, USA

Before you watch

A Label the pictures with these words.

architect   living roof   solar panel

1

2

3

_____   _____   _____

While you watch

B Watch the video and circle the words you hear.

1 The first idea was to make the roof like a flying garden / carpet.
2 This Mega Green Museum's impact on the environment must be very low / little.
3 The more you look, the more you realise how simple / complicated the building is.
4 Openings in the front will let cool wind / air flow into the museum.
5 All the materials must be green / recycled materials.
6 The solar cells are like little leaves in the forest / park.

After you watch

C Complete the summary of the video below using these words.

animals   centre   flowers   happy   roof   simple   sun   world

The California Academy of Science is the largest green museum in the
(1) _____. The museum was built in the (2) _____
of Golden Gate Park in San Francisco and is home to thousands of
(3) _____ and beautiful sea creatures. The architect Renzo Piano
designed this building with a very low impact on the environment. At first
the building seems (4) _____, but it is really quite complicated.
The living roof is covered with many (5) _____ and plants.
Cool air enters the front of the building and warm air exits through the
(6) _____. They used only recycled materials to create it, and
there are around 60,000 solar panels that take energy from the
(7) _____. When Renzo visited the building, he felt very
(8) _____.

Ideas Focus

- Do you think public buildings should be green? Why? / Why not?
- Is your school green? Why? / Why not?
- How could your school have less impact on the environment?

Vocabulary

A Complete the dialogues with the words in capitals in the correct form.

1 'What's it like outside?' 'It's terrible! It's cold and _____!' **RAIN**

2 'Is it hot where you are?' 'Hot? It's _____!' **BOIL**

3 'How's the weather in Greece?' 'It's great. It's warm and _____.' **SUN**

4 'Is it snowing in Berlin?' 'Yes, it is and it's _____.' **FREEZE**

5 'What's the weather like?' 'It's very _____ here.' **WIND**

6 'Are you enjoying London?' 'Not really. It's _____ every day!' **CLOUD**

B Complete the words in the sentences.

1 There was too much rain and now there's a f _ _ _ d.

2 Can you hear the t _ _ _ _ _ r? It's getting closer!

3 There was a b _ _ _ f _ _ _ and it burnt down the forest.

4 There is a d _ _ _ _ _ t and the farmers are wondering when it will rain.

5 From the window we could see the l _ _ _ _ _ _ _ g flashing in the sky.

6 Where will the explorers find water to drink in the d _ _ _ _ t?

7 It took them three days to climb to the top of the m _ _ _ _ _ _ n.

8 There are many unusual plants and animals in the r _ _ _ _ _ _ _ _ t.

C Circle the correct words.

1 Why are you cutting down / out that tree? What's wrong with it?

2 Many different kinds of birds live in / on the trees in this forest.

3 If the river dries off / up, what will happen to the fish?

4 It's scary to think how many animals are at / in risk of disappearing.

5 There is a serious problem and we need to deal for / with it now.

6 Of course kangaroos live in / on the land! Where else would they live?

7 Who forgot to turn off / out the tap in the kitchen this morning?

8 Because of the storm, the fishermen at sea were at / in danger.

9 What will happen when we run out from / of oil on this planet?

10 It was very hot yesterday, but today the temperature has gone down / off.

11 All the rain we had did a lot of damage for / to many buildings.

12 They used off / up all the fresh water, and now there is no more.

D Choose the best answer, *a*, *b* or *c*.

1 A pretty _____ landed on our picnic table in the park.
   a snail   b fly   c butterfly

2 If you don't _____ the flowers every day, they will die.
   a water   b grow   c plant

3 Be careful! That dog is _____ and it could bite you.
   a aggressive   b massive   c furry

4 The dinosaurs became _____ a very long time ago.
   a scary   b extinct   c strange

5 Europeans sailed across the _____ to South America.
   a lake   b river   c ocean

6 _____ is great! I go to the beach, and I don't go to school!
   a Winter   b Summer   c Autumn

7 A line of small black _____ quickly walked across the floor.
   a snails   b bees   c ants

8 Every morning, my _____ wakes me up by singing!
   a canary   b guinea pig   c hamster

Review 6 — Units 11 & 12

Grammar

A Circle the correct words.

1 Hamsters aren't as cute like / as cute as puppies.
2 I think that big spiders are scarier from / than bees.
3 Which do you think is worse / more worse – a flood or a fire?
4 Ants work more hard / harder than many other insects.
5 You should drive more careful / more carefully on icy roads.
6 Are hamsters furry than / as furry as rabbits?
7 A crocodile can run more quickly / quicker than you realise.
8 Today isn't hot as / hotter than it was yesterday.

B Complete each sentence with the correct superlative form of the word given.

1 Which is _____ place to go for a summer holiday? (good)
2 I think today is _____ day of the year! (wet)
3 Is Everest _____ mountain to climb? (dangerous)
4 Did you know that the cheetah runs _____ of all the big cats? (fast)
5 It rains here _____ in the month of December. (frequent)
6 Which animal is _____ in the jungle? (loud)
7 Do tortoises move _____ of all the animals? (slow)
8 We have three kittens and the black one eats _____. (hungry)

C Complete the sentences with the adjectives in the correct order.

1 cute • French • little
  I've got a _____ bulldog.
2 brown • scary • long
  Mum found a _____ snake in the garden!
3 London • grey • miserable
  It was another _____ day.
4 round • wooden • pretty
  Before the bush fire, there were some _____ cabins here.
5 metal • big • square
  What's inside that _____ box?
6 old • Italian • red
  Grandpa still drives his _____ sports car.

D Complete the dialogues with the correct adjective form of the word given.

1 A: Were you really lost in the rainforest? What was it like?
  B: It was _____! (fright)
2 A: Are you looking forward to visiting the Amazon?
  B: Yes, I'm very _____ about it. (excite)
3 A: How long did it take you to climb the mountain?
  B: A week! We were all so _____ when we got to the top. (tire)
4 A: Did you enjoy your trip to the zoo?
  B: Not really. It was quite _____ actually. (disappoint)
5 A: Look at all the snow that fell last night!
  B: That's _____. How am I going to get to work? (annoy)
6 A: Oh, no! They're going to build a road through the forest.
  B: Yes, I was _____ when I read about it. (shock)

Grammar Reference

Unit 1

1.1 Present Simple

Affirmative
I/we/you/they work.
He/she/it works.

Negative
I/we/you/they **don't** work.
He/she/it **doesn't** work.

Questions
Do I /we/you/they work?
Does he/she/it work?

Short Answers	
Yes, I/we/you/they/**do**.	**No**, I/we/you/they **don't**.
Yes, he/she/it **does**.	**No**, he/she/it **doesn't**.

We use the Present Simple for
- facts.
  Ice feels cold.
- routines or habits (often with adverbs of frequency).
  Parents often take photos of their children.
- permanent states.
  My daughter lives in Switzerland.

Note: Time expressions that refer to **repeated actions** are often used with the Present Simple. For example, *every day/week/month, once a week, twice a year, at weekends, at night, in the morning*, etc.

1.2 Adverbs of frequency

Adverbs of frequency show how often something happens. They come before the main verb, but after the verb *be*.
Sue often arrives late for school.
Jane is never late for school.
Common adverbs of frequency are: *always, usually, often, sometimes, rarely, never*

1.3 Present Continuous

Affirmative
I **am** (**'m**) work**ing**.
He/she/it **is** (**'s**) work**ing**.
We/you/they **are** (**'re**) work**ing**.

Negative
I **am** (**'m**) **not** work**ing**.
He/she/it **is not** (**isn't**) work**ing**.
We/you/they **are not** (**aren't**) work**ing**.

Questions
Am I work**ing**?
Is he/she/it work**ing**?
Are we/you/they work**ing**?

Short Answers	
Yes, I am.	**No**, I'm not.
Yes, he/she/it is.	**No**, he/she/it **isn't**.
Yes, we/you/they are.	**No**, we/you/they **aren't**.

Spelling: take → tak**ing**
sit → si**tting**
stu**dy** → stud**ying**

We use the Present Continuous for
- actions that are happening at the time of speaking.
  I'm having an English lesson now.
- actions that happen around the time of speaking.
  I'm studying the Present tenses this week.
- temporary situations.
  My mother isn't working this week.

Note: We use these common expressions with the Present Continuous: *at the moment, now, right now, for the time being, at present, this morning/afternoon/evening/week/month/year, today*, etc.

Note: Stative verbs, which describe states e.g. *like, love, believe, know, think* are not used in continuous tenses.

Unit 2

2.1 Past Simple

Affirmative
I/he/she/it/we/you/they work**ed**.

Negative
I/he/she/it/we/you/they **didn't** work.

Questions
Did I/he/she/it/we/you/they work?

Short Answers	
Yes, I/he/she/it/we/you/they **did**.	**No**, I/he/she/it/we/you/they **didn't**.

Spelling: dance → danc**ed**, travel → trave**lled**, stu**dy** → stu**died**, play → pla**yed**

Note: Some verbs are irregular and do not follow these spelling rules. See a list of irregular verbs on page 180 & 181. It's a good idea to learn irregular verbs with the same pattern in the past tense together, e.g., *cut, hit, hurt, put* and *shut* all stay the same in the simple past. *Blow, draw, fly, grow, throw* all have simple past forms that end 'ew', (*blew, drew, flew, grew, threw*).

We use the Past Simple for
- something that started and finished in the past.
  Dad met Mum in 1982.
- past routines and habits (often with adverbs of frequency).
  Dave often played basketball at weekends.
- actions that happened one after the other in the past, for example when telling a story.
  The bell rang and the children went into their classrooms.

Note: Some common time expressions that are often used with the Past Simple are *yesterday, last night/week/month/summer, a week/month/year ago, twice a week, once a month, at the weekend, in March, in the morning/afternoon/evening, at night, on Thursdays, on Monday mornings*, etc.
I looked at old family photos last night.

Grammar Reference

2.2 *Used To*

Affirmative
I/he/she/it/we/you/they **used to** work.

Negative
I/he/she/it/we/you/they **didn't use to** work.

Questions
Did I/he/she/it/we/you/they **use to** work?

Short Answers	
Yes, I/he/she/it/we/you/they **did**.	**No**, I/he/she/it/we/you/they **didn't**.

We use *used to* + bare infinitive for
- actions that we did regularly in the past, but that we don't do now.
  *My sister **used to ride** her bike to school.*
- states that existed in the past, but that don't exist now.
  *Jim's hair **used to be** curly, but now it's straight.*

2.3 Past Continuous

Affirmative
I/he/she/it **was** work**ing**.   We/you/they **were** work**ing**.

Negative
I/he/she/it **was not** (**wasn't**) work**ing**.   We/you/they **were not** (**weren't**) work**ing**.

Questions
Was I/he/she/it work**ing**?   **Were** we/you/they work**ing**?

Short Answers	
Yes, I/he/she/it **was**. **Yes**, we/you/they **were**.	**No**, I/he/she/it **wasn't**. **No**, we/you/they **weren't**.

Spelling: write → writ**ing**, travel → trave**lling**, study → stud**ying**

We use the Past Continuous for
- actions that were in progress at a specific time in the past.
  *I **was playing** with my sister at 5 o'clock yesterday afternoon.*
- two or more actions that were in progress at the same time in the past.
  *Helen **was talking** and her friend **was listening**.*
- giving background information in a story.
  *The family **was having** dinner and **discussing** their day.*
- an action that was in progress in the past that was interrupted by another action.
  *Dad **was making** breakfast when he heard the good news.*

Note: Some common time expressions that are often used with the Past Continuous are *while, as, all day/week/ month/year, at ten o'clock last night, last Sunday/week/ year, this morning*, etc.
*The children **were playing** on the beach **all day**.*

Unit 3

3.1 Present Continuous for the future

We use the Present Continuous to talk about
- future arrangements.
  ***We are visiting** our cousins on Saturday.*

Note: Time expressions that refer to **the future** are often used with the Present Continuous when we are talking about the future. For example, *tomorrow, next week/ month/weekend, tonight, in a week/a few days.*

3.2 Prepositions of time

We use **at** with
- times of day:
  *We eat **at** 1 o'clock.*
  *We go to the dining room **at** lunchtime.*

- the following expressions:
  at the weekend
  at night
  at the moment
  at Christmas

We use **in** with
- longer time periods:
  in June
  in winter
  in the morning/afternoon/evening
  in 1990
  in the 1990s

- a period of time to show how long something takes:
  *He cooked dinner **in** 30 minutes*

- a period of time to show how long before something will happen:
  *I'm leaving **in** five minutes. (I'm leaving in five minutes from now.)*

We use **on** with
- days and dates:
  on Monday
  on Monday morning
  on Friday night
  on 25th March

3.3 Prepositions of place

We use **at** with
- relative positions:
  at the back/the front/the top/the bottom/the end

- general ideas:
  at the table
  at the door
  at the cinema/the theatre
  at the station/the airport
  at the office
  at someone's house
  at home

at school
at work
at a basketball match

We use **in** with
containers:
in my handbag
in a bucket
in a pan

rooms, buildings, countries, towns, places with limits:
in the kitchen
in his car
in the departure lounge
in the park
in hospital
in prison
in England
in London

water:
in the river/sea/pond/lake

other things that contain something:
in his book
in the text
in the picture
in a row/queue

We use **on** with
surfaces:
on the floor/wall/ceiling
on the blackboard/the page
on the road
*Lunch is **on** the table.* (Note: we sit **at** a table)
Sit on this chair.

transport:
on a bus/plane/boat/ship

floors:
on the ground/first/second floor
(Note: we say *in the basement/attic*)

parts of an object:
on the front of the T-shirt
on the back of his hand
on the end of his nose

left and right:
on the left of the shop
on the right of the Post Office
drive on the right

3.4 Prepositions of direction

We use **from** to show
• where something started:
*He came home late **from** school.*
*I brought you something **from** the shops.*
*Go **from** A to B.*

We use **to** to express movement
• from one place to another:
*go **to** school*

*come **to** London*
*bring a present **to** the party*
*give/lend something **to** someone*

We use **into** to show
• that something has entered a place:
*The teacher came **into** the room.*
*The bird dived **into** the sea.*
*A bee flew **into** the car.*

We use **onto** to show
• that something has moved to a position on something:
*The cat jumped **onto** the wall.*
*He threw his clothes **onto** the bed.*
(Compare: *The boy jumped **on** the bed.* (The boy was on the bed and started jumping). This shows position, not direction.)

We use **towards** to show
• that something is moving in a particular direction:
*The dog ran **towards** the cat.*

3.5 Prepositional Phrases

We use common prepositional phrases
• to talk about time:
*He sleeps **in the middle of** the day.*
*They are tired **at the end of** the week.*

• to talk about place:
*The teacher stands **in front of** the class.*
*She found her keys **at the bottom of** her bag.*
*The bookshelf is **on the left of** the television.*

Unit 4

4.1 *Will*

Affirmative
I/he/she/it/we/you/they **will** play.
Negative
I/he/she/it/we/you/they **will not (won't)** play.
Questions
Will I/he/she/it/we/you/they play?

Short Answers	
Yes, I/he/she/it/we/you/they **will**.	**No**, I/he/she/it/we/you/they **won't**.

We use **will** for the future
• for decisions made at the time of speaking.
*The fridge is empty. I**'ll buy** some food.*
• promises.
*She**'ll buy** some presents; she promised.*
• threats.
*Don't leave your toys on the table; I**'ll throw** them away.*
• to talk about future facts.
*The supermarket **will close** at six.*
• after verbs like *think, believe, be sure, expect,* etc. and words like *probably, maybe,* etc.
*I hope they**'ll deliver** the groceries soon.*
• to offer to do something for someone.
*I**'ll help** you do the shopping.*

Grammar Reference

• to ask someone to do something.
Will you put the milk in the fridge, please?

4.2 Be Going To

Affirmative
I **am ('m) going to** help. He/she/it **is ('s) going to** help. We/you/they **are ('re) going to** help.

Negative
I **am ('m) not going to** help. He/she/it **is not (isn't) going to** help. We/you/they **are not (aren't) going to** help.

Questions
Am I **going to** help? **Is** he/she/it **going to** help? **Are** we/you/they **going to** help?

Short Answers	
Yes, I am.	**No**, I'm not.
Yes, we/you/they are.	**No**, we/you/they aren't.
Yes, he/she/it is.	**No**, he/she/it isn't.

We use *be going to* for
• future plans and intentions.
Nancy's going to cook lunch on Sunday.
• predictions for the near future based on present situations or evidence.
The child is playing near the water. He's going to get wet.

Note: Some common time expressions that are often used with *will* and *be going to* are *this week/month/summer, tonight, this evening, tomorrow, tomorrow morning/afternoon/night, next week/month/year, at the weekend, in January, in a few minutes/hours/days, on Thursday, on Wednesday morning,* etc.

4.3 Countable Nouns

Most nouns are countable and have singular and plural forms.
banana → bananas
We usually use *a* or *an* with singular countable nouns.
a pear
an apple

We can use *some, any* or a number (e.g. *three*) with plural countable nouns.
*Here are **some** apples.*
*Are there **any** pears?*
*There are **six** eggs.*

We use singular or plural verb forms with countable nouns depending on whether we are talking about one or more items.
*He usually eats **an egg** for breakfast.*
***Eggs** are tasty.*

Remember
Some countable nouns don't end in -s. Remember to use a plural verb form with them.
***Children** often don't like vegetables.*

4.4 Uncountable Nouns

Some nouns are uncountable. They do not have plural forms.

advice	knowledge
biology	luggage
cheese	medicine
chocolate	milk
equipment	money
food	music
fruit	research
fun	rubbish
furniture	salt
health	time
history	traffic
homework	water
information	weather

We always use singular verb forms with uncountable nouns.
*Fruit **is** usually healthy.*
*Money **is** hard to earn.*

Remember
Some uncountable nouns end in -s. Remember to use a singular verb form with them.
The news is terrible.
Maths is easy.

4.5 Quantifiers

We use *some* with both uncountable and plural countable nouns in affirmative sentences and in requests or offers.
*John's bought **some** biscuits.*
*Could I have **some** milk, please?*
*Would you like **some** advice?*

We use *any* with both uncountable and plural countable nouns in negative sentences and in questions.
*Cate doesn't want **any sugar** in her tea.*
*Are you watching **any films** this weekend?*

We use *a lot of/lots of* with both uncountable and plural countable nouns.
*This shop sells **lots of** coffee.*
*Diana's got **a lot of** cold drinks in the fridge.*

We use *a little* with uncountable nouns and *a few* with plural countable nouns in affirmative sentences.
*There was **a little** tea left in the jar.*
*There were **a few** children at the park.*

We use *much* with uncountable nouns and *many* with plural countable nouns in negative sentences and in questions.
*How **much** milk do you drink every morning?*
*There aren't **many** carrots in the fridge.*

Unit 5

5.1 Present Perfect Simple

The Present Perfect Simple is formed with the verb *have* and the past participle.

Affirmative
I/we/you/they **have ('ve)** work**ed**.
He/she/it **has ('s)** work**ed**.

Negative
I/we/you/they **have not (haven't)** work**ed**.
He/she/it **has not (hasn't)** work**ed**.

Questions
Have I/we/you/they work**ed**?
Has he/she/it work**ed**?

Short Answers	
Yes, I/we/you/they **have**.	No, I/we/you/they **haven't**.
Yes, he/she/it **has**.	No, he/she/it **hasn't**.

Spelling: work → work**ed**
dance → danc**ed**
study → stud**ied**
stay → stay**ed**
travel → travel**led**

Note: Irregular verbs do not follow these spelling rules. See a list of irregular verbs on pages 180 & 181.

We use the Present Perfect Simple for
something that started in the past and is still true now.
I have slept in this room since I was three.
something that happened in the past but we don't say when.
We have taken a lot of family photos.
something that happened in the recent past.
The door is wet because he has just painted it.
experiences.
We have built a garage.

Note: Time expressions that connect the past to the present are often used with the Present Perfect Simple. For example, *already, still, just, never, ever, yet, for, for ages/a long time, since.*
We have used this computer since 2010.

5.2 Have been & Have gone

The Present Perfect Simple form of the verb *be* is *have been*.
I have been here since 8 o'clock.
The Present Perfect Simple form of the verb *go* is also *have been* when it means 'to go and come back'.
I have been to Paris but I have never been to Rome.
The Present Perfect Simple form of the verb *go* is also *have gone* when it means 'to go and still be there'.
The children have gone to Paris but they will be back on Monday.

5.3 For & Since

We often use *for* and *since* with the Present Perfect Simple. *For* refers to a period of time and *since* refers to a point in time.
I have worn glasses since 2000.
I have worn glasses for years.

5.4 Possesssive 's

We use *'s* to show that
- something belongs to someone.
  Mary's house is big.
- something has a particular relationship with someone or something else.
  Mary is Mike's wife.

We use *'s* after singular nouns.
- *Here's the dog's breakfast.*
- *This is Jack's laptop.*

We use *'s* after irregular plural nouns.
- *The shop sells men's shoes.*
- *The children's room is very big.*

We use *s'* with regular plural nouns.
- *The shop sells girls' shoes.*
- *The twins' room is very big.*

We use *s'* after names that end in *-s*.
- *This is Charles' son.*
- *Those are Mr Potts' sons: Tim and Phil Potts.*

5.5 Possessive Adjectives & Possessive Pronouns

Subject Pronoun	Possessive Adjective	Possessive Pronoun
I	my	mine
you	your	yours
he	his	his
she	her	hers
it	its	–
we	our	ours
you	your	yours
they	their	theirs

We use possessive adjectives before nouns to show that something belongs to someone or has a particular relationship with someone.
That's the dog's bed. That's its bed.
This is my sisters' room. It's their room.
We use possessive pronouns to show that something belongs to someone. Possessive pronouns replace a possessive adjective and a noun, or the possessive form and a noun.
That is my bedroom. It's mine.
This is Dad's car. It's his.

Unit 6

6.1 Demonstratives

We use *this* + singular noun or uncountable noun to show that something is near us in space or time.
This is my town; I love living here.
This traffic is terrible because everyone is going to work.
We use *these* + plural noun to show that something is near us in space or time.
These buildings are new; there used to be a field here.
We use *that* + singular noun or uncountable noun to show that something is further away from us in space or time.

That island over there is called Hydra.
I spent *that* money at the market yesterday.
We use **those + plural noun** to show that something is further away from us in space or time.
Those children should not go near that unfriendly dog!

6.2 The Indefinite Article: *A/An*

We use *a* before a consonant sound.
a city
a university

We use *an* before a vowel sound.
an underground station
an hour
an ATM

We use *a / an*
- with singular countable nouns.
  *Dora is **an** explorer.*
- to mention something for the first time. (When we refer to it again, we use *the*.)
  *I live on **an** island. (**The** island is called Spetses.)*
- to show job, status, etc.
  *She's **a** mother of four.*

6.3 The Definite Article: *The*

We use *the* with singular and plural countable nouns and uncountable nouns, to talk about something specific when the noun is mentioned for a second time.
*Look! There's **a** dog in the road. Is **the** dog lost?*

We also use *the* before
- unique nouns.
  *Who was the first man on **the** moon?*
- names of cinemas, theatres, ships, hotels, etc.
  *We're going to **the** Royal Theatre tonight.*
  *When did **the** Grand Hotel open?*
- names of rivers, deserts, mountain ranges, and names or nouns with *of*.
  *Where are **the** Himalayas?*
  ***The** Thames goes through London.*
- countries or groups of countries whose names are plural.
  *He lives in **the** United Kingdom.*
  *She is from **the** Philippines.*
- musical instruments.
  *Do you play **the** guitar?*
- nationalities.
  ***The** French are proud of their cooking.*
- the following words: *beach, countryside, station, jungle,* etc.
  *Did you enjoy your day at **the** beach?*
- morning, afternoon, evening.
  *Terry is arriving in **the** evening.*

We do not use *the* before
- proper nouns.
  ***Pat** is **Ruth**'s brother.*
- names of sports, games, colours, days, months, drinks, holidays, meals, and languages (not followed by the word *language*).
  *My dad wears **green** when he plays **rugby**.*
  *Did you make your mum **breakfast** on **Mother's day**?*

Note: When we refer specifically to a meal, a colour, a drink, etc. then we use *the*.
***The** breakfast that you made yesterday was delicious.*
***The** tea you made was perfect.*

- subjects of study.
  *Do you prefer **maths** or **history**?*
- names of countries, cities, streets (BUT: *the High Street*), squares, bridges (BUT: *the Golden Gate Bridge*), parks, stations, individual mountains, islands, lakes, continents
  ***London** is the capital of **England**.*
  *We stayed in a **hotel** on **East Street**. It's near **Green Park**.*
- bed, church, school, hospital, prison, university, college, court when we talk about something related to the main purpose of the place. (*Work* never takes *the*.)
  *Harry is in **prison**.*
  *Harry's mum has gone to **the prison** to visit Harry.* (Harry's mum is not in prison; she's gone to visit.)
- means of transportation in expressions like *by car*, etc. (BUT: *in the car*).
  *We travelled **by underground**.*

Unit 7

7.1 Zero Conditional

If clause	Main clause
present simple	present simple

We use the zero conditional to talk about the result of an action or situation that is always true. We can use *when* instead of *if*.
*If you **ride** a motorbike, you **need** a helmet.*
*When you **ride** a motorbike, you **need** a helmet.*

7.2 First Conditional

If clause	Main clause
present tense	will + bare infinitive

We use the first conditional to talk about the results of an action or a situation that will probably happen now or in the future.
*If you **play** against that team, you'**ll** certainly **win**!*
*If you **take** music lessons, you'**ll learn** to read music.*
We can use *can, could, may* or *might* in the main clause instead of *will*. We can also use an imperative.
*If you like word games, you **might enjoy** Scrabble.*
*If you want to learn something new, **try** origami.*

7.3 Gerunds

We form gerunds with verbs and the *-ing* ending. We can use gerunds
- as nouns.
  ***Painting** is a popular hobby.*
- after prepositions.
  *Jack is interested **in learning** photography.*
- after the verb *go* when we talk about activities.
  *Sam **goes cycling** at the weekends.*

We also use gerunds after certain verbs and phrases.

enjoy
finish
hate
's no good
's no use
's (not) worth
keep
like
love
miss
practise
prefer

The fans **enjoyed meeting** their favourite band!
It's no good shouting! He can't hear you.

7.4 Infinitives: Full Infinitives

We form full infinitives with *to* and the verb. We use full infinitives

- to explain purpose.
  We went to the stadium **to watch** the match.
- after adjectives such as *afraid, scared, happy, glad, sad,* etc.
  She was **scared to sing** in front of the school.
- after the words *too* and *enough*.
  It was **too** difficult **to win** the chess game.
  He wasn't good **enough to be** in the team.

We also use full infinitives after certain verbs and phrases.

ask
begin
choose
decide
fail
forget
hope
invite
learn
need
offer
plan
prepare
start
want
would like

He **wanted to play** the piano.
Her parents **agreed to pay** for music lessons.

7.5 Bare Infinitives

We use bare infinitives after

- modal verbs.
  If she tries, she **can improve** her voice.
- *had better* to give advice.
  You **had better remember** the dance.
- *would rather* to talk about preference. We often use the word *than*.
  I **would rather watch** the talent contest **than** enter it.

Unit 8

8.1 *Can*

We use *can* + bare infinitive
- to talk about general ability in the present and the future.
  George **can** ride a bike and he's only three.

- for requests.
  Can I **borrow** your football?
- for permission.
  Yes, you **can borrow** my helmet.

8.2 *Could*

We use *could* + bare infinitive
- to talk about general ability in the past. (past form of *can*)
  Martina **could play** tennis when she was six.
- for polite requests.
  Could you **wait** here, please?

8.3 *May*

We use *may* + bare infinitive
- for polite requests. (with *I* and *we*)
  May I **come** in?
- for polite permission.
  Yes, you **may use** my bike.

8.4 *Would*

We use *would* + bare infinitive
- for polite requests.
  Would you **fix** my bike, please?

8.5 *Shall*

We use *shall* + bare infinitive
- for offers.
  Shall I **teach** you to play tennis?
- for strong intentions.
  I **shall win** this time!

8.6 *Should*

We use *should* + bare infinitive
- to give advice.
  You **shouldn't ride** without a helmet.
- to ask for advice.
  Should runners **eat** before the race?

8.7 *Must*

We use *must* + bare infinitive
- to say that something is necessary.
  Visitors **must pay** to swim in the hotel pool.
- to talk about obligations.
  You **must wear** a helmet on a motorbike.

8.8 *Mustn't*

We use *mustn't* + bare infinitive to talk about something that is not allowed.
Players **mustn't be** late for the match.

8.9 *Have To*

We use *have to*
- to say that something is necessary.
  You **have to** win to get first prize.
- to talk about obligation.
  Pete **has to** play every day to become a better player.

8.10 *Mustn't & Don't Have To*

There is an important difference between *mustn't* and *don't have to*. We use *mustn't* to say that something is not allowed, whereas we use *don't have to* to show that there is no obligation or necessity.

*You **mustn't** push another player.*
*You **don't have to** play a team sport, you can choose something else.*

8.11 Needn't

We use *needn't* + bare infinitive to say that something is not necessary.
*You **needn't buy** a tennis racket, you can have mine.*

Note: We can also use *need* as an ordinary verb. It has affirmative, negative and question forms and it is usually used in the Present Simple and the Past Simple. It is followed by a full infinitive.
*Our team **needs to score** a goal.*
*I **don't need to buy** a new bike. My dad gave me one!*
*__Do__ you **need to be** fit to run a mile?*

Unit 9

9.1 Relative Pronouns

We use relative pronouns in relative clauses which give us information that we need in order to be able to understand who or what the speaker is talking about. When the relative pronoun is the subject of the verb, we use *who* or *that* to refer to people and *which* or *that* to refer to things.

*That's the man **who/that** gave us directions.*
*Those are the cabins **which/that** have the best view.*

When *who*, *which* or *that* is the object of the relative clause, we can omit the relative pronoun.
*__This__ is the place (**which/that**) we visited.*
*She's **the waitress** (**who/that**) they paid.*
We can replace *who* with *whom* when it is the object of the verb, but this is more formal.
*She's **the receptionist** (**whom/who/that**) we asked about our bill.*

9.2 Adverbs

Adverbs describe verbs. We form adverbs by adding *-ly* to adjectives: *careful → carefully, quiet → quietly*. For adjectives that end in *-y*, change the *-y* to *-i* and add *-ly*. Some adjectives that end in *-e* lose the *-e*: *true → truly, terrible → terribly*. Others do not: *sure → surely*.

Irregular Adverbs
Note: Some words like *hard, late, straight* and *fast* are both adjectives and adverbs. Irregular adverbs include the word *well*.
*She's a good dancer. She dances **well**.*
Other words *friendly, lovely, silly,* and *ugly*, even though they end in *-ly* are not adverbs but adjectives.
With the verb *be*, we use adjectives, not adverbs.

Unit 10

10.1 The Passive Voice

We use the passive when
- the action is more important than who or what is responsible for it (the agent).
  *The passports **are checked** by the police.*

- we don't know the agent, or it is not important.
  *Tickets **are booked** online.*

We change an active sentence into a passive sentence in the following way.
The object of the verb in the active sentence becomes the subject of the verb in the passive sentence. The verb *be* is used in the same tense of the main verb in the active sentence, together with the past participle of the main verb in the active sentence.
*They **park** the cars on the pavement. The cars **are parked** on the pavement.*

In this example we do not know who parks the cars – it is not very important so we do not include this information in the passive sentence.

Note: When it is important to mention the agent in a passive sentence, we use the word *by*. When we want to mention a tool or material in the passive sentence, we use the word *with*.
*Prisoners **built** the Yungas Road.*
*The Yungas Road **was built by** prisoners.*
*The photo **was taken with** a smart phone.*

10.2 The Passive Voice: Present Simple

The passive is formed with the present simple of the verb *be* and a past participle.

Tense	Active	Passive
Present Simple	make/makes	am/are/is made

10.3 The Passive Voice: Past Simple

The passive is formed with the past simple of the verb *be* and a past participle.

Tense	Active	Passive
Past Simple	made	was/were made

Unit 11

11.1 Comparative & Superlative Adjectives & Adverbs

We use the comparative to compare two people or things. We usually form the comparative by adding *-er* to an adjective or adverb. If the adjective or adverb has two or more syllables, we use the word *more*. We often use the word *than* after the comparative.
*Hot weather is sometimes **more dangerous than** cold weather.*
*The snow fell **more heavily** on the mountain **than** in the city.*

We use the superlative to compare one person or thing with other people or things of the same type. We usually form the superlative by adding *-est* to the adjective or adverb. If the adjective or adverb has two or more syllables, we use the word *more*. We use the word *the* before the superlative.
*What is **the hottest** month of the year?*
*The storm affected the fishing village **the most seriously**.*

Spelling: big → big**ger**/big**gest**, brave → brav**er**/brav**est**, tidy → tid**ier**/tid**iest**

Some adjectives and adverbs are irregular and form their comparative and superlative in different ways.

Adjective/Adverb	Comparative	Superlative
good/well	better	the best
bad/badly	worse	the worst
many/more	more	the most
much	more	the most
little	less	the least
far	farther/further	the farthest/furthest

Note: Some words like *hard*, *late*, *straight* and *fast* are both adjectives and adverbs.

Other words like *friendly*, *lovely*, *silly*, and *ugly*, even though they end in *-ly* are not adverbs but adjectives. The words *hardly* (= barely) and *lately* (= recently) are not the adverbs of *hard* and *late*.

1.2 Other comparative structures

We use *as + adjective/adverb + as* to show that two people or things are similar in some way.
*Fog is **as dangerous as** snow for drivers.*

We use *not as/so ... as* to show that one person or thing as less of a quality than another.
*British summers aren**'t as hot as** Greek summers.*

Unit 12

12.1 Ordering adjectives

Sometimes more than one adjective is used in front of a noun.
*He is a **tall, young** man.*
*We bought a **round, white, Japanese** vase.*

Opinion adjectives
Some adjectives give a general opinion, which could describe anything.
*He's a **good** farmer.*
*She's a **wonderful** friend.*
*It's a **special** day.*

Other adjectives give a specific opinion to describe particular nouns:
***useful** insect*
***long** life*
***clever** gorilla*

Usually a more general opinion adjective comes before a more specific opinion:
an ***amazing, useful*** insect
a ***wonderful, long*** life
an ***interesting, clever*** gorilla

When we use two or more adjectives in front of a noun to describe a person or thing, we usually put them in this order.

general opinion	great	beautiful
size	little	long
age	old	new
shape	square	rectangular
colour	red	white
nationality	Chinese	Egyptian
material	wooden	cotton
noun as adjective	music	bath
NOUN	box	towel

Generally, the adjectives with the strongest connection to the noun go closer to the noun than the ones with weaker connections (opinions, not facts). Of course we don't often use more than two or three adjectives before a noun.
*We visited the **fascinating famous London Natural History Museum** on a **horrible rainy** day.*
*They put their **old brown cardboard boxes** in the **ugly huge blue plastic recycling** bin.*

12.2 Adjectives ending *-ing* and *-ed*

These adjectives are formed from verbs like: *bore, interest, amuse, fascinate, tire, amaze, excite* and *frighten*.
Adjectives that end in *-ed* describe how someone feels. They have a passive meaning.
*The children **are fascinated** by science. The children are **fascinated**. The **fascinated** children watched the scientist with open mouths.*

Adjectives that end in *-ing* describe the effect something has. They have an active meaning.
*The museum **fascinates** the children. The museum is **fascinating**. We took the children to the **fascinating** Science Museum.*

Remember
We do not say 'I am boring' because this means that the speaker bores other people!
*The lesson is **boring**.*
*The pupils are **bored**.*

Email

When writing an email,

- make it clear why you are writing.
- be friendly and use informal language.
- don't use *texting* language (for example, *ur* for *you're* and *lol* for *laugh out loud*).

Plan

Greeting
Hi...! / Hello...! / Dear ...,

Paragraph 1
Begin with polite phrases. Thank the reader for his/her email or ask about him/her and say why you are writing.
How are you?
Thanks for your email.
I'm writing to ...

Paragraph 2
Give more details about why you are writing.
I'd like to ... / I'm thinking of ... / We're going to ...

Paragraph 3
Give more information.
And ... / Also, ...

Signing off
See you soon! / See you on Saturday! / Hope to see you soon. / Write back soon! / I look forward to seeing you.
Love, ...

Email checklist

- Have you followed the plan? ☐
- Have you used grammatically correct forms? ☐
- Have you checked for spelling and punctuation mistakes? ☐
- Did you use informal language, such as short forms of verbs? ☐
- Is your writing style suitable for the situation and the reader? ☐
- Did you use linking words? ☐

Formal email

When writing a formal email,

use formal language and full forms.
make it clear why you are writing.
make sure you focus on the subject you're writing about.

Plan

Greeting
Dear Sir / Madam, Dear Mr ..., Dear Mrs ..., Dear Ms ...

Paragraph 1
Explain why you're writing.
I'm writing to ... / I'm emailing to ...

Paragraphs 2 & 3
Give more details on what you are writing about and what you want to find out or do.
I'd like to ... / Is it possible for me to ...? / Can you tell me ...? / Could you give me ...?

Paragraph 4
Suggest what needs to be done next.
Could you let me know as soon as possible? / Can you send me an email with more information? / I look forward to hearing from you. / I look forward to meeting you.

Signing off
Kind regards / Best regards

Formal email checklist

Have you followed the plan? ☐
Have you used grammatically correct forms? ☐
Have you checked for spelling and punctuation mistakes? ☐
Have you used formal language and full forms? ☐
Have you used a suitable greeting and sign-off? ☐

Poster or advert

When writing a poster or advert,

- include all the important information about your event in the advert or poster.
- use imperatives to persuade the reader.
- remember to give contact details.

Plan

Paragraph 1
Say what the event is and give details about when and where it will happen and any costs.
Dance lessons every Wednesday, 5.00 p.m. to 7.00 p.m. / Sports centre / School Fair, Saturday 11th June on the school sports field. / Tickets are £2 per person. / £5.00 per lesson.

Paragraph 2
Persuade people to come.
Come along and get fit! / Come and try it! / Why don't you come and see for yourself! / How about trying something new!

Contact details
Give the name, number and / or email of the person to contact about the event.
Contact Dave on 0298 9746927. / Email me at helen.benn@foxmail.com for more details. / Call the school on 03495 757393 for more information.

Poster or advert checklist

- Have you followed the plan? ☐
- Have you checked for grammar, punctuation and spelling mistakes? ☐
- Have you included all the important information ☐
- Have you used imperatives to persuade the reader ☐
- Have you given contact details ☐

Reply to an invitation

When writing a reply to an invitation,

read the invitation carefully and decide if you will accept or decline.
say thank you for the invitation in the first paragraph.
use polite phrases to accept or decline.
use modal verbs to help you be more polite.
if you decline, explain why.
finish by talking about the event or another future meeting.

Plan

Paragraph 1
Say thank you for the invitation. Choose formal or informal language, depending on who invited you and to what.
Thanks for the invitation to your party. / Thank you very much for the kind invitation to your daughter's wedding.

Paragraph 2
Say if you can come or not.
I would love to come. / I'm afraid I can't come. / Unfortunately, I can't come.

Paragraph 3
If you decline, explain why.
I'm on holiday on that day. / I'm visiting my parents that weekend.

Paragraph 4
If you accept, ask a question or talk about the event.
Can I bring a partner? / Should I bring anything? / It's going to be a great party!

Paragraph 5
Talk about the future to finish.
I'm really looking forward to seeing you! / Can't wait to see you there! / Sorry I can't come, but hopefully see you soon. / Let's try to meet up soon.

Reply to an invitation checklist

Have you followed the plan? ☐
Have you used grammatically correct forms? ☐
Have you checked for spelling and punctuation mistakes? ☐
Have you clearly accepted or declined the invitation? ☐
Have you explained why, if you cannot go? ☐
Have you used modals to help you sound polite? ☐

Postcard

When writing a postcard,

- open and close your postcard in a friendly way.
- use informal language.
- use linking words and phrases to join your ideas.
- explain the good points about your holiday.

Plan

Opening
Use an informal greeting.
Dear Eric, Hi Eric

Paragraph 1
Write about the holiday and explain what you have done so far.
We're having a lovely/terrible time. Rome is a great city! / We've had some great food! / The weather is wonderful/awful!

Paragraph 2
Write what your future plans are.
We're going to visit a museum tomorrow.

Paragraph 3
Ask a question.
When are you going on holiday? / How is your holiday going?

Closing:
Use an informal phrase for closing the postcard.
Bye. See you soon.
David

Postcard checklist

- Have you followed the plan?   ☐
- Have you used informal language that is grammatically correct?   ☐
- Have you checked for spelling and punctuation mistakes?   ☐
- Have you asked a question?   ☐
- Have you included all the information you were given?   ☐

Report

When writing a report,

think of a suitable title for your report.
use formal language.
remember to use headings to organise your report.
allow yourself time to plan your report.
think about the advantages and disadvantages of each option.
each part of your report should be separated from the next with clear paragraphs.

Plan

Paragraph 1
Say why you are writing the report.
The purpose of this report is to ... / This is a report on ...

Paragraph 2
Give any important background information about the situation and the report.
At the moment, ... / This report is based on results from ...

Paragraph 3
Present the findings.
60% of the people interviewed said ... / 20% of sales were ...

Paragraph 4
End the report by concluding and recommending future action.
In conclusion, ... / To sum up, the main recommendations/suggestions are ... / As can be seen from this report, ...

Report checklist

- Have you followed the plan? ☐
- Have you used grammatically correct forms? ☐
- Have you checked for spelling and punctuation mistakes? ☐
- Have you used formal language and the full forms of verbs? ☐
- Have you used linking words correctly? ☐
- Have you made suggestions and/or recommendations? ☐

Speaking Reference

Talking about yourself

My favourite subject is …
In my free time I usually …
I've got one sister, she's older / younger than me …
I don't have any pets.
I've got a cat called Jasper.
I spend a lot of time with my (grandma).
I always (play football / watch TV) with my (dad / friends).

Describing a person

She's … tall / blonde/quiet.
He's got … red hair / braces.
She usually wears … jeans / black.
He's really funny … but he gets angry if …
He understands me / listens to my problems.
She loves … animals / parties / volleyball.
He doesn't like … homework / shopping / winter.

Asking for details about events

Where is it?
When time does it start / finish?
What should / shall I bring?
Is there a phone number / an email address?
Can I take my friend / boyfriend / girlfriend / partner?
Can you repeat that / say that again, please?
Can you spell that, please?

Eating out

What time does the restaurant open?
Can I book a table?

Taking an order

What would you like to order?
Any drinks?
I'm afraid we don't have …

Ordering food and drink

Can I have / I'd like / I'll have the pasta, please?
Do you have any garlic bread?
What kind of ice-cream do you have?
How much is a bottle of sparkling water?
Can we have the bill, please?

Describing my bedroom

My bedroom room is great because …
I don't really like my bedroom because …
I've got a computer / laptop / printer / TV …
The walls are white and I've got red curtains.
I keep my … on my bookshelves / in my wardrobe.
I really love my posters of …
My room is usually tidy / untidy … because …

Asking for directions

Where is the …? / I'm looking for …
Is there a bank near here?
Where is it exactly?

Giving directions

It's at the end of the road.
It's opposite / next to / behind the school.
It's at the crossroads.
Go straight on.
Go / Turn right / left (at the traffic lights / at the roundabout).
Take the first (turning on your) right / left.

Checking understanding

Did you say 'turn right'?
I'm sorry. I didn't understand.
Could you repeat that, please?
I'm not sure what you mean.

Giving detailed information

The competitions starts at 8 p.m. / 10 a.m. / 8.30 a.m.
The exhibition starts on the 1st of May / 22nd October / 4th January.
It finishes on the 15th April / 20th June / 1st September.
The website address is …
You can enter if you are aged between … and … years old.
You can win a laptop / iPod / guitar.

Asking about likes

Do you like doing sport inside or outside?
Do you prefer doing sport alone or in a team?
Do you enjoy running?

Giving advice

Why don't you …?
You should …
You needn't / don't have to…
You could try …
You have to …

Responding to advice

That's a good idea.
I don't think that's a good idea because …
Or perhaps I could …

Asking about a holiday

Where did you go?
Where did you stay?
What was the weather like?
What activities did you do?
Did you enjoy the holiday?

Describing a holiday

We went to a place called Trapani.
It was in the countryside / near the beach / in the city.
It was a really modern / noisy / busy city.
It was really quiet and boring.
It was amazing!

Asking for travel information

What time does the train / bus / plane leave?
Where does it leave from?
Which stop do I need?
How far is … from …?

How long does it take to get from … to …?
How much is the fare for a … ticket?
Which metro line do I need for the airport?

Giving travel information
The airport is 30km away.
The port is 5km from the town centre.
Trains run every half hour.
… leaves from gate 22 / platform 2.
… departs at 8 a.m.
The taxi fare is €20.

Asking questions about the weather
When will there be snow?
Will it rain on Monday?
Which city has the warmest weather?
What will the temperature be in Prague?
Which city has the best weather?

Describing differences
On Saturday, Madrid will be colder than Athens.
There will be more rain in Oslo than in Stockholm.
Miami will be hotter than Chicago.

Describing similarities
London is as sunny as Rome today.
It's cold and wet in Paris and Amsterdam.

Wh- questions
Where is the … ?
Where can I buy …?
Why do people waste so much food?
What can you buy in your local shops?
What is the cost of …?

Other questions
How much food is wasted …?
Is there a website …?

Unit 3, page 39

Mel and Luke's wedding questions

- date?
- what / time?
- take / my partner?
- where / wedding?
- where / eat?
- email?

Unit 4, page 51

Unit 6, page 77

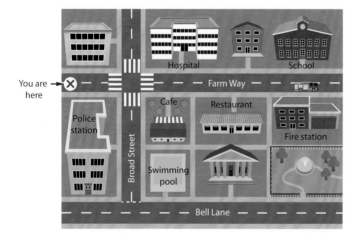

Unit 7, page 91

Photography exhibition questions

- where?
- dates?
- who / enter?
- what / win?
- website?

Unit 11, page 143

Weather forecast questions

- where / weather forecasts for?
- which city / colder / Monday? / temperatures?
- which city / hotter / Tuesday? / temperatures?
- when and where / storm?
- which city / best weather in your opinion? / Why?

Unit 12, page 155

Farmers' Market questions

- where?
- what time?
- what / buy there?
- why / buy there?
- why / good for the environment?

Unit 3, page 39

Tom's birthday party questions
- where?
- date?
- time?
- phone number?
- what / bring?

Unit 4, page 51

Dave's Café
Open from 7 am till 5 pm

Snacks
Selection of 20 mixed olives	3 euros
Garlic bread	4 euros
Cheese sandwich	4 euros
Small pizza	6 euros
Chips	5 euros

Desserts
Chocolate brownie	4 euros
Strawberry tart	5 euros

Drinks
Coffee: Cappuccino, Americano, Espresso, Latte	2 euros
Orange juice	2 euros
Sparkling water	1:50 euros
Still water	1:50 euros

Takeaway lunches available.
Call Rachel on 07452 766868.

Unit 6, page 77

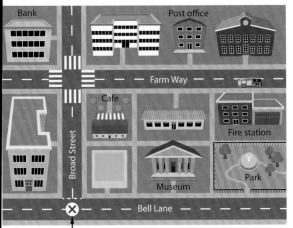

Bank
Post office
Farm Way
Café
Broad Street
Fire station
Museum
Park
Bell Lane
You are here

Unit 7, page 91

Talent competition questions
- where?
- date?
- for teenagers?
- website?
- what / win?

Unit 10, page 129

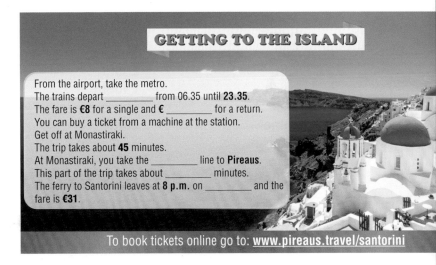

GETTING TO THE ISLAND

From the airport, take the metro.
The trains depart _____ from 06.35 until **23.35**.
The fare is **€8** for a single and € _____ for a return.
You can buy a ticket from a machine at the station.
Get off at Monastiraki.
The trip takes about **45** minutes.
At Monastiraki, you take the _____ line to **Pireaus**.
This part of the trip takes about _____ minutes.
The ferry to Santorini leaves at **8 p.m.** on _____ and the fare is **€31**.

To book tickets online go to: **www.pireaus.travel/santorini**

Unit 11, page 143

Weather forecast questions
- where / weather forecasts for?
- which city / warmer / Monday? / temperatures?
- which city / colder / Tuesday? / temperatures?
- when and where / rain?
- which city / best weather in your opinion? / Why?

Unit 12, page 155

Food Waste questions
- how much food / waste / UK?
- cost / wasted food / per UK family?
- why / waste food?
- what kind / food / waste the most?
- website / more information?

Irregular Verbs

Infinitive	Past Simple	Past Participle
be	was/were	been
beat	beat	beaten
become	became	become
begin	began	begun
bite	bit	bitten
blow	blew	blown
break	broke	broken
bring	brought	brought
broadcast	broadcast	broadcast
build	built	built
burn	burnt	burnt
buy	bought	bought
can	could	–
catch	caught	caught
choose	chose	chosen
come	came	come
cost	cost	cost
cut	cut	cut
deal	dealt	dealt
do	did	done
draw	drew	drawn
dream	dreamt	dreamt
drink	drank	drunk
drive	drove	driven
eat	ate	eaten
fall	fell	fallen
feed	fed	fed
feel	felt	felt
fight	fought	fought
find	found	found
fly	flew	flown
forecast	forecast	forecast
forget	forgot	forgotten
get	got	got
give	gave	given
go	went	gone
grow	grew	grown
have	had	had
hear	heard	heard
hide	hid	hidden
hit	hit	hit
hold	held	held
hurt	hurt	hurt
keep	kept	kept
know	knew	known
lead	led	led
learn	learnt	learnt
leave	left	left
lend	lent	lent
let	let	let

Infinitive	Past Simple	Past Participle
lie	lay	lain
light	lit	lit
lose	lost	lost
mean	meant	meant
make	made	made
meet	met	met
pay	paid	paid
prove	proved	proven
put	put	put
read	read /red/	read /red/
ride	rode	ridden
ring	rang	rung
rise	rose	risen
run	ran	run
say	said	said
see	saw	seen
sell	sold	sold
send	sent	sent
set	set	set
shake	shook	shaken
shine	shone	shone
show	showed	shown
shoot	shot	shot
shut	shut	shut
sing	sang	sung
sink	sank	sunk
sit	sat	sat
sleep	slept	slept
slide	slid	slid
smell	smelt	smelt
speak	spoke	spoken
speed	sped	sped
spend	spent	spent
stand	stood	stood
steal	stole	stolen
stick	stuck	stuck
stink	stank	stunk
sweep	swept	swept
swim	swam	swum
take	took	taken
teach	taught	taught
tell	told	told
think	thought	thought
throw	threw	thrown
understand	understood	understood
wake	woke	woken
wear	wore	worn
win	won	won
write	wrote	written

NATIONAL GEOGRAPHIC
L E A R N I N G

Close-up A2
Student's Book

Angela Bandis
Diana Shotton

Publisher: Gavin McLean

Editorial Manager: Claire Merchant

Commissioning Editor: Kayleigh Buller

Editor: Cathy Rogers

Head of Production: Celia Jones

Content Project Manager: Melissa Beavis

Manufacturing Manager: Eyvett Davis

Text/Cover Designer: MPS Limited

Compositor: MPS Limited

Audio Producer: James Richardson

Recorded at: Soundhouse Studios

Acknowledgements

The Publisher has made every effort to trace and contact copyright holders before publication. If any have been inadvertently overlooked, the publisher will be pleased to rectify any errors or omissions at the earliest opportunity.

For product information and technology assistance, contact us at
Cengage Learning Customer & Sales Support, cengage.com/contact

For permission to use material from this text or product,
submit all requests online at **cengage.com/permissions**
Further permissions questions can be emailed to
permissionrequest@cengage.com

ISBN: 978-1-4080-9684-0

National Geographic Learning
Cheriton House, North Way, Andover, Hampshire, SP10 5BE
United Kingdom

National Geographic Learning, a Cengage Learning Company, has a mission to bring the world to the classroom and the classroom to life. With our English language programs, students learn about their world by experiencing it. Through our partnerships with National Geographic and TED Talks, they develop the language and skills they need to be successful global citizens and leaders.

Locate your local office at **international.cengage.com/region**

Visit National Geographic Learning online at **NGL.Cengage.com/ELT**
Visit our corporate website at **www.cengage.com**

Printed in the United Kingdom by Ashford Colour Press Ltd.
Print Number: 10   Print Year: 2022